IMAGES
of America

WAUCONDA

I0806415

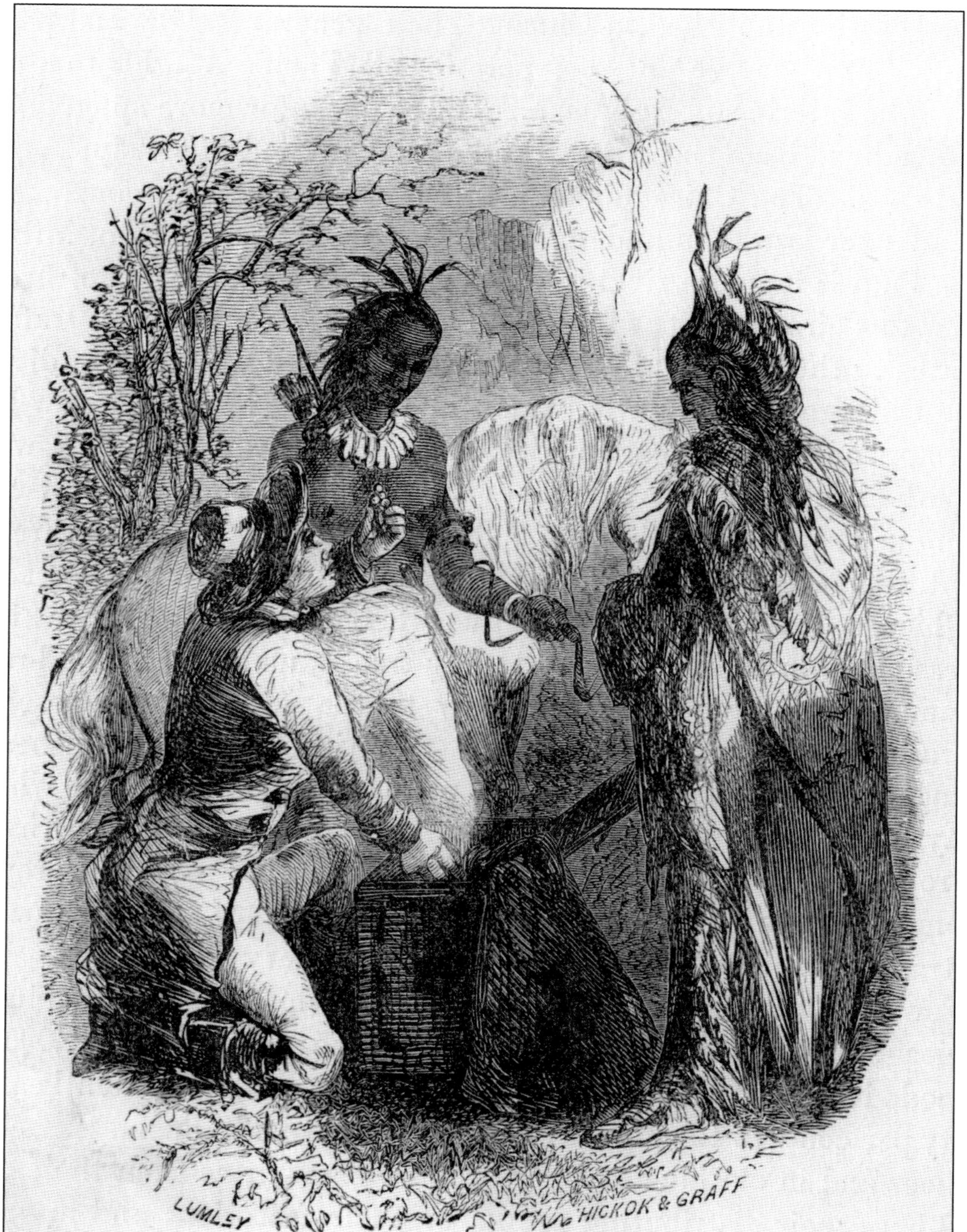

Native Americans and a white settler are depicted trading in a sketch from *The Past and Present of Lake County, Illinois* by Elijah Haines, published in 1877.

On the Cover: Around 1911, boaters arrive at Kuebker's Landing with the day's catch. Mertie Kuebker Cook inherited the property after her father's death in 1925, and she and her husband, Homer T. Cook, changed the name to Cook's Boathouse. Later, it was known as Farman's by the Sea and Lindy's Landing, the name it has today. (Courtesy of the Lake County Discovery Museum.)

IMAGES
of America

WAUCONDA

Kathy Catrambone and Marianne Folise

ARCADIA
PUBLISHING

Copyright © 2011 by Kathy Catrambone and Marianne Folise
ISBN 978-0-7385-8317-4

Published by Arcadia Publishing
Charleston, South Carolina

Printed in the United States of America

Library of Congress Control Number: 2011936870

For all general information, please contact Arcadia Publishing:
Telephone 843-853-2070
Fax 843-853-0044
E-mail sales@arcadiapublishing.com
For customer service and orders:
Toll-Free 1-888-313-2665

Visit us on the Internet at www.arcadiapublishing.com

This book is dedicated to the people of Wauconda, both past and present.

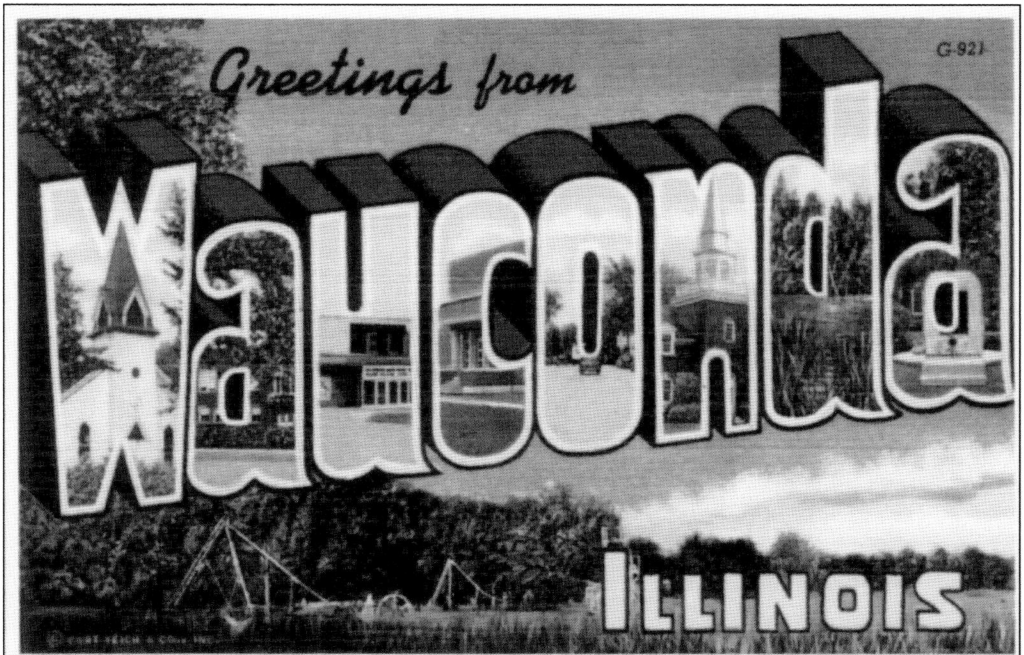

A 1950 Curt Teich Company postcard depicts selected views of Wauconda in its letters. Teich's work is highly collectible, and the national Curt Teich Postcard Archives are kept in the Lake County Discovery Museum.

CONTENTS

ACKNOWLEDGMENTS

The authors are grateful to all who were willing to spend time with us, sharing their stories, photographs, and historical knowledge. Many of these people are descendants of some of the oldest families of the community. The experience of working on this book rekindled the authors' treasured memories of times spent with family and friends, growing up and spending summers in Wauconda.

Heartfelt gratitude goes to Doris Aimers-Voss; Cindy Francisco Bilisko; Ira Bliss; Steve Boehmer; Jim Broughton; Neville and Kathie Carr; Angela Catrambone; David Dato; Barbara Parelius Davenport; Fred Dierker; Mary Ann Dierker Andrew; Aaron Aggarwal, manager of Bulldogs Grill; Diana Dretske, collections coordinator at the Lake County Discovery Museum; Steve Freund; Jeanne Guilfoyle; Jan Prior Hironimus; Donna Wellman Kennebeck; the Kisselburg family; Dr. Joe Lincoln; Kelly Lincoln; Audrey Lincoln Painter; Dolly Leuder Lewis; Gayle Nolan Libreri; Lyle and Louise Matthews; Rosemary Mers; Lynn McAllister, reference librarian, Wauconda Public Library; Don Meyer; Barbara Peck Pawlak; Mary Ellen Thomas Perry; Annie Fisher Peterson; Jacque Ross Peterson; Dan Quick; Mary Reilly Bastien; Kathy Reilly; Deanna Wiemuth Rogers; Gail Baseley Schendel; Sandy Schraml; Sue Serratore; Paul Smith; Ron K. Vaughn Sr.; Jackie Victor; Richard A. Warfield; and Katie Manyluk Wolter.

Introduction

Township 44, Range 9, in the county of Lake, was simply called home by Native American Woodland tribes that inhabited the pristine prairie. They were the Winnebago and Potawatomi, who passed land from generation to generation. They did not know the concept of private land ownership when the US government ordered them to move west of the Mississippi River because of the Treaty of Chicago in 1833 (ratified in 1835).

The United Nations of Chippewa, Ottawa, and Potawatomi signed the treaty and sold five million acres to the United States, including the last tracts of Native-occupied Great Lakes land. Native Americans ceded their land throughout Lake County to the federal government. An Englishman, Charles Latrobe, wrote about the event in his book *The Rambler in North America*, published in London in 1836: "Even though convinced of the necessity of their removal, my heart bled for them in their desolation and decline."

When white settlers arrived, the area was known as Rice's Prairie. It later became Bangs Lake settlement for Justus Bangs, the area's first settler; and then, in 1850, it was known as the township of Wauconda.

"Wahcondah" is a word used by Sioux-speaking tribes, meaning "great spirit." Others called it "spiritual place" or "spirit water." The story goes that La Fayette Mills, a young schoolteacher, encountered the name in James Fennimore Cooper's *The Prairie*. He suggested the word "Wauconda" to Bangs, who liked it and presented a petition to the township commissioners who, following the wishes of the residents, approved the name. Another well-known theory—that Wauconda was named for an Indian chief buried somewhere along the southern shore of Bangs Lake—is not considered to be accurate.

Settlers were drawn to the area for the fertile farmland with its bountiful lakes, rivers, and streams, which were perfect for fishing, trapping, and hunting wild game.

Bangs, responsible for laying the foundation for Wauconda, was aptly named the "prince of pioneers." He was a farmer, businessman, and philanthropist. Among his accomplishments were building and opening the first general store and many of Wauconda's other principal buildings, some of which still stand.

Word of the good fortune in Illinois spread throughout New England. Many settlers, most of them white Protestants from Vermont, Massachusetts, and New York, made their way to the Midwest via covered wagon or sailing vessels through the Erie Canal and Great Lakes. They purchased land from the federal government for $1.25 an acre according to a decree by Pres. James Polk. Many settlers were related by either birth or marriage. In 1840, Bangs's longtime friend and brother-in-law Andrew Cook and his wife, Mary Oaks, sister of Louisa Oaks Bangs, arrived. They purchased 380 acres of land along the west shore of Bangs Lake. Their first home was a log cabin, and Cook's main occupation was farming.

Two brickyards were located in the vicinity; one was on the Cook property near the lake. In the early 1850s, he constructed and occupied the first brick house in the township from bricks he made himself. The two-story Cook House now houses the Wauconda Historical Society.

The first stage route from Chicago to Janesville, Wisconsin, went through Wauconda. Ambrose Bangs, then about 14, became the stage driver for about eight years. It took a week to make the round trip. Some of these early roads were known as McHenry Road, Rand Road, and Old Plank Road, which, like all plank roads, was a toll road.

In 1839, the area's first school was built on land Bangs donated. R.S. Crosby and local residents built it from logs found in nearby woods. Books were few in those days, and the primary sources of learning were Cobb's speller, some second- and third-grade readers, an arithmetic primer, and the Bible. A few years later, the Little Red Schoolhouse was built where the Methodist/Episcopal church stood. The teachers were La Fayette Mills and his wife. Then the Wauconda Academy was built in 1856, and Euphemia Valentine was the first teacher.

In April 1850, the first town meeting of Wauconda was called to order, and the first public officials were elected. The town's population at the time was 200. Bangs was elected justice of the peace in 1854 and served for 12 years, as well as county supervisor for two terms and postmaster for several terms. The increasing size of the town necessitated moving the burial ground to a more remote area, and Bangs donated a piece of land for it.

In 1838, a Baptist community was established, and a Methodist church was organized in 1853. From the fall of 1856 until 1870, the two congregations shared a church building. They came together again in 1915 to establish the Federated Church. As Irish immigrants moved into the area, Roman Catholics worshipped in a log house east of town, where Transfiguration Cemetery resides. The first of three Transfiguration Church buildings was constructed within the village limits in the summer of 1877.

On February 28, 1867, a charter was granted for a railroad linking Palatine, Lake Zurich, and Wauconda called the Palatine, Lake Zurich and Wauconda Railroad (PLZ&W). Service to Wauconda finally started on May 10, 1913. However, persistent financial woes, maintenance problems (giving the train its nickname, "the Palatine, Lake Zurich, and Walk the Rest of the Way"), and road improvements making automobile travel easy doomed the railroad to failure in less than 12 years.

Local residents voted to incorporate Wauconda as a village on August 18, 1877. The election was held at the Pratt House, which today is the Lakeside Inn; the vote passed 49 to 24. The population at the time was 390. The first trustees were elected on September 18, 1877, and six days later the trustees elected Robert Harrison as village president. On September 29, 1877, they adopted two liquor ordinances as the village's first laws. Voters passed the first tax levy on January 2, 1878, for $300 to build an office and a calaboose.

At the beginning of the 20th century, the quaint village became known as a summer resort and cabin community for vacationing Chicagoans. Beaches and cottages were established in the 1910s, and the "summer people" started coming, creating a new identity for Wauconda.

The village attracted city dwellers looking to escape the changing city, especially in the 1950s and 1960s. Many of the new residents were ex-soldiers from the city's west and northwest sides who had purchased property from the old-timers and built cottages. They converted the cottages to permanent residences, a trend that continued for about 30 years, and set Wauconda on its modern-day path.

One

Early Settlers

New Englanders arrived after the 1833 Treaty of Chicago, lured by the government's promise of cheap land. A poem in an 1833 Boston newspaper stated, "Come leave the fields of childhood worn out by long employ / and travel west and settle in the state of Illinois."

Homesteaders staked claims to good farmland, built log cabins, and waited for the government to survey the land so they could buy it for the promised price of $1.25 an acre. One of these men was Justus Bangs. Born December 16, 1806, in Montague, Massachusetts, Bangs traced his roots to passengers aboard the *Anne*, which arrived in Plymouth, Massachusetts, from England in 1623—three years after the first pilgrims arrived. Bangs grew up in Vermont, and as he was nearing 30, he and his nephew Elihu Hubbard traveled to Michigan and Chicago; Bangs was not impressed with either. In Chicago, he met a man who knew his brother David. He escorted them to Meacham's Grove (now Bloomingdale). After a short residence there, the search continued for the Fox River and land.

They spent one night at Diamond Lake, where they camped with Native Americans. The next morning, they followed the Indians' trail to Mechanics Grove (now Mundelein). There, Daniel Marsh told them about a tract of land near a lake where he had fished the day before. They followed Marsh's log tracks and found the lake. Bangs once wrote, "The lake and surroundings were more beautiful than anything I had seen. I had found my home." The lake would later bear his name. In June 1836, he and his friends built two log cabins on the south shore of the lake: one for Bangs and one for Hubbard. Thomas and Jeremy Slocum soon followed.

Bangs returned to Vermont to recover from an injury and sent his parents and two sisters to hold his claim in Illinois. In 1839, he returned to Wauconda, bringing his wife, Louisa Oaks, whom he married in January 1829, and their sons Andrew C. and Ambrose A.

Family and friends joined them. Names of settlers before 1850 included Oaks, Cook, Hubbard, Kimball, Hill, Todd, Harrison, Wells, Seeber, Mills, Sherman, Martin, Hawkins, Davlin, and Murray. Most were related by blood or marriage. Several marriages occurred between three of the families: Asa Oaks married Ruby Bangs, Luke Oaks married Bethiah Bangs, Louisa Oaks married Justus Bangs, and her sister Mary Oaks married Andrew Cook.

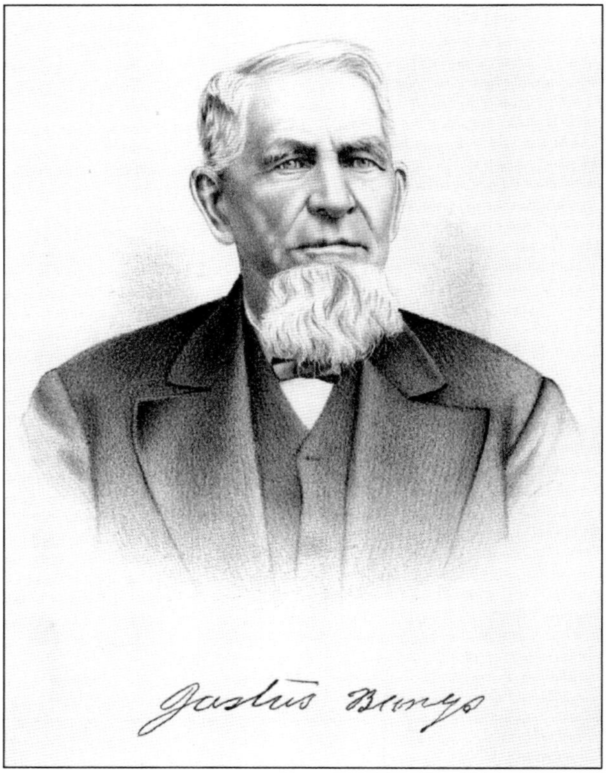

Justus Bangs, who started it all, lived to be 89 years old. Upon his December 13, 1895, death, it was said, "His memory will be revered not only as the founder of Wauconda, but also for his many generous acts and deeds of kindness, which win more true love than any public benefit." Bangs's family history can be traced to the original Pilgrim settlers of America. (Courtesy of the Lake County Discovery Museum.)

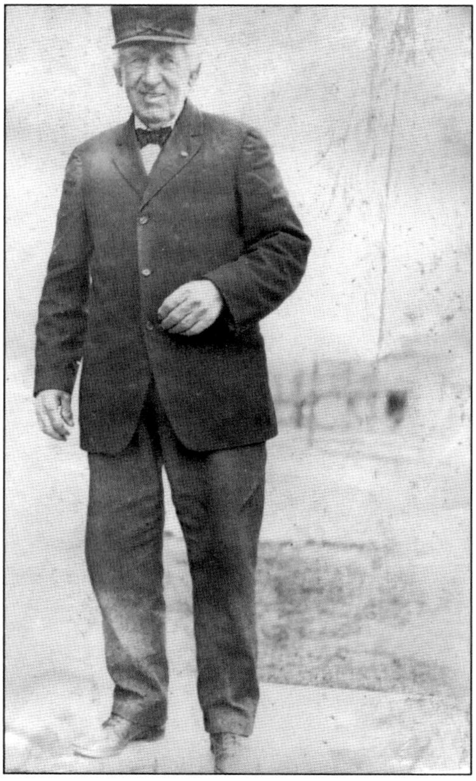

Ambrose Bangs, one of Justus and Louisa Bangs's two sons, was born in 1831. At 14, he became the driver of the stagecoach from Wauconda to Janesville, Wisconsin. In 1853, he left home and married Eliza Hill of New York. In 1862, he entered the military and was assigned to Company B, 96th Illinois Infantry and served during the Civil War. Captured and held prisoner in the Battle of Chickamauga, Georgia, he returned to Wauconda and later become a farmer engaging in grain and livestock. (Courtesy of the Lake County Discovery Museum.)

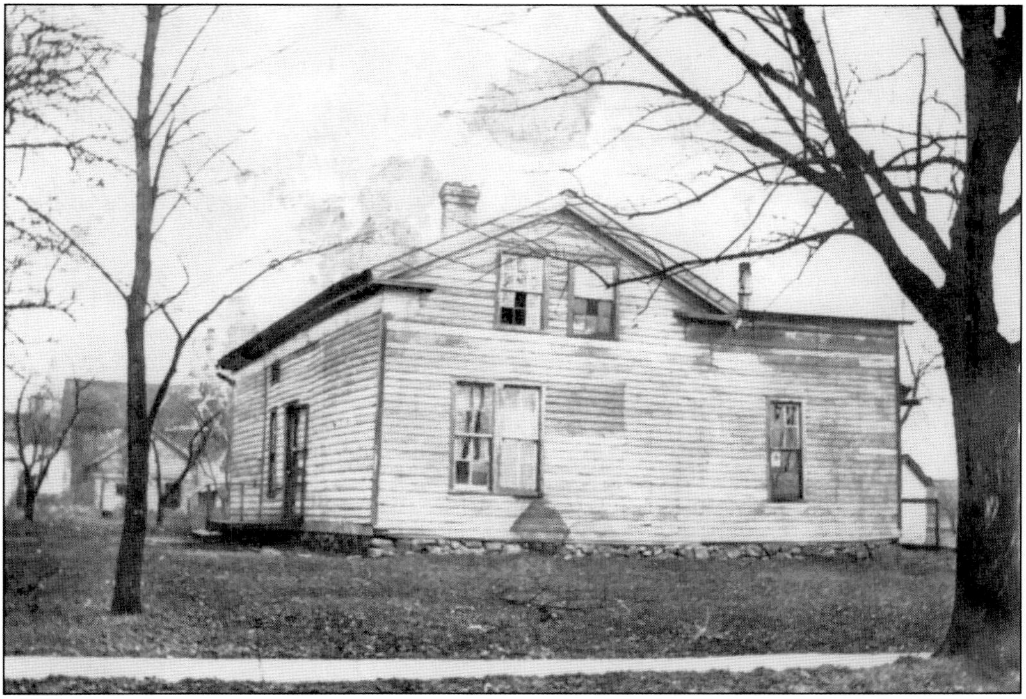

Justus Bangs built this, his second house, in 1842 at the corner of Main and Bangs Streets. He and his first wife, Louisa, lived here until she died on May 25, 1851, at 45. He left the house after marrying Caroline Cone in 1852. The house was torn down in 1899, and the property was used to widen Main Street. Caroline and Justus were both friends of the Rand family of Des Plaines, who invited each of them to their house for a weekend. Caroline, at 36, was considered well beyond her years to marry. She and Justus met on Friday and liked each other. Justus proposed on Saturday evening, and they were married the following week on Sunday, January 22, 1852. (Courtesy of the Lake County Discovery Museum.)

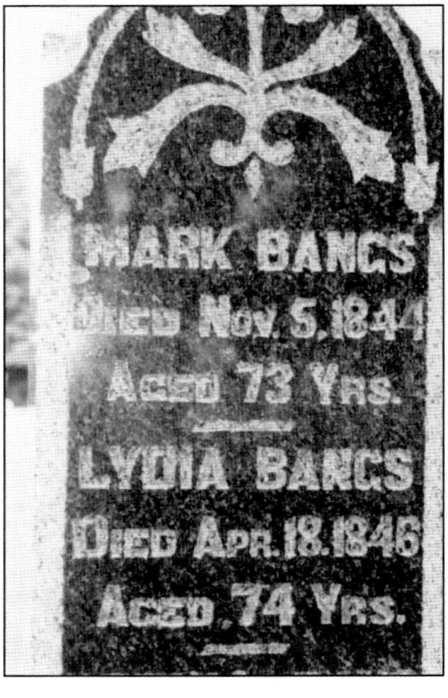

Justus Bangs's father, Mark Bangs, was born in Harwich, Massachusetts, on September 10, 1771. The elder Bangs was known to have held strict temperance attitudes. He married Lydia Whitney of Conway, Massachusetts, on February 9, 1792. She was known as a lady of culture and refinement and a devoted member of the Baptist Church. They lived a full, rich life, raising 12 children. Both are buried at Wauconda Cemetery. (Courtesy of Marianne Folise.)

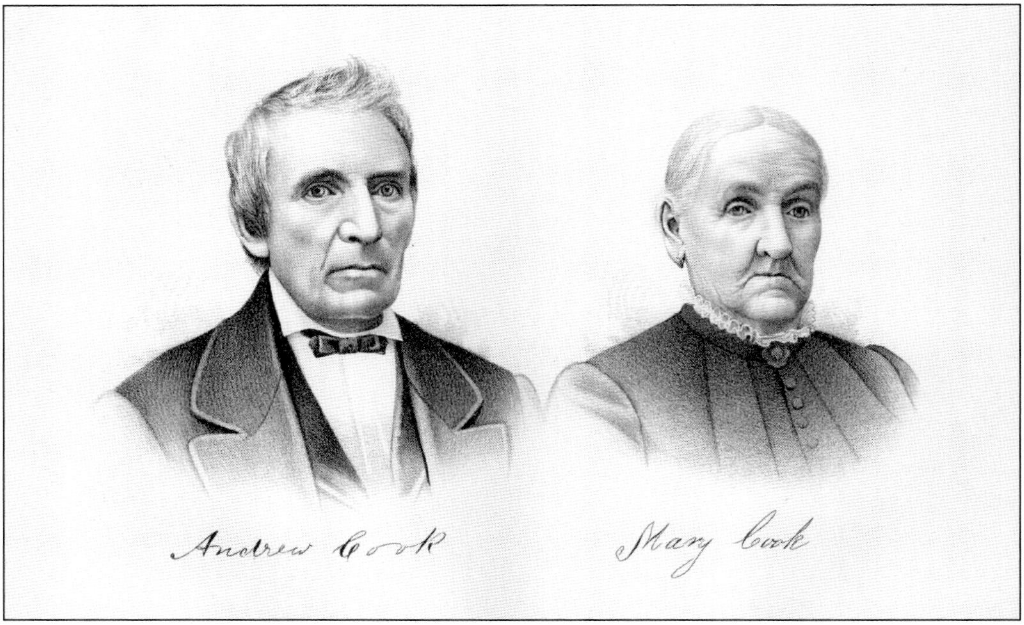

Andrew Cook and Mary Oaks Cook, in-laws of Justus Bangs, married in 1830 in Vermont. Their union bore them 13 children; 9 lived to adulthood. In 1839, they arrived in Wauconda and purchased 380 acres at $1.25 an acre. Their first dwelling was a log cabin, which they replaced in 1850 with the first brick house in the area. Cook made the bricks himself. Two brickyards were in the vicinity; one on the Cook farm was near the lake. A limestone kiln was located on the banks of the lake on the Kimball property in the area that is now Main and Liberty Streets. The house was a two-story structure with nine rooms and a porch on the east side facing the lake. Some Winnebagos, who remained along the Fox River, often visited. Cook became wealthy and played a prominent role in political affairs, holding school and township government offices. Village trustees held their first meeting at the home in 1850. Below is a current picture of the house. (Above, courtesy of Lake County Discovery Museum; below, Marianne Folise.)

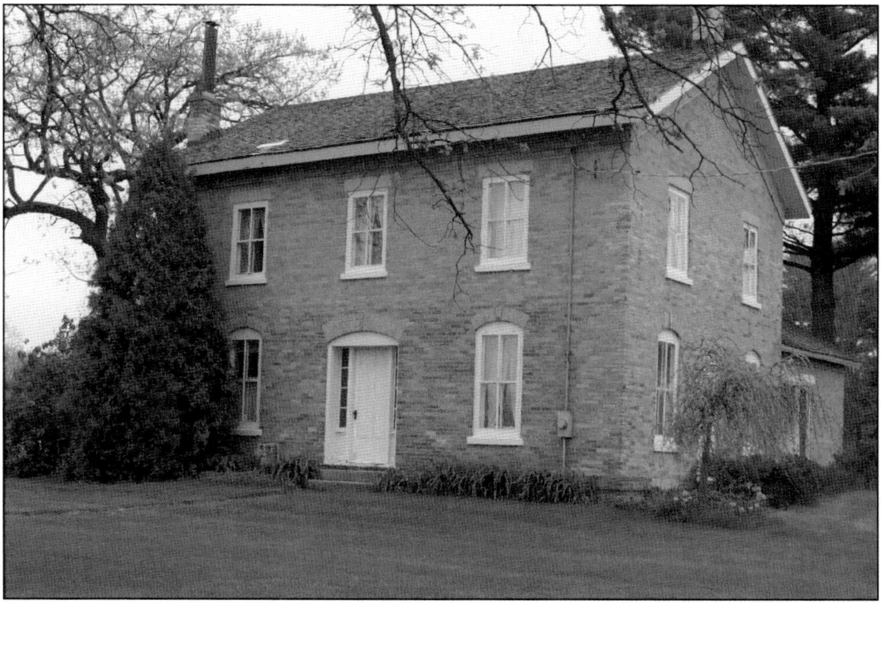

1850-1901: Andrew Cook builds the house. He and his wife, Mary Cook, live in the house until their deaths. He dies in 1884; she, in 1901.

1901-1906: William and Lucy Cook Clough and Lucy's brother, Arthur Cook, live in the house until Arthur dies in 1906.

1907-1919: Still owned by the Cook family, the house is rented to John J. and Anna Brown, who live there with their two children.

1920-1936: House is rented to Raymond Lusk, great-grandson of Andrew and Mary Cook.

1940-1947: Homer T. Cook sells the house to a Mr. DeWolf, who rents it to Ronald Paddock, long-time director of the Wauconda National Bank, and his family.

1947-1950: Mr. DeWolf sells the house to Roger and Emily Parelius, who have two children, Barbara and Roger. The new owners renovate the house, adding an apartment upstairs. The first renters were Russell and Beatrice Lutz; later, Ray and Myrtle Boekup.

1950-1977: Roger and Emily Parelius sell the house to Ralph and Doris Madea, who live in the house until 1977.

1977: Ralph and Doris Madea sell the house, which is in need of repair, to the Wauconda School District. The high school is adjacent to the property. The School District leases it to the Wauconda Township Historical Society, which restores the building to resemble its original layout.

1992: The Illinois State Historical Society designates the house a historic site.

This is a timeline of the history and inhabitants of the Cook House at 711 North Main Street. (Courtesy of Lynn McAllister and Barbara Parelius Davenport.)

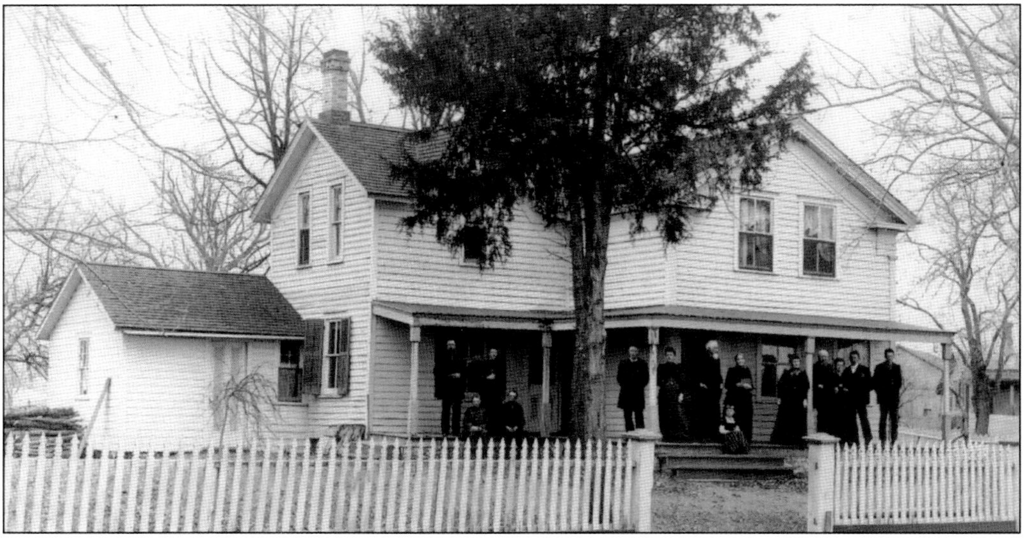

Peter Mills built the Andrew Oaks house, now the site of Kisselburg Funeral Home, in the mid-1800s. Mills settled in Wauconda in 1836 and was the maternal great-grandfather of Harry and Della Kirwan, whose family owned Kirwan's Tavern, a fixture on Main Street (see chapter four for more). Upon Mills's death in 1864, the house was sold to Andrew Oaks, brother-in law of Justus Bangs and Andrew Cook. This 1893 photograph was taken at the golden wedding anniversary celebration of Andrew and Phoebe Oaks, pictured in center with their family, and Mr. and Mrs. B.S. Hammond. On the left is the Henry Werden family, and on the right is the Matthew Smith family. Seated is Ruth Smith (right). (Courtesy of the Kisselburg Home.)

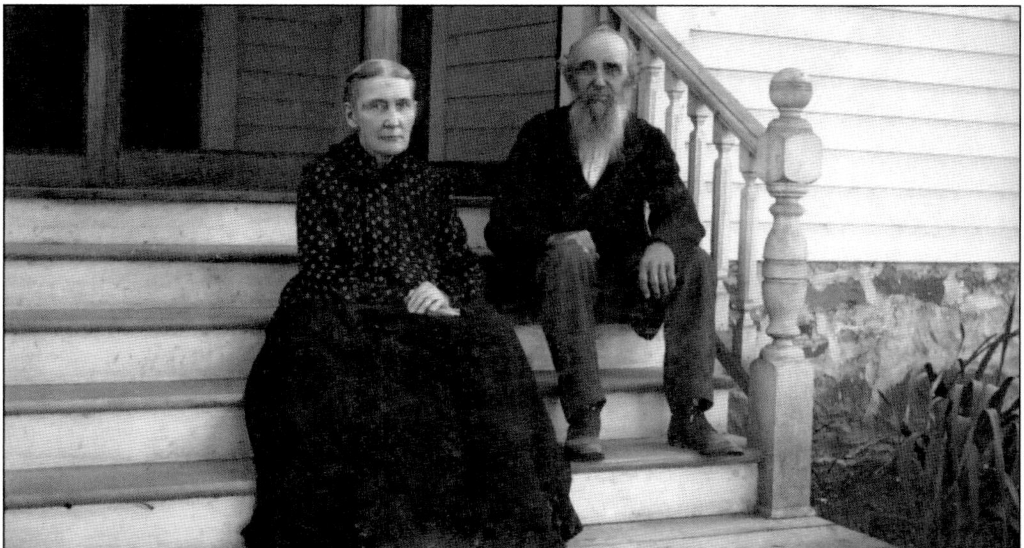

Morris Seth Hill (right) was born May 24, 1823, in New York. He came to Wauconda with his parents, Seth and Deborah Ann (Clark) Hill, in 1844. He married Terrissa Mills (left), also of New York, on May 24, 1849. They engaged in farming in Wauconda. His paternal grandfather was Reuben Hill, a Revolutionary War hero, who is buried in the Wauconda Cemetery (see chapter nine for more). Terrissa was a cousin to La Fayette Mills, who drew the first plat of the village of Wauconda and was the town's first teacher. Mills was the first township clerk, a schoolteacher, and the man who suggested the village's name to Justus Bangs. (Courtesy of Jacque Ross Peterson.)

Two

PROMINENT FAMILIES

It would be impossible to include all the men and women who were prominent in Wauconda's history. So this chapter honors some of the dedicated, hardworking people who are representative of all who served the community. They carried on what Justus Bangs and his contemporaries started.

These people showed persistence, ingenuity, and sometimes sheer guts to achieve what they did in life. They worked hard to attain their station and served their neighbors and Wauconda as a whole. They left their mark on the village for future generations to build upon. Many of these people had a rich ancestral history, ranging from hearty New England pioneers who could trace their roots to the adventurous people who left their homes to chart unknown territory in search of a better life.

This chapter is a tribute to all the men and women of the generation who bore, raised, and nourished future generations of Wauconda residents.

Of note, this history would be lost without the tireless efforts of Doris Marie Claypool Aimers-Voss. She recorded hundreds of hours of oral history and transcribed the tapes, which can be found in the reference department of the Wauconda Public Library.

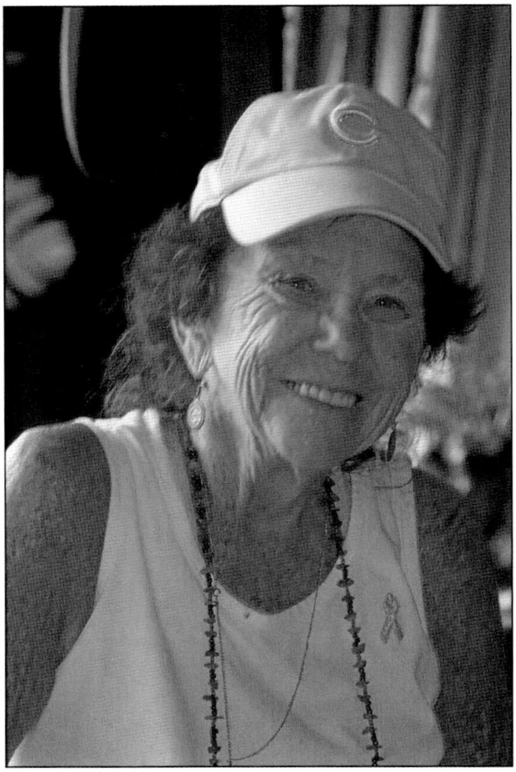

Doris Marie Claypool Aimers-Voss was transplanted from city to country in 1944 in time to start high school. Her parents owned and operated Inez and Bill's, a grocery store and tavern, in Williams Park. Later, they moved the tavern business to Main Street. She taught fourth grade in Wauconda. She married Al Aimers in 1951, and they had three children and five grandchildren. While raising her children, she earned her master's and PhD at Northern Illinois University in DeKalb. She then taught sixth grade in Wauconda until her retirement in 1994. She lost her husband to Amyotrophic Lateral Sclerosis (ALS, or Lou Gehrig's Disease) in 1986, and 10 years later she married Firmin Voss. (Courtesy of Marianne Folise.)

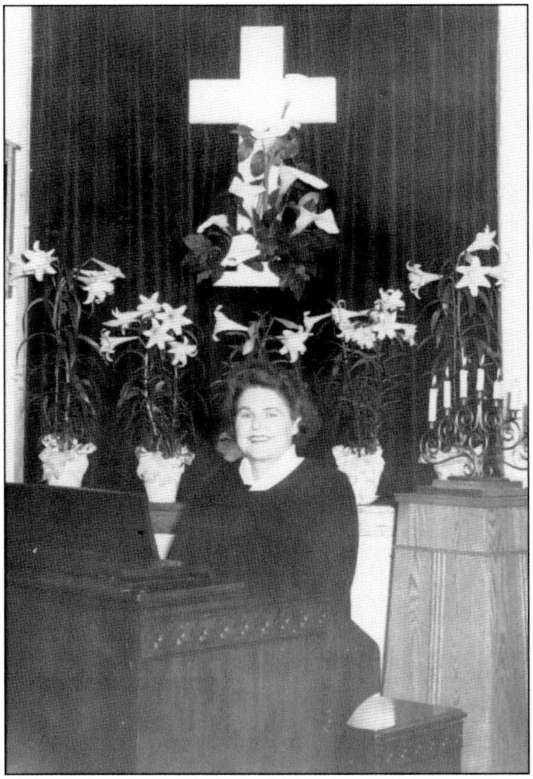

Pictured playing the organ at Wauconda Federated Church is Mary Murphy Lueder, born on March 17, 1911. Her great-grandfather was Justus Bangs. In 1915, her grandfather Dennis Murphy built the Palace Theater, where Mary pushed pedals on the organ while silent films were shown. She married Roland Lueder in 1934 and in 1955, after many years as a homemaker, began a 23-year career teaching at Wauconda Junior High School. She played the organ and gave piano lessons into her 98th year. She died on December 4, 2009, and is buried in Wauconda Cemetery. (Courtesy of Dolly Lueder Lewis.)

Dr. John A. Ross, pictured here in 1948 with his wife, Celista, came from Davenport, Iowa, and set up a practice in Wauconda in 1922. Office calls were $1.50, and house calls were $3. He often received payment in chickens, vegetables, and home-baked goods. He had a lasting effect on the history of Wauconda. From 1925 to 1937, Dr. Ross served as village trustee, and he was mayor from 1938 until his death in 1949 at the age of 73. It was said that Dr. Ross had a special charm and personality, and his presence in or out of the sick room "would be a lift to one's spirit." (Courtesy of Jacque Ross Peterson.)

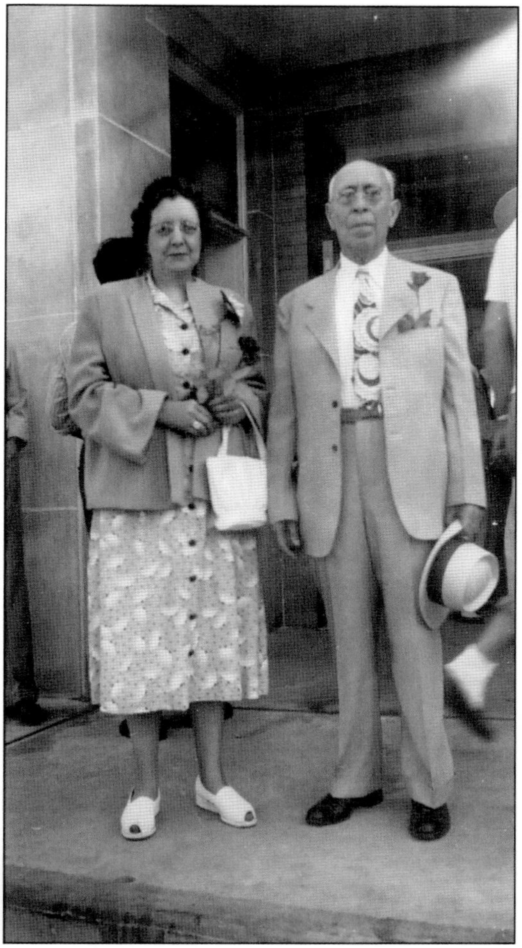

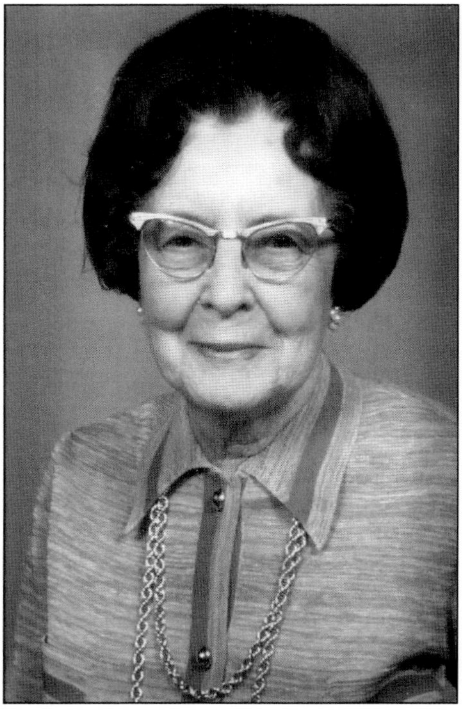

Celista Ross and her physician husband had a daughter, Jacqueline ("Jacque"), born in 1924. Celista helped with the patients and cared for the many babies who were born in their home. She was active in the Eastern Star and president of the Ladies Auxiliary of the Wauconda Federated Church. (Courtesy of Jacque Ross Peterson.)

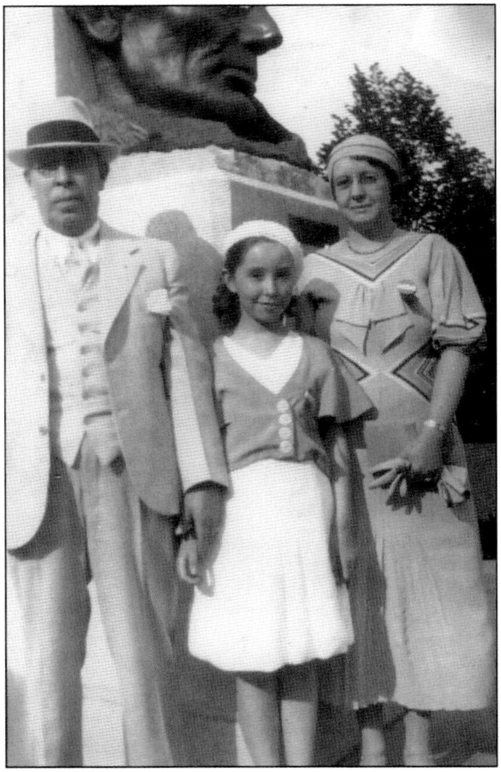

At left, Dr. John and Celista Ross and their daughter Jacque enjoy a trip to Springfield, Illinois, in May 1934. Below, Jacque and Lt. Robert P. "Bob" Peterson pose on their wedding day, October 8, 1943, at the Federated Church (see chapter nine for more). They have two children, Patricia Jean and John Ross. Jacque attended school in Wauconda and taught dance at her own studio while in high school. She graduated from business school in Chicago. (Both courtesy of Jacque Ross Peterson.)

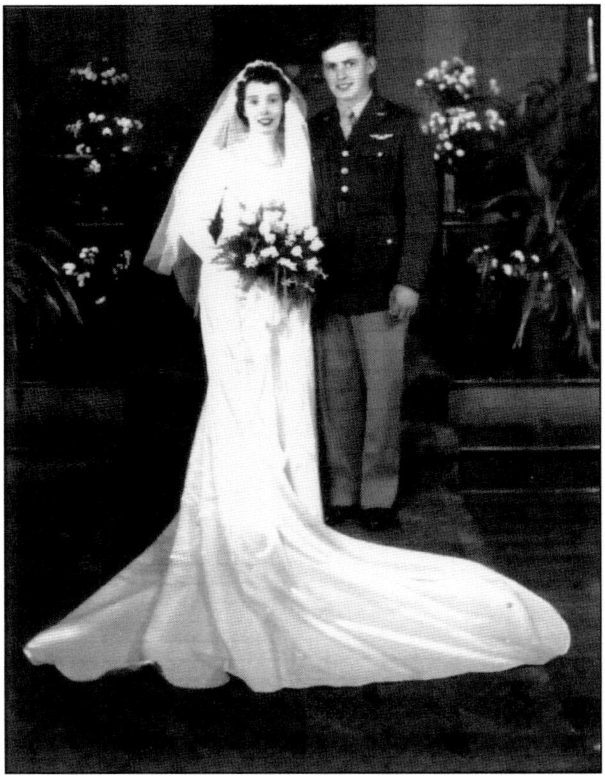

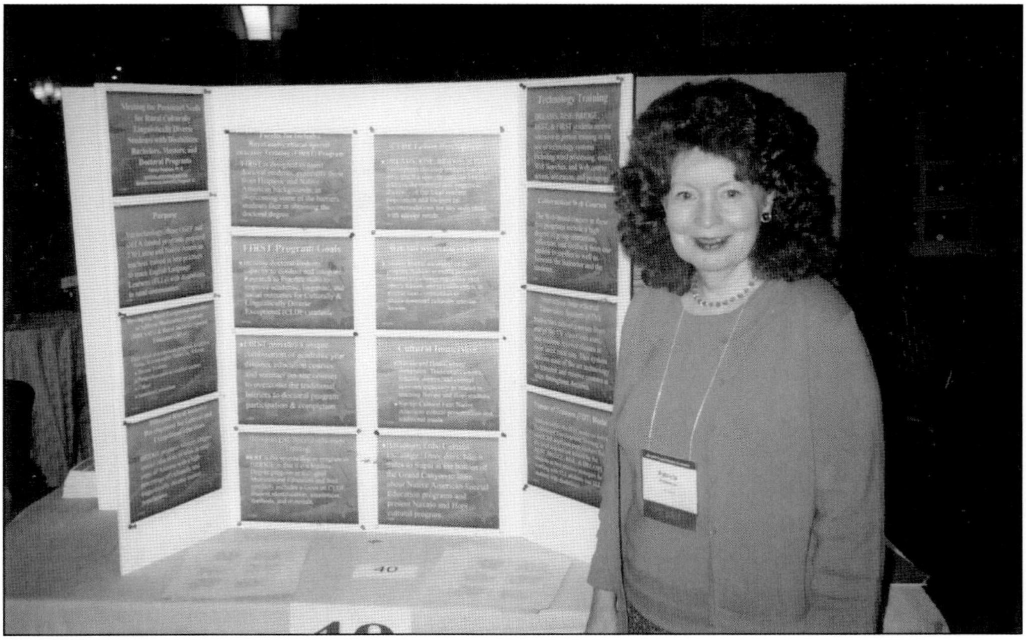

Dr. Patricia Jean Peterson is a professor of special education and bilingual special education at Northern Arizona University in Flagstaff. She and her husband, Stephen Showalter of Virginia, have one son, Robb, who attends North Central College in Naperville, Illinois. She lectures in the United States and abroad about special education. She has written and received more than $5 million in grants, which have enabled 1,000 students from diverse backgrounds to become teachers. (Courtesy of Jacque Ross Peterson.)

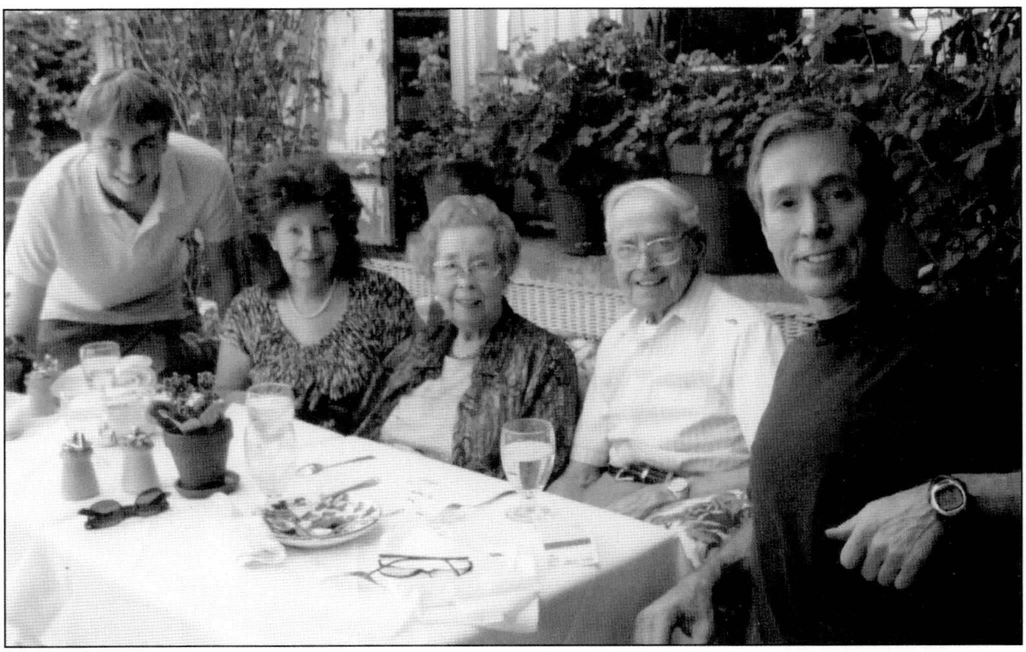

The Peterson family is seen having lunch at the Ivy in Beverly Hills, California, in 2009. From left to right are grandson Robb, daughter Patricia Jean, Jacque, Bob, and son John Ross. (Courtesy of Jacque Ross Peterson.)

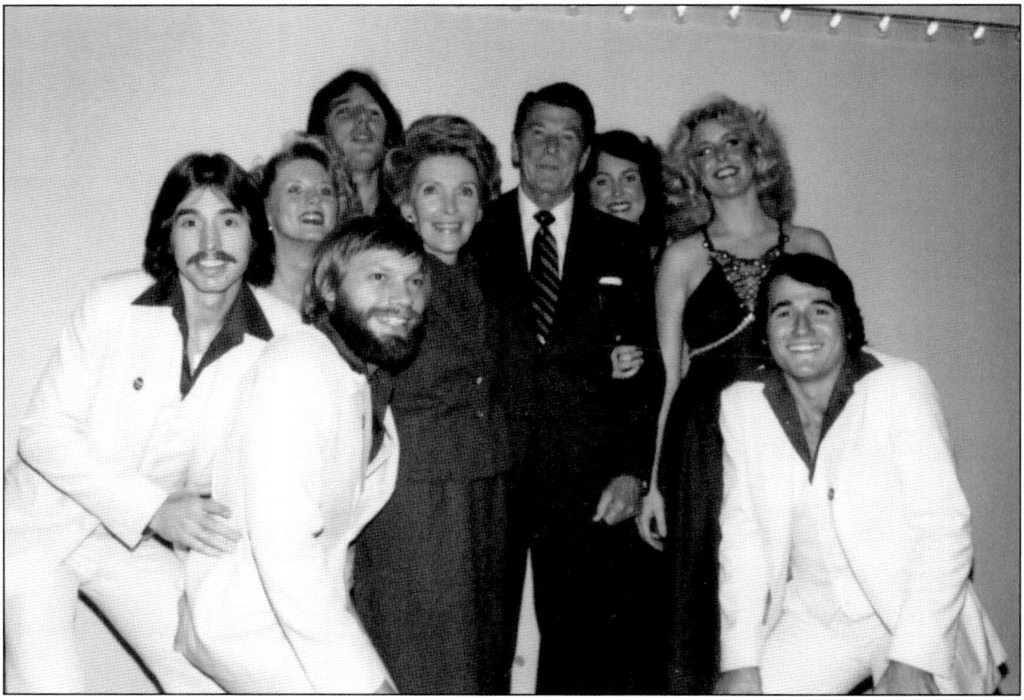

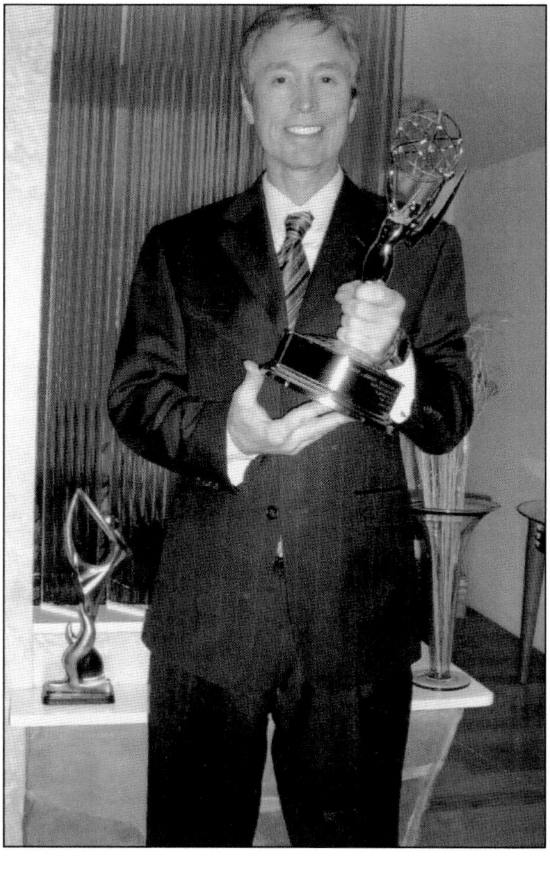

In this picture, John Ross Peterson (far left) poses with the Serendipity Singers, Pres. Ronald Reagan, and First Lady Nancy Reagan. Ross started his musical career playing coronet in the Wauconda High School Band. In 1976, he replaced the last original member of the Serendipity Singers, which traveled globally. For 15 years, his mother, Jacque Ross Peterson, was its manager. After directing the group for 20 years, John Ross went on to become an Emmy Award–winning producer. (Courtesy of Jacque Ross Peterson.)

John Ross Peterson holds his 2008 Daytime TV Emmy Award for producing a two-hour special, *America's Invisible Children: The Homeless Education Crisis in America*. In 2009, he received a second nomination, and in 2010 he was a producer and musical director for the Daytime TV Emmy Awards show. He also created several adventure-orientated TV series. He established the Montana Grizzly Encounter near Bozeman, a zoo that protects grizzlies. (Courtesy of Jacque Ross Peterson.)

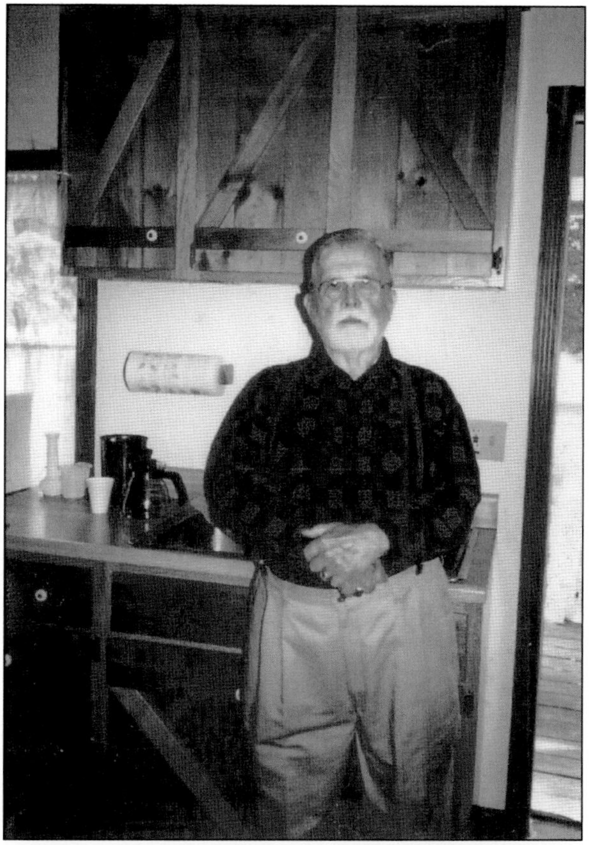

Dr. Lawrence E. Foulke, pictured at right in 1999, practiced medicine in Wauconda for 32 years. He studied at the University of Illinois School of Medicine and interned at Ravenswood Hospital, both in Chicago. He and Merle White married in 1938 and had two sons, Gifford and Douglas. In the 1930s, Dr. Foulke joined the Army and served in the Medical Corps Reserves, becoming doctor for the Civilian Conservation Corps; he was called to active duty in 1942. Discharged in 1946, he purchased a house, pictured below, that was built in 1872 on the Hubbard estate. Part of the house became his office. When the practice grew, he built an office at 363 Main Street, a few doors from the home. He retired in 1978. He once said, "I was a country boy who was educated in the city but returned to the country to practice medicine and live." He died in 2007 at the age of 99. (At right, courtesy of Cindy Francisco Bilisko; below, Marianne Folise.)

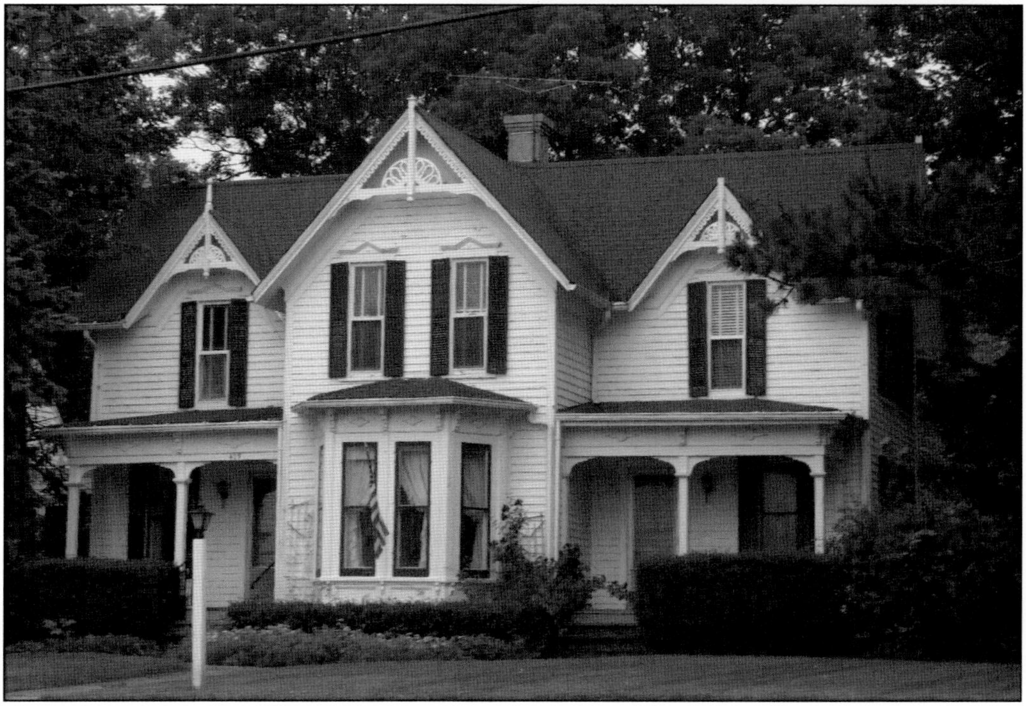

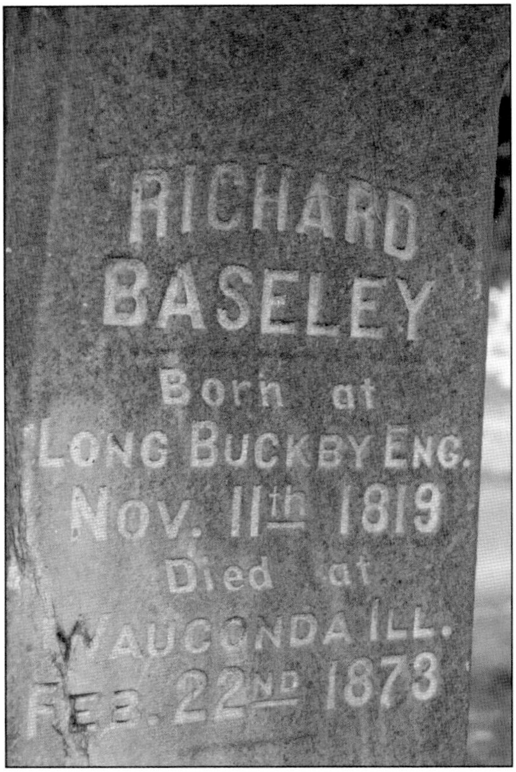

Richard Baseley and Sarah A. Case were born in England: he in 1819 and she in 1825. They married in 1847, and two years later they crossed the Atlantic to New York City. The couple traveled west via the Erie Canal and Great Lakes to Waukegan and arrived with $1 to their names. They traveled on foot to Diamond Lake, settling there for six years until 1856, when they came to Wauconda. They were soon identified with the growth and interests of the village. Their first home was Daniel Hubbard's 1836 log cabin. Richard worked to benefit the community, especially fostering quality education, and he was a staunch Whig. Devoted members and supporters of the Methodist Church, the Baseleys had six sons and two daughters. The eldest died in infancy, while the others became industrious adults and respected members of society. Richard died in 1873 and Sarah in 1891. (Both courtesy of Marianne Folise.)

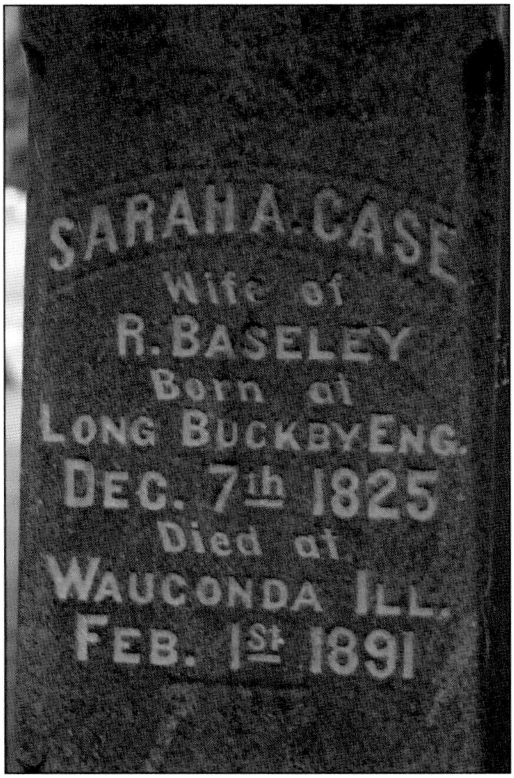

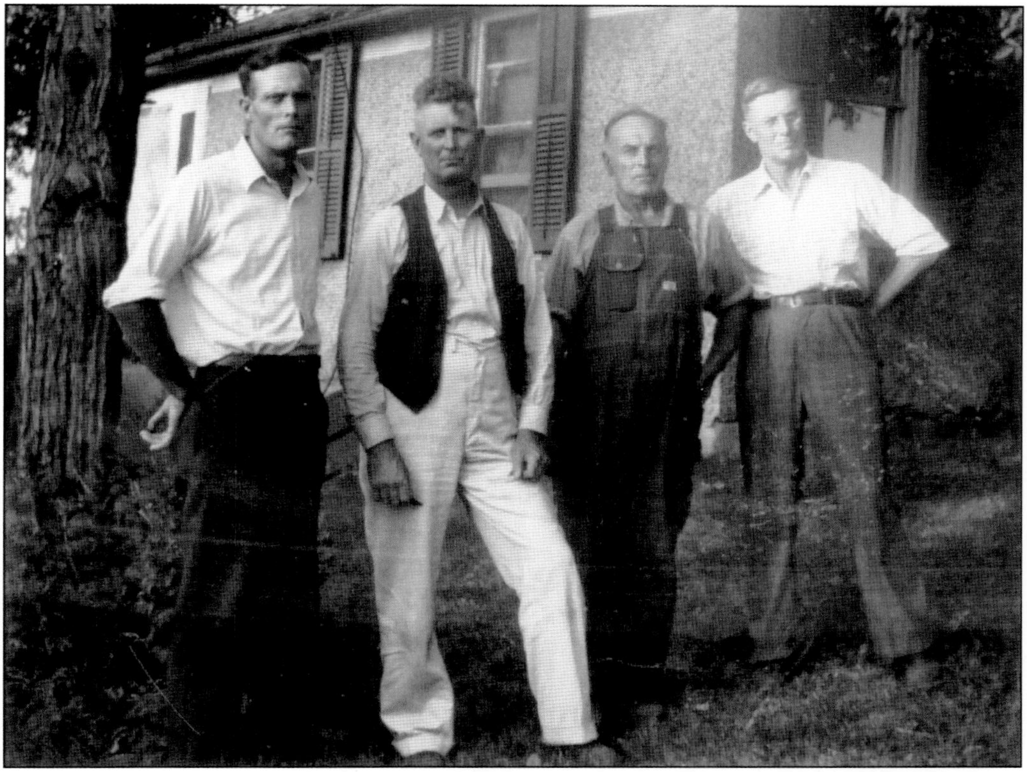

Four of Richard and Sarah Baseley's grandchildren are seen above in this 1930s photograph. From left to right are Art, Albert, Claude, and Henry "Hank." A member of an earlier generation, A.S. Baseley, son of Richard and Sarah, was paid $32 a month in 1892 to care for Wauconda's fire equipment, streetlamps, sidewalks, and streets. Below, more of the members of the Baseley clan pose for a 1920s photograph. Identified are John Andrew, Harry, William Sr., Joe, and Mayse Baseley. (Both courtesy of Gail Baseley Schendel.)

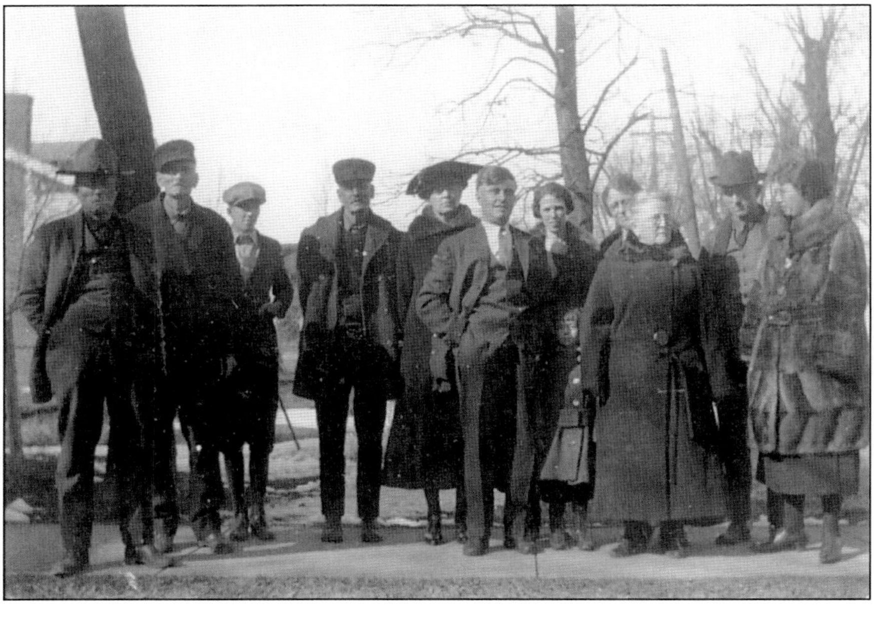

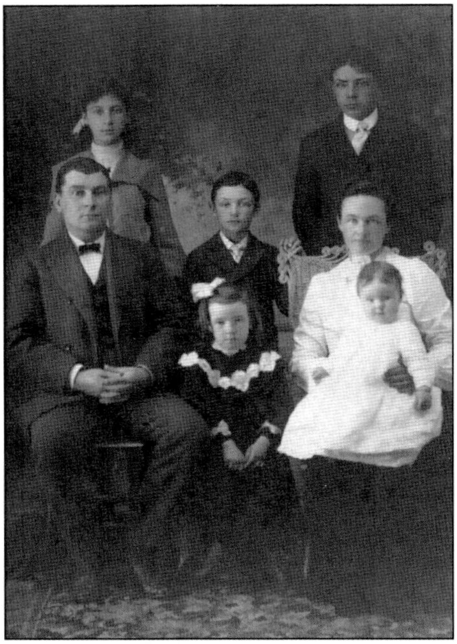

Posing in this family portrait are George M. Broughton and his wife, Catherine Blackburn Broughton, holding baby Lois. The two youngsters in the middle are George Earl "Pete" and Gertrude. Standing on the left is Edna, and on the right is Lyle. George was part-owner of the well-known Blackburn and Broughton Hardware Store on Main Street, and he passed the business on to Lyle. (Courtesy of Jim Broughton.)

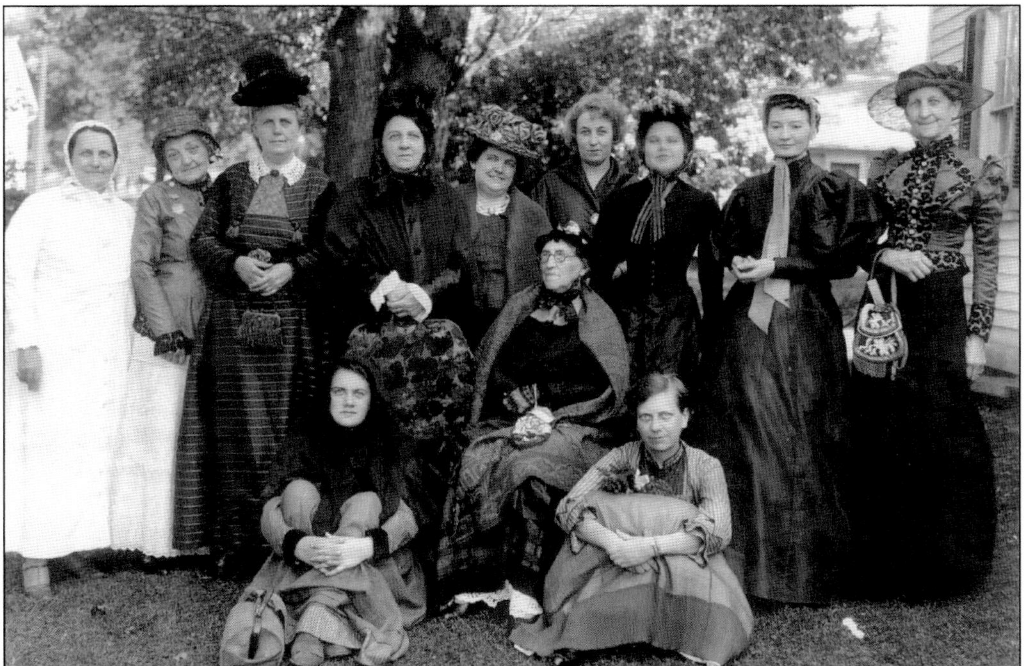

Members of the Wauconda Women's Club commemorate the centennial of the 1836 settlement of what would become Wauconda. Pictured are, from left to right, (first row) unidentified, Justus Bangs's daughter Fannie Bangs Pratt, and Women's Club president Alice Kennedy Carr; (second row) Bangs's granddaughter Caroline Pratt Einhorn, Fannie Wells Gilbert, unidentified, Bangs's granddaughter Nina Pratt Tomiskey, Bangs's granddaughter Winnie Pratt Murphy, Frances Kent Banks, Bangs's great-granddaughter Mary Murphy Lueder, Gerrie Smith, and Lil Tidmarsh, wife of the local druggist. (Courtesy of Neville Carr.)

Margot Pietsch Lincoln is 14 in this 1942 photograph with her pony Silver in the Tamarack area of Wauconda. She lost her mother at the age of seven and moved to Wauconda with her father, Conrad Pietsch, a 1917 German immigrant who became a civil engineer. She worked on the Roney farm and grew up friends of the Lincoln girls and married George upon his return from World War II. In her 50s, after raising 10 children, she became a nurse. (Courtesy of the Lincoln family.)

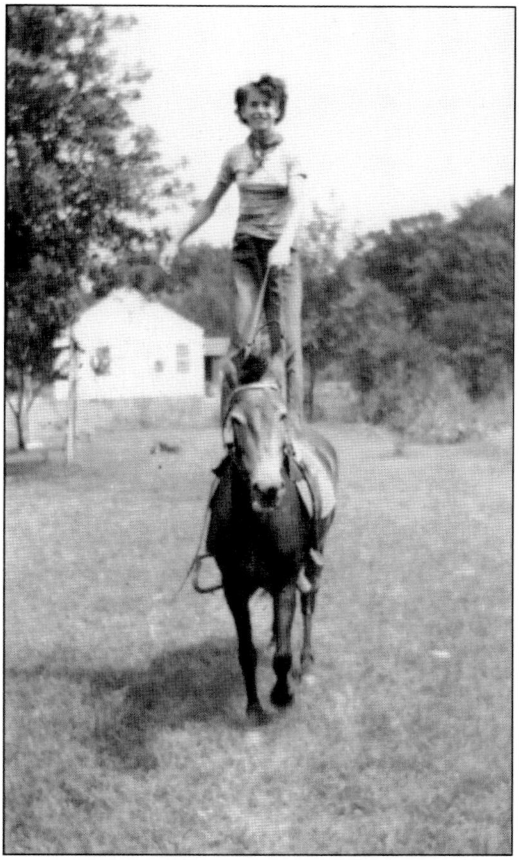

George and Margot Lincoln pose with their 10 children in 1993 at their only daughter's wedding. They are, from left to right, (first row) David, chef; George, father; Elizabeth, nurse practitioner; Margot, mother; and Pat, salon owner and the seventh son of the seventh son; (second row) Aaron, a lawyer; Tim, Abbott Lab manager; Joe, dentist; Scott, nurse/MD; Mike, carpenter; Randy, retired LTC military officer; and Brian, mason foreman. (Courtesy of the Lincoln family.)

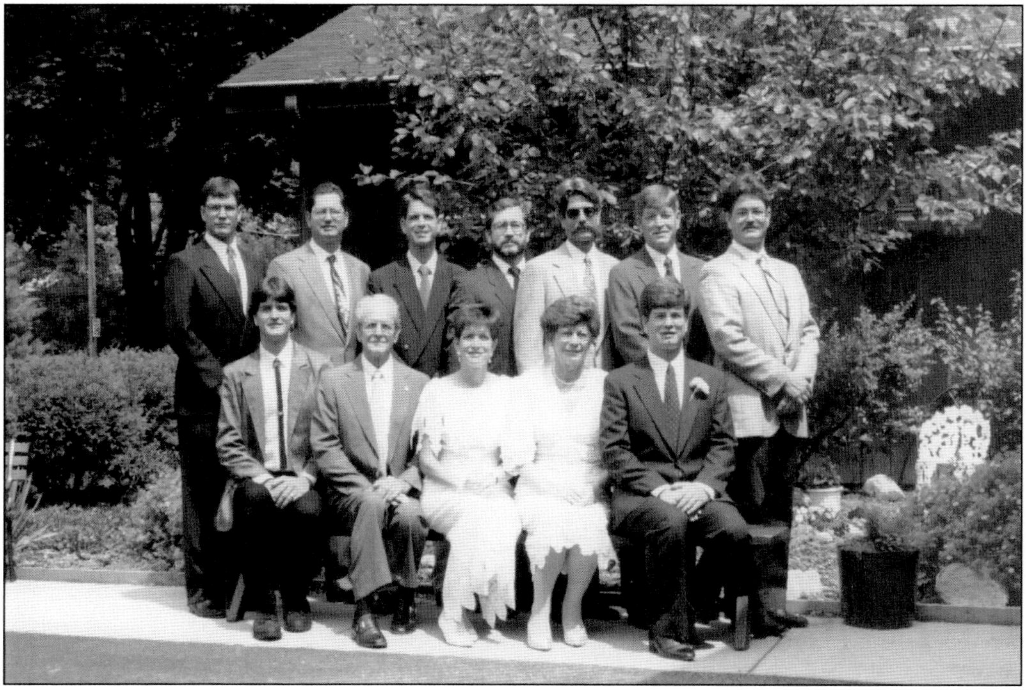

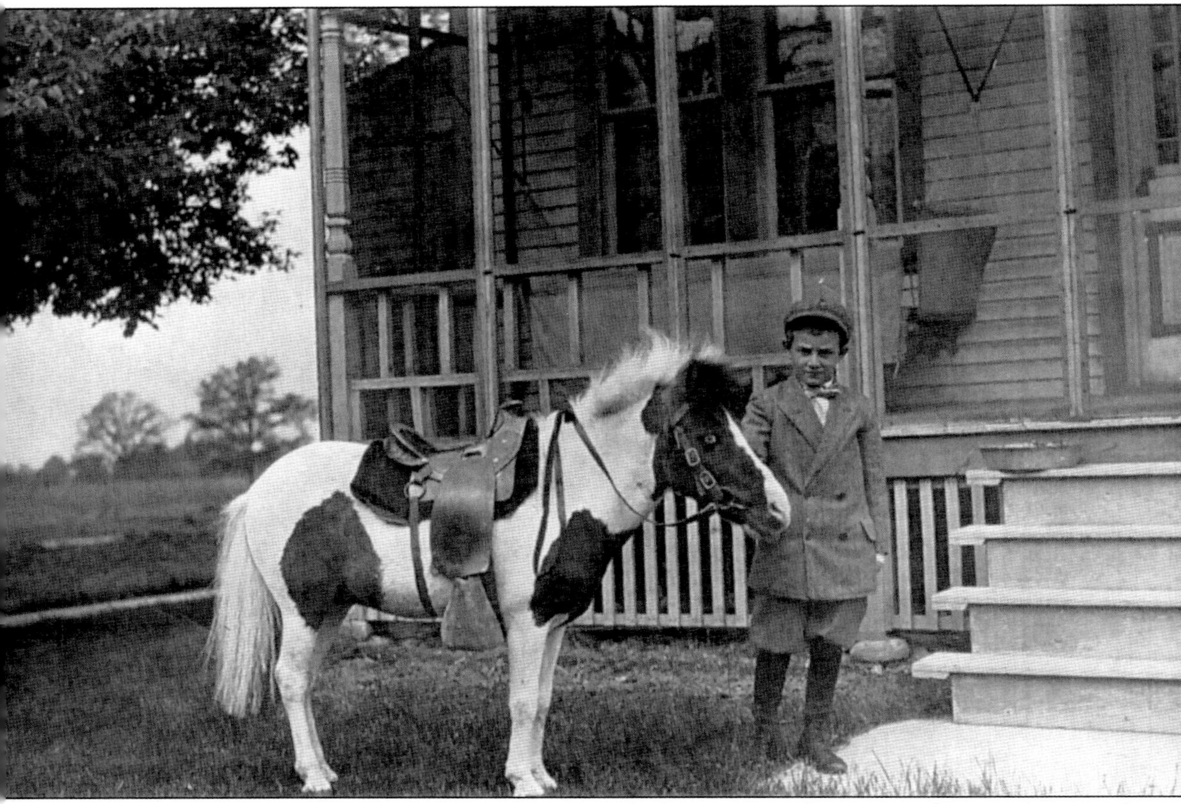

James F. Carr and his pony Pedro are photographed in 1911 on the corner of Bangs Street and Maple Avenue. James was the youngest child of Frank L. Carr and Lizzie Neville Carr. Frank bought the *Wauconda Star* in 1908 and renamed it the *Wauconda Leader*; he was the publisher for seven years. Little James also became a prominent Wauconda business leader. (Courtesy of Neville Carr.)

Pictured at right in 1930 are James F. Carr and his wife, Alice Kennedy Carr. Born February 8, 1904, James was a lifelong Wauconda resident and business leader who helped to shape the village in the 20th century. He established Carr's Sweet Shop on Main Street, was chief fundraiser in the purchase of Wauconda Fire Department's first fire truck in the 1930s, and developed the Hubbard Woods subdivision. He was the founder, builder, and, for many years, director of Wauconda National Bank. From 1935 to 1955 he served as village postmaster; in 1955, he established Carr's Insurance and Real Estate. He was also a member the Wauconda Historical Society and Lions Club. Alice was a member and president of the Wauconda Women's Club. The couple was active in the Federated Church. They had two children—Susan and Neville—four grandchildren, and several great-grandchildren. Alice died on September 26, 1993, at the age of 87. James died Christmas Day in 1999 at the age of 95. Pictured below is the couple looking dapper in 1988. (Both courtesy of Neville Carr.)

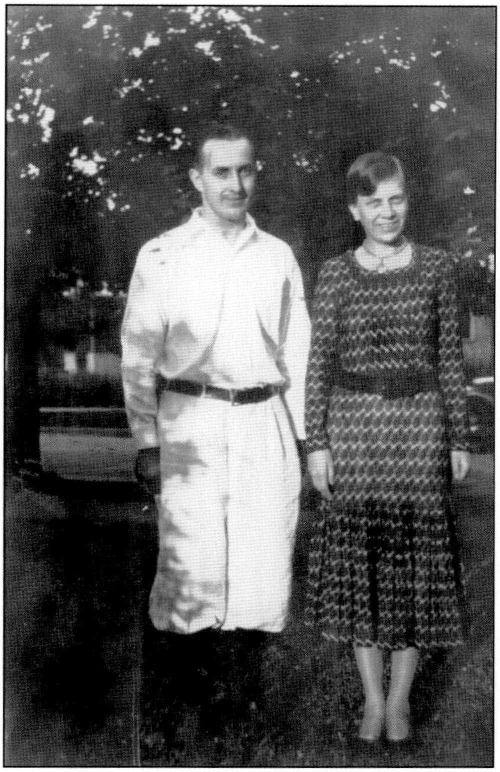

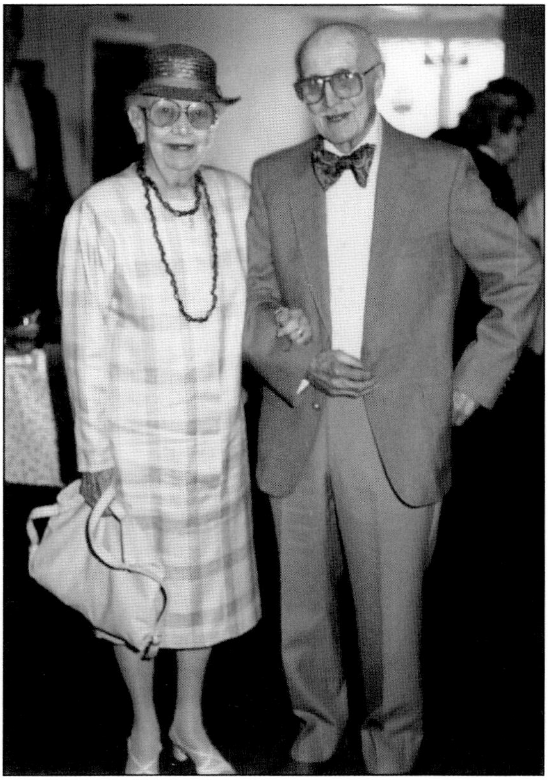

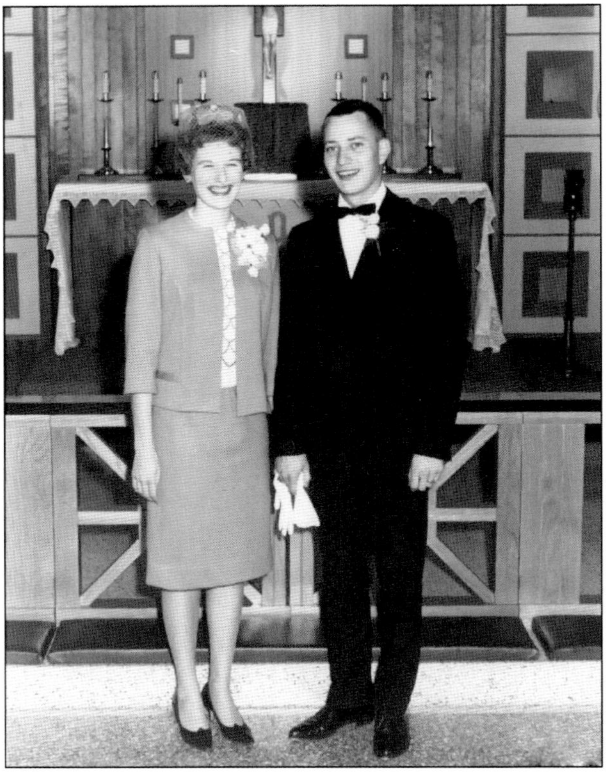

Neville Carr and Kathie Broughton Carr stand at the altar of Transfiguration Church on their wedding day on September 25, 1963. They met at Wauconda High School and have fond memories of growing up in the village in the 1950s. Their parents were local business and community leaders. The Carrs had their own real estate business and have three children and seven grandchildren. Neville has a wealth of knowledge and love of the village's history. (Courtesy of Neville Carr.)

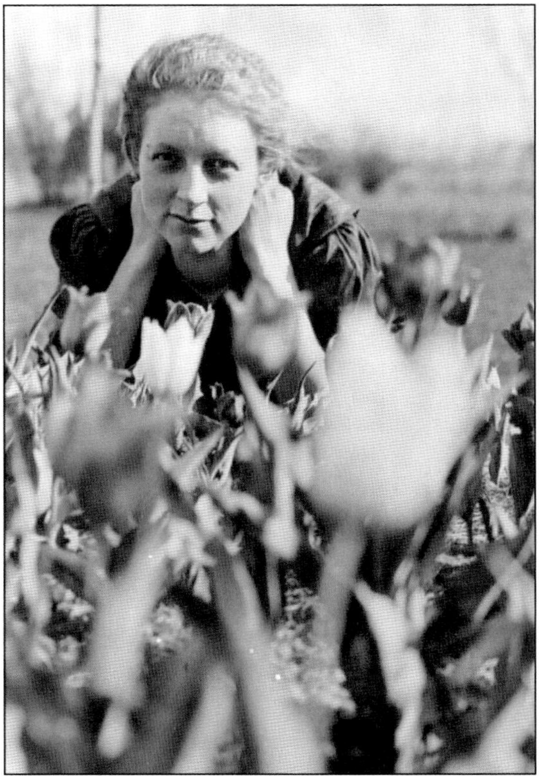

In this c. 1914 photograph is Grace Toynton Harris, who was known for her photography skills as a young woman. She was an active member of the Federated Church (for more see chapter eight). (Courtesy of Mary Ellen Thomas Perry.)

Della Kirwan was born in Wauconda on March 31, 1898. In 1900, her father, Arthur, opened Kirwan's Tavern on the corner of Main and Mill Streets. Upon his death in 1939, his son Harry took over the family business until his death in 1957. Della's roots go back to Peter Mills, her great-grandfather, who settled in the area in 1836. She died on June 9, 1993, at the age of 95. (Courtesy of Jacque Ross Peterson.)

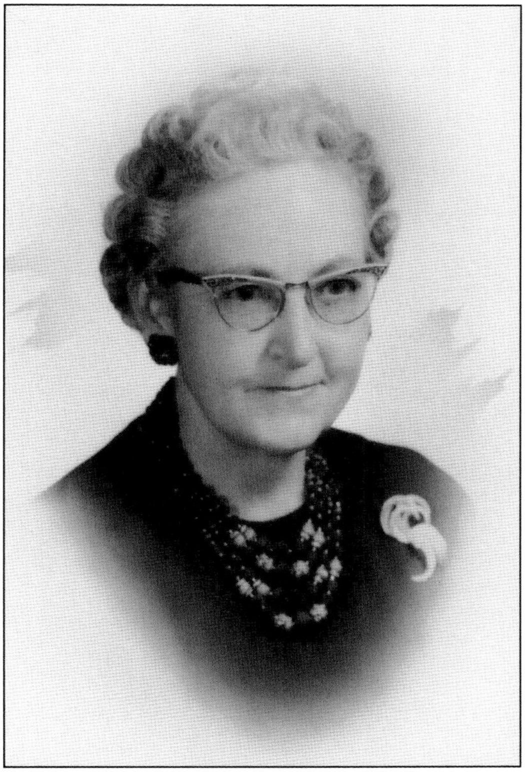

Celebrating Belle Taggert's birthday are, from left to right, Ruth Croydon, whose husband, Oliver, painted the altarpiece, "Christ in the Garden of Gethsemane" at the Federated Church; her niece Margaret Duers; an unidentified lady; Mr. and Mrs. Snetzinger; and an unidentified man. Belle and Margaret had a small boardinghouse in the Duers's home at 350 South Main Street. They charged adults $5 per week for room and board and $3 for children. The home was torn down and replaced by the Marlene Apartments. (Courtesy of Jacque Ross Peterson.)

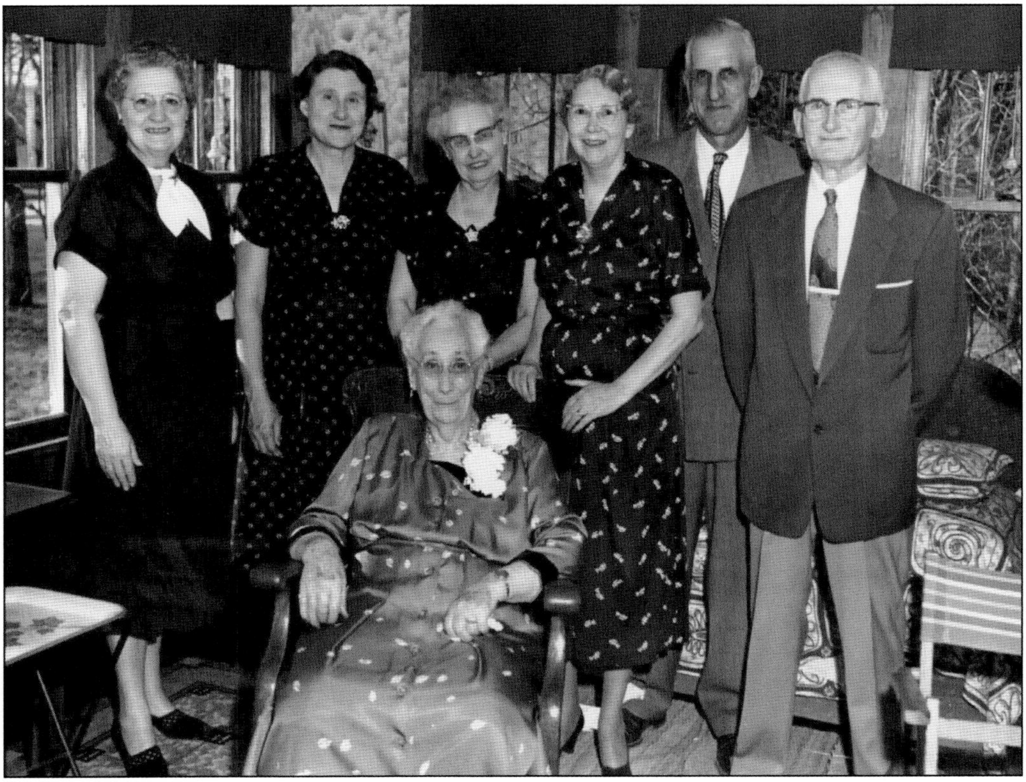

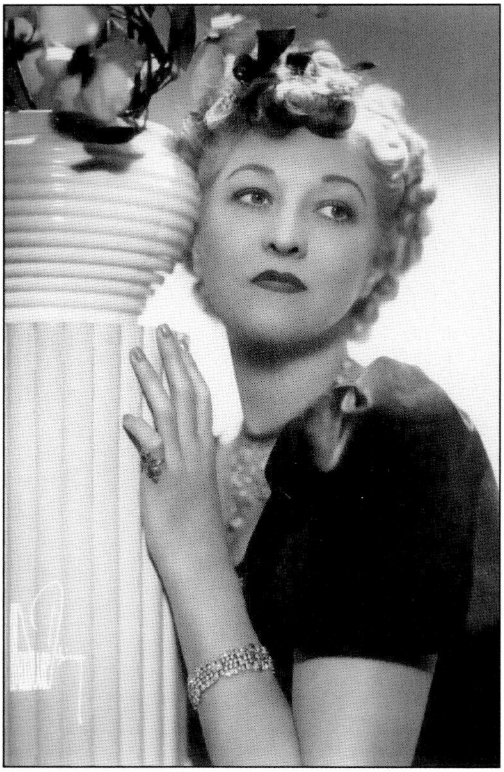

Florence Schubert Bliss (right) graduated from the American Conservatory of Music in Chicago at the age of 16. She had an illustrious career as a singer. She moved to Wauconda in 1940 as a widow with her two sons, Hugo and Ira (pictured below). In 1942, she married Harry Kirwan, who was running the family business, Kirwan's Tavern. She taught music at Wauconda High School and gave private lessons in her home. Ira (below, right) followed in his mother's musical footsteps, directing a band, The Playboys, for 30 years. He also played saxophone, clarinet, and violin. Ira graduated from the University of Illinois, Chicago, and became an architect. His work includes the Wauconda Fire Station, Kisselburg Funeral Home, and Wauconda Township Office Building. He was a building and zoning official for the village, served on the zoning board, and is still called upon as a consultant. In 1963, Ira took over Kirwan's. He has been a member and officer of the Lions Club and American Legion and past president of the chamber of commerce. Hugo (below, left) went into the insurance business. (Both courtesy of Ira Bliss.)

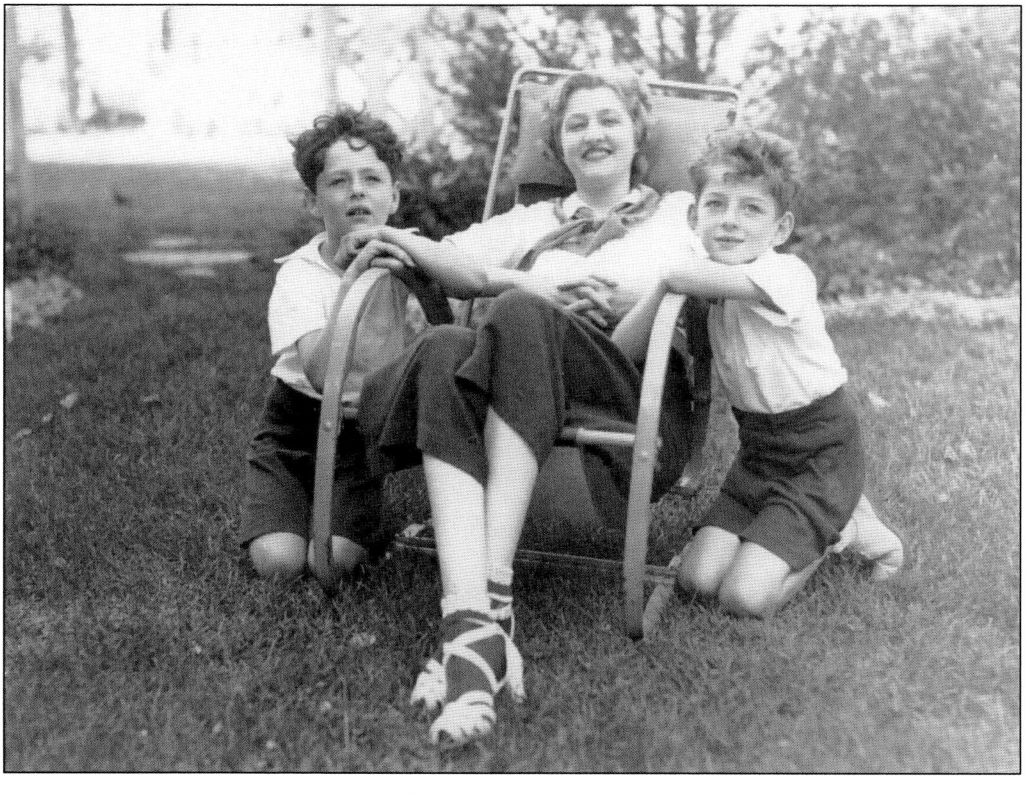

Three

Early Main Street and the Railroad

"No barns on Main Street" was Justus Bangs's edict to guard the natural beauty when establishing his settlement in 1850.

The first Main Street ran along the banks of the lake; however, Hampton Colgrove, who lived in the north part of town, petitioned to have the street relocated to where it is today. In its early days, the dirt street had to be sprayed with water to control the dust. As Wauconda's population and business community grew, Main Street had to be widened, although perhaps no one could foresee the bumper-to-bumper traffic the beaches of Bangs Lake would attract in the mid-20th century. On June 5, 1899, village officials threatened to condemn land belonging to the estate of Justus Bangs (who died in 1895) so the street could be widened. Mr. and Mrs. Clarence L. Pratt, Bangs's daughter and son-in-law, sold the property necessary for the village project.

Cement sidewalks began replacing wooden ones in 1906, silencing the click-clack sound of ladies' heels on the wood. Youngsters on roller-skates had a new play area, but in 1908 an ordinance declared sidewalks off limits to skates.

Electric streetlights were installed on December 3, 1885. In the 1920s, a large electric sign spelling out "Wauconda" spanned the width of the street. It was dismantled because upkeep was too expensive.

Main Street had been the lifeline for business and government throughout Wauconda's history. The calaboose (local jail) was on the street, as were the doctor's office, dry goods store, beach, bus station, and silent movie theater. The Pratt House, a stagecoach stop, became the Lakeside Inn hotel. The village hall, in its reincarnations, has always been on Main Street. The street is enjoying new activity generated by businesses such as Bliss Wine and Gifts, Bulldogs Grill, Frank's Karma Café, Honey Hill Coffee Co., and a reinvigorated Lindy's Landing.

For a short time, visitors arrived by train when Wauconda was a stop on the Palatine, Lake Zurich and Wauconda (PLZ&W) Railroad. Bangs jumped onboard the idea of a train as early as 1852. The first train pulled into the station on May 10, 1913, and was greeted by cheering crowds. Its run was short-lived; plagued by money and operational woes and competition from improving automobile transportation, the train ceased running on August 14, 1924.

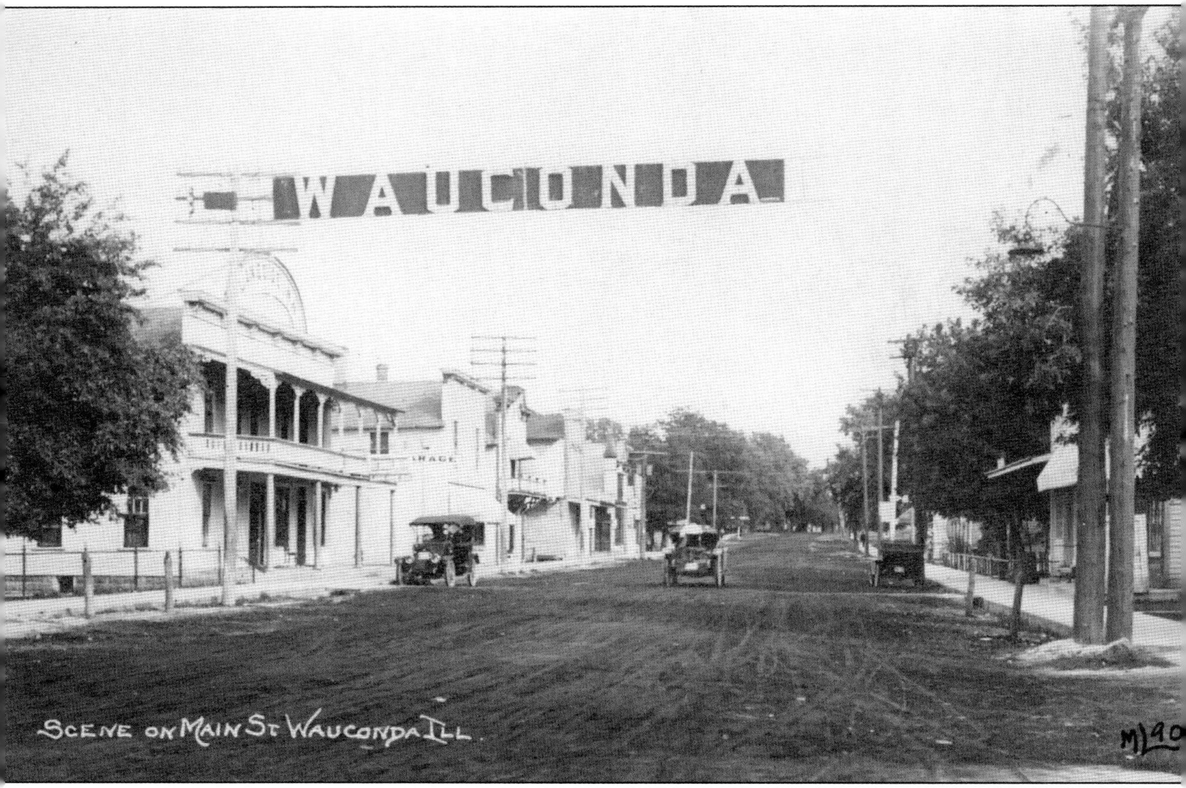

An electric sign stating "Wauconda" stretched across Main Street in the 1920s—there was no mistaking where a person was. The sign was taken down after upkeep and maintenance strained the village's budget. (Courtesy of Lake County Discovery Museum.)

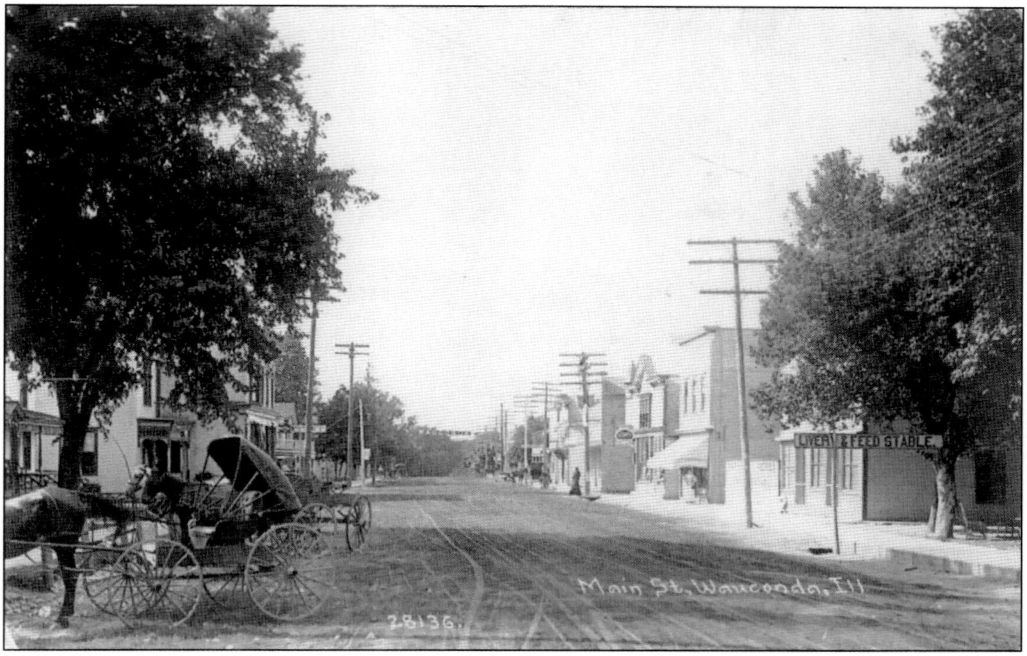

Here is another view of Main Street looking north. (Courtesy of Lake County Discovery Museum.)

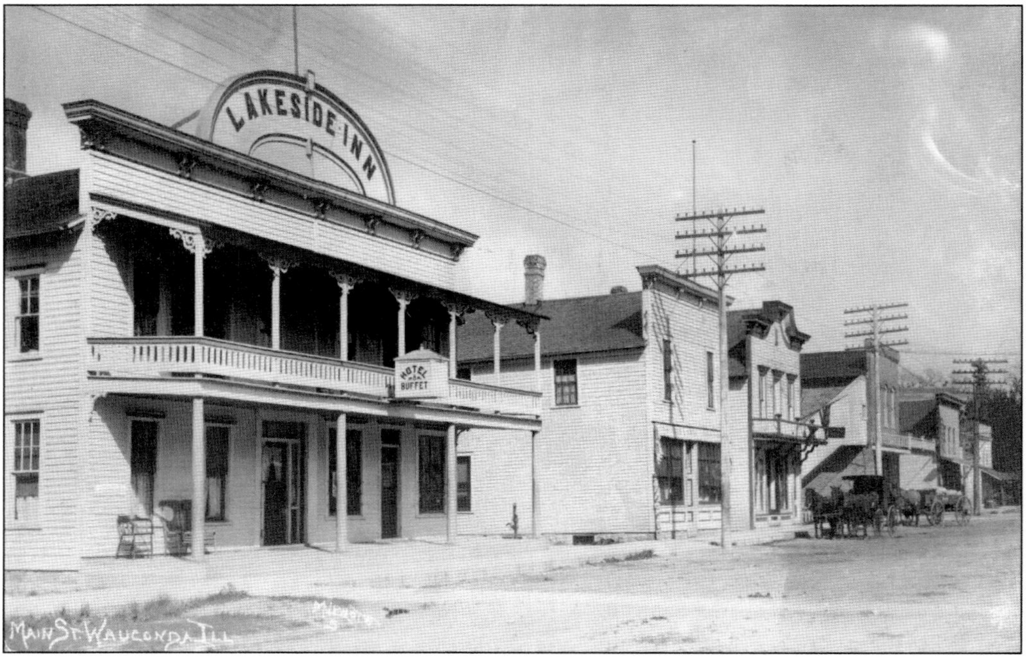

The Lakeside Inn, a prominent structure on Main Street, was one of Justus Bangs's original buildings. It was earlier the Pratt House, a stagecoach stop. (Courtesy of Lake County Discovery Museum.)

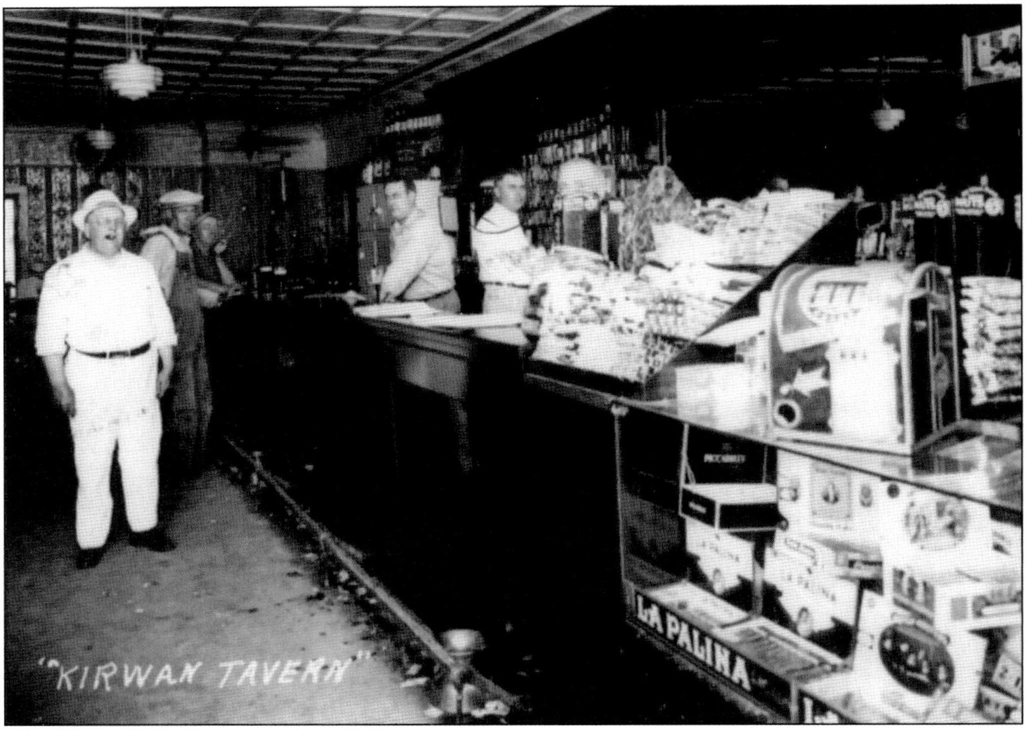

Kirwan's Tavern was a mainstay on Main Street for 88 years (for more see chapter four). (Courtesy of Ira Bliss.)

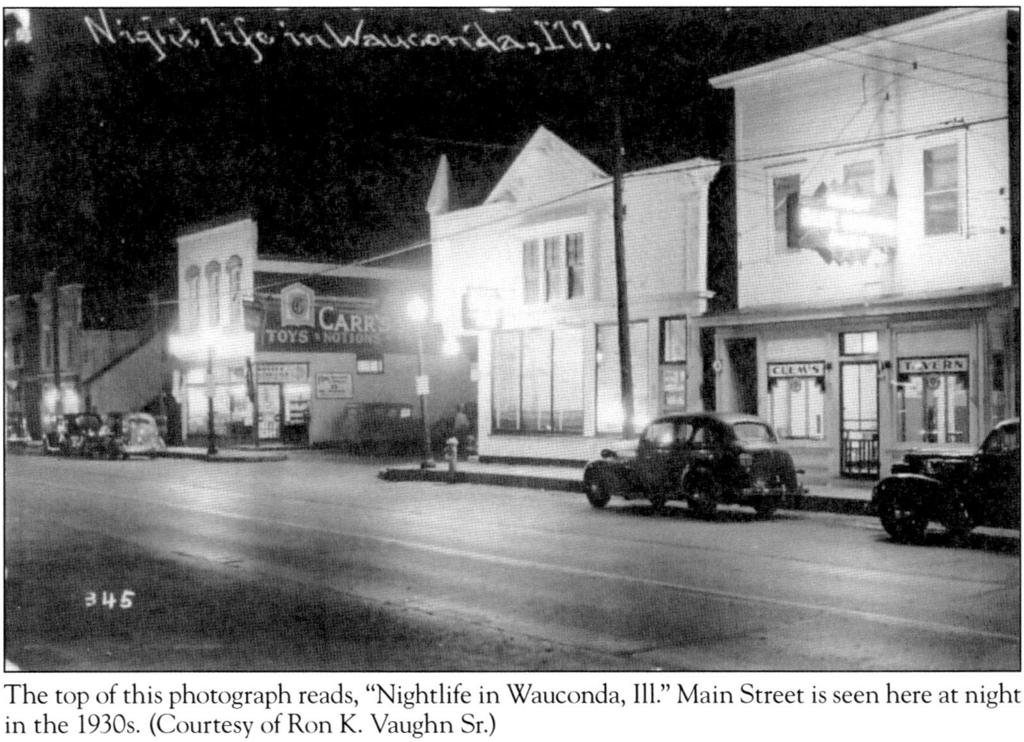

The top of this photograph reads, "Nightlife in Wauconda, Ill." Main Street is seen here at night in the 1930s. (Courtesy of Ron K. Vaughn Sr.)

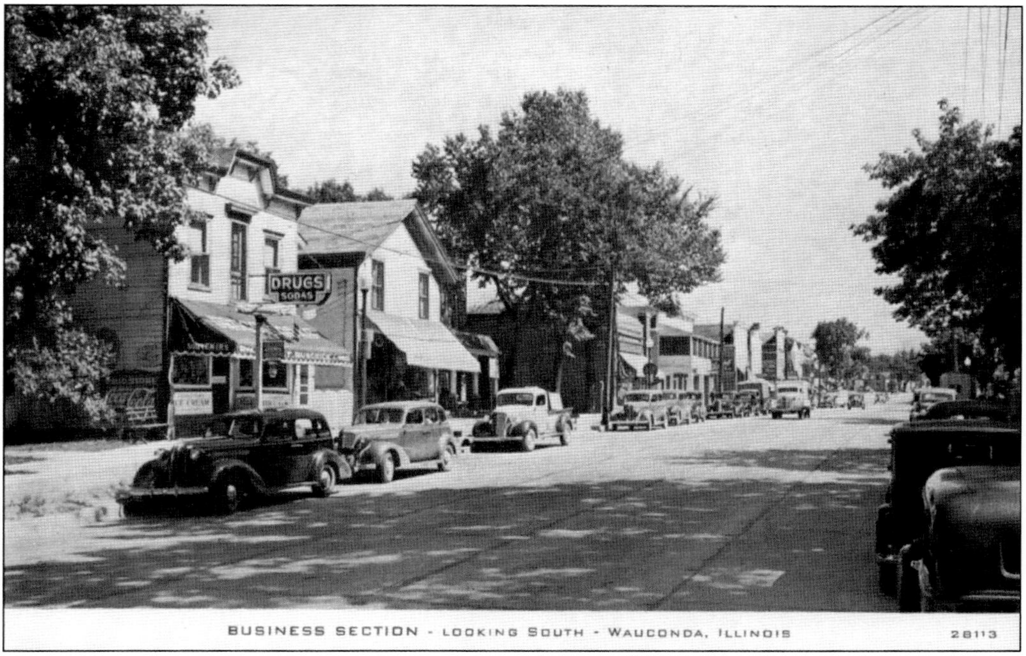

Main Street took on a different look around 1935 (above), as well as the 1960s (below). (Both courtesy of Kelly Lincoln.)

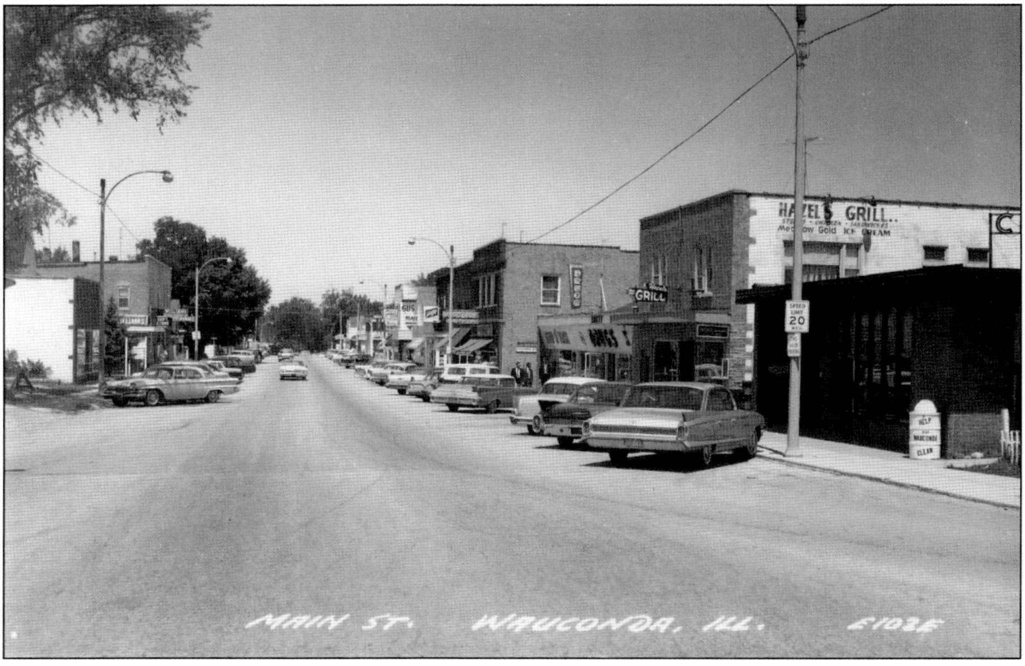

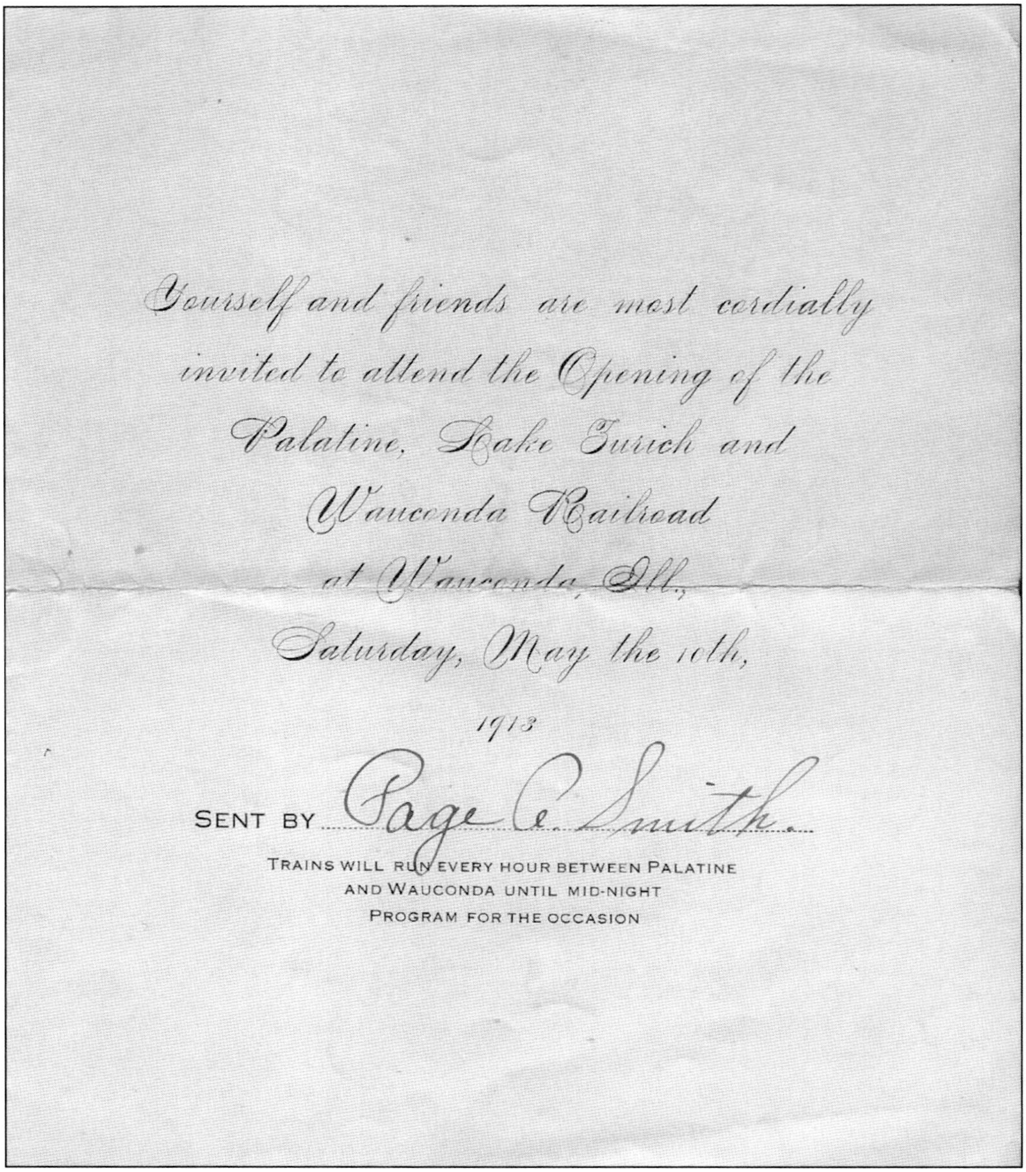
Yourself and friends are most cordially invited to attend the Opening of the Palatine, Lake Zurich and Wauconda Railroad at Wauconda, Ill., Saturday, May the 10th, 1913

SENT BY Page C. Smith

TRAINS WILL RUN EVERY HOUR BETWEEN PALATINE AND WAUCONDA UNTIL MID-NIGHT

PROGRAM FOR THE OCCASION

Wauconda's official Railroad Day was celebrated on Saturday, May 10, 1913, forty-four years to the day when a golden spike was hammered into the track completing the Transcontinental Railroad. The PLZ&W sent this engraved invitation to its stockholders for the celebration.

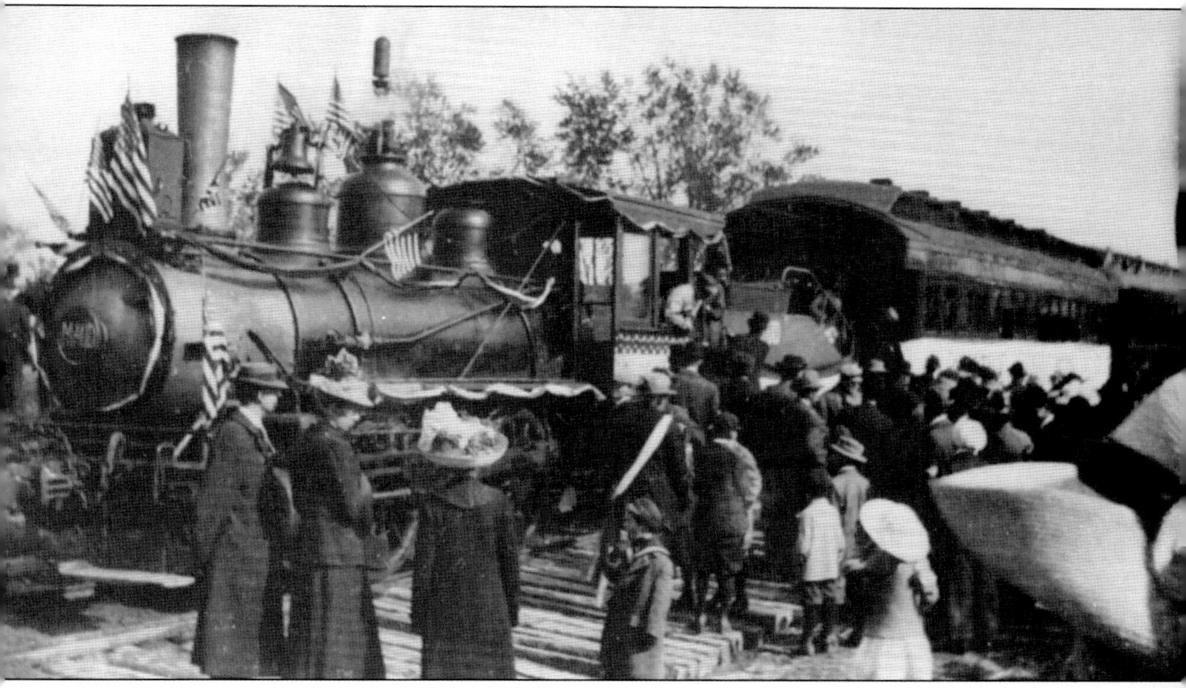

Engineer Jim Humphrey leans out of *Old Maud*'s cab to talk with people in the crowd during Railroad Day; however, the large crowd upset the timetable for the planned festivities. The train was to be greeted at Wauconda by a salute of dynamite by H.M. Davis, one of the town's early stage drivers, and the locomotive while ringing of fire, church, and school bells. The Wauconda version of the program called for the first train to arrive at 11:00 a.m. Because of the large crowds, Palatine sent an earlier train. When it arrived, the train contained ordinary passengers who were mistaken for the expected dignitaries and was greeted with a din. Several more trainloads of visitors arrived before the Palatine dignitaries closed their shops at 1:00 p.m. and boarded the train. The lead car carried a large banner, "Palatine Commercial Association." This train was pulled by *Molly*, and it carried the company officers. The Palatine military band played during the journey. When they reached Lake Zurich, they found the village deserted. They continued and stopped one mile south of Wauconda at the E.J. Cook farm, where Humphrey coupled *Old Maud* to the train in *Molly*'s place and finally pulled into town at 2:10 p.m. Chagrined Wauconda residents repeated the noisy reception, this time sans dynamite, with *Old Maud* adding its whistle to the celebration.

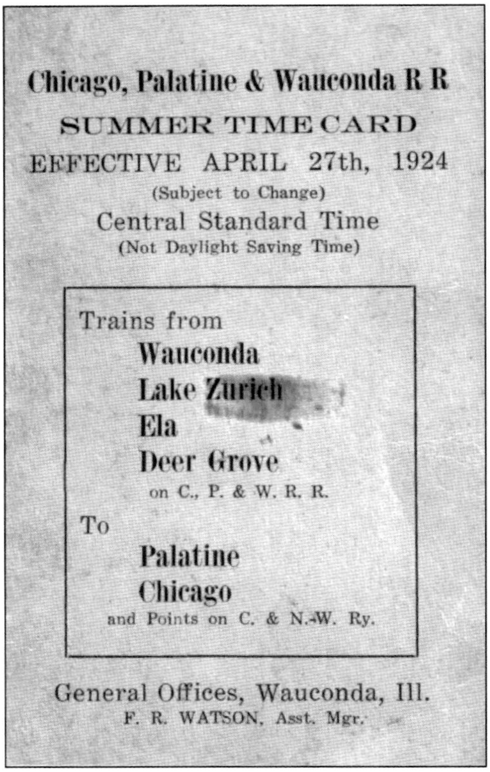
Chicago, Palatine & Wauconda R R
SUMMER TIME CARD
EFFECTIVE APRIL 27th, 1924
(Subject to Change)
Central Standard Time
(Not Daylight Saving Time)

Trains from
Wauconda
Lake Zurich
Ela
Deer Grove
on C., P. & W. R. R.
To
Palatine
Chicago
and Points on C. & N.-W. Ry.

General Offices, Wauconda, Ill.
F. R. WATSON, Asst. Mgr.

This is the last summer schedule for train service to Wauconda on the former PLZ&W, which assumed the name of Chicago, Palatine & Wauconda Railroad Co. on April 6, 1921. Throughout its short history, the railroad had financial and logistical troubles and in later years competition from the automobile and truck, new forms of motor transportation. Its death knell was the unseasonably cold July 4, 1924, holiday, the coldest since 1891. People failed to take the train to the local beaches. In response to a government order, the railroad quietly, and unofficially, suspended service without notice on August 14, 1924. No trace of the railroad exists today, although it has been said if one looks hard enough some remnants of track can be seen. The depot is now the home of the Wauconda Police Department.

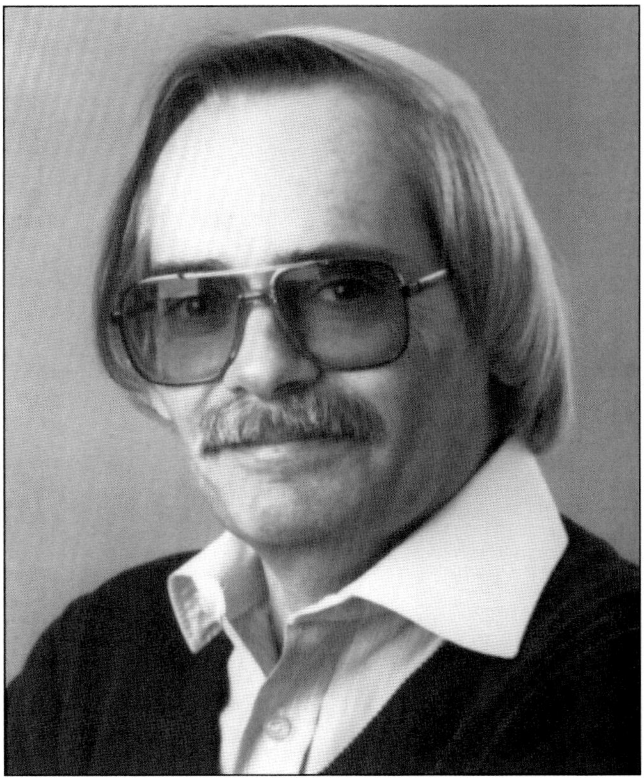

Richard Whitney wrote *Old Maud: The Story of the Palatine, Lake Zurich & Wauconda Railroad*, the definitive book about an interesting piece of Wauconda's history. Originally from Delaware, the noted rail fan and his wife, Sharon, lived in Wauconda for more than 20 years. From the time he saw the letters PLZ&W on an old power company's right-of-way map, he spent nearly 30 years absorbing as much information about the line as he could. His 1992 book is in the collection of the Wauconda Public Library.

Four

Businesses

Farmers, who needed clothing, household goods, and whatever food they did not grow, were the business community's first customers. They traded produce for merchandise, and to capture that trade Justus Bangs built the first general store in 1845, which operated for 30 years. Closely following him was Luther Kimball with a general store at Main and Mill Streets.

Most of the early businesses were wood-framed buildings connected by wooden sidewalks. Kimball's business burned down and was replaced by Robert Harrison's brick general store; the building's owners included C.L. Pratt, the Golding Brothers, the Prior brothers, Albert Pick (who later owned the Pick-Congress Hotel in Chicago), James F. Carr and Neville Carr, and Hollis Prior. The Bulldogs Grill is the current tenant.

In 1855, the Creamery, a cheese factory, was built. At the height of Wauconda's dairy-farming business, the area had three creameries. In 1858, the current Lakeside Inn was the Pratt House and had prominence as a stagecoach stop.

Reuben and Mary Hill opened a farm-equipment and hardware store in the early 1860s. Jim Spencer had a saw and gristmill where farmers could bring grain to be ground into flour on Mill Street near the lake. The village had a foundry and Grantham's Ice House.

In 1875, shoppers could buy stoves, farm goods, and guns at Brewster and Johnson's. F.R. Harrison owned Wauconda Drug Store. Henry Maiman was a tailor and sold gentlemen's fine furnishings.

By 1900, shops included Graham's Drug Store, Otto Welter Jewelers, Price Brother's General Merchandise, Gustav Fidler's Butcher Shop, Carl Erikson's Shoemaker, Maiman's Dry Goods, and Kirwan's Tavern. Later, a movie theater showed silent films and then became A & P Grocery. Dahm's Market later became Dickson's Market. Arthur Kirwan and Miles Fuller built a blacksmith shop.

In 1913, J. H. Patterson opened Wauconda's first lumberyard on the southwest corner of Main and Liberty Streets.

In 1948, Wauconda National Bank opened its doors—the first bank since 1931. William C. and Maxine Kisselburg brought their family funeral home to Wauconda in 1949.

In 1956, the emphasis shifted from Main Street to the Wauconda Shopping Center on Liberty Street. Business expansion continued west beyond the shopping center, with another shopping center whose biggest tenant is Jewel-Osco, and west toward Island Lake. McDonald's opened near Jewel in 1986. After a decades-long absence, Dairy Queen returned 2011.

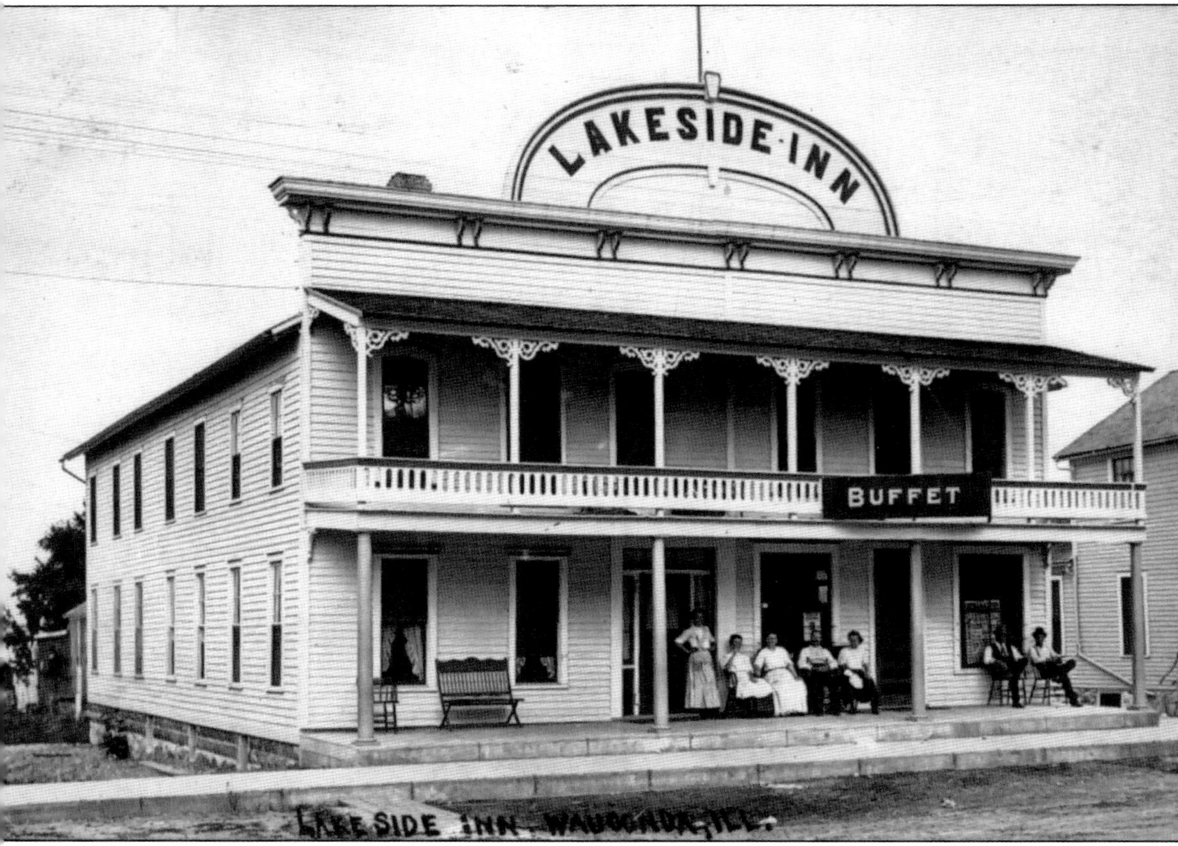

Justus Bangs hired Louis Todd to build the Lakeside Inn as a hotel in 1847. Seven years later, at Bangs's urging, John and Lydia Pratt moved from Stamford, Vermont, with 19 people. The Pratts took over the hotel and renamed it the Pratt House. It also was a stagecoach stop and a popular location for local elections. It was there that local residents voted to incorporate Wauconda as a village on August 18, 1877. In 1858, it reclaimed its original name. The Pratts' daughter and son-in-law, Mary Pratt Murphy and Dennis Murphy, purchased the hotel from the Pratts in the early 20th century. It had more owners and names before once again returning to its original name. The Lakeside Inn, with its original bar, served customers into 2011. This photograph is from around 1910. (Courtesy of the Lake County Discovery Museum.)

Loretta "Pat" Broughton is one of the Lakeside Inn waitresses in this 1930s photograph. (Courtesy of Jim Broughton.)

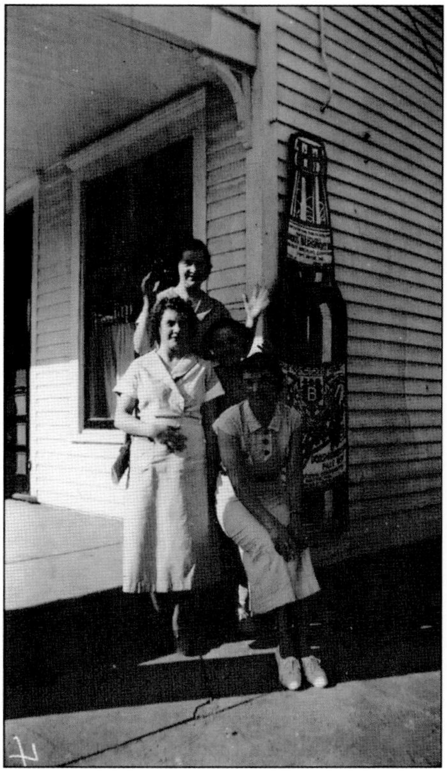

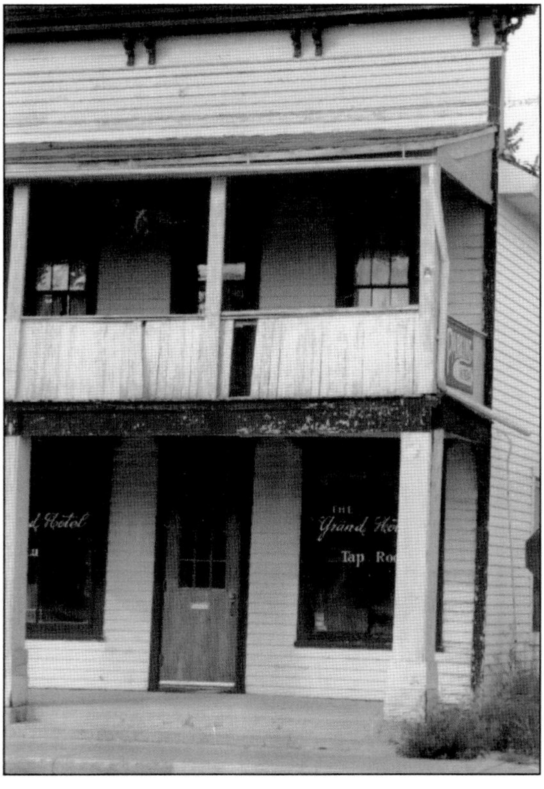

In the 1980s, the building fell into disuse, but it was rescued and revived under several ownerships and names. The words, "The Grand Hotel," can be seen on the windows. After being refurbished, it was called the Grand Hotel again, and later O'Traina's. Later, it bore the name Justus Bangs gave it. The Lakeside Inn is at 110 South Main Street. (Courtesy of Angela Catrambone.)

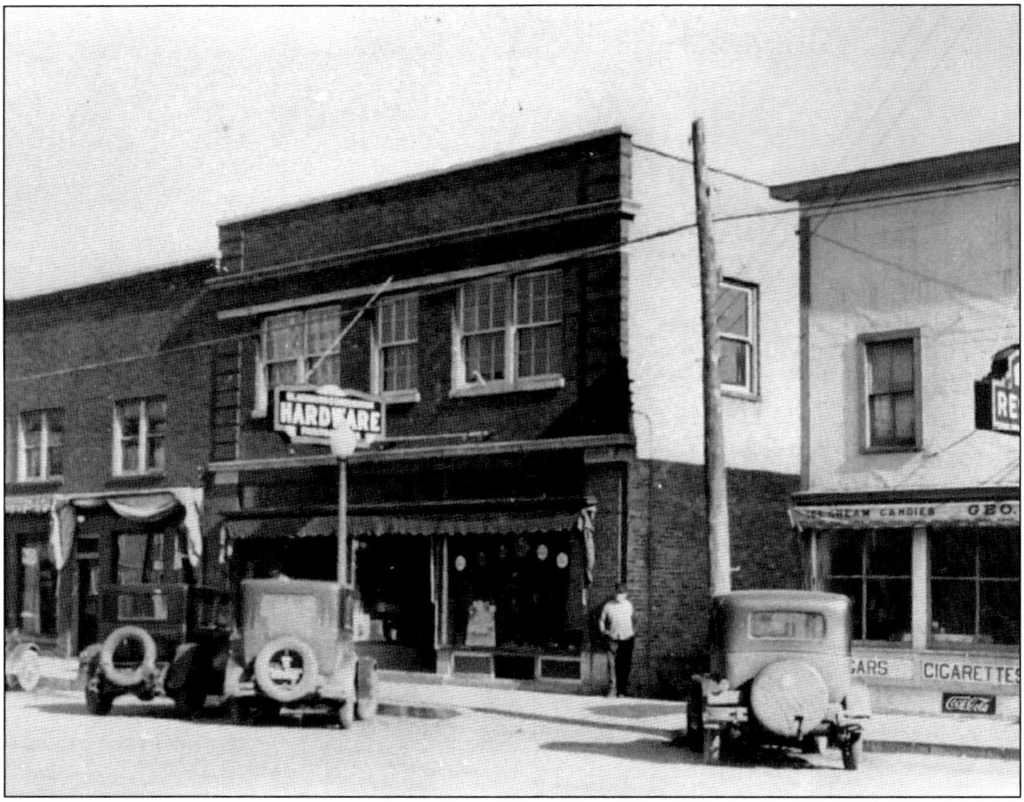

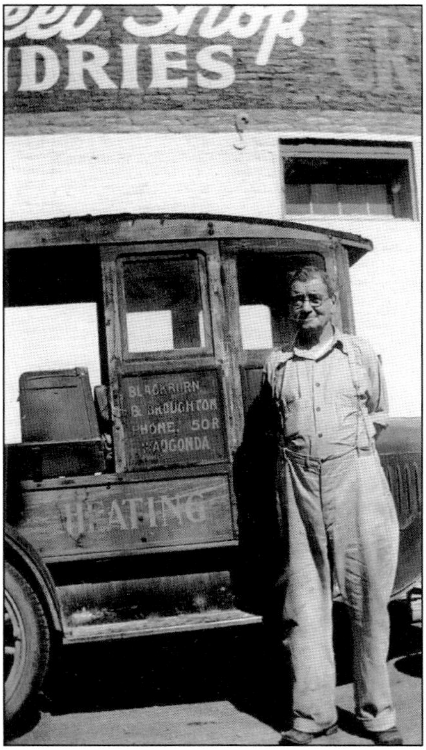

Cousins George Blackburn and George M. Broughton opened a hardware store in 1910 on Mill Street and moved it to Main Street in 1917, where it was known as Blackburn and Broughton Hardware Store. They sold hardware supplies, farm implements and supplies, and kitchen needs such as stoves. In 1927, the original frame building was replaced by a brick structure at the same location, 210 South Main Street, as shown above. Lyle Broughton, son of George M., worked there as a young man until his 1956 retirement. One year earlier, Glen Blackburn, George's son, bought out Lyle. Glen had worked at the store since 1936 and was the last family member to own and operate the hardware store after more than 70 years business. It has been an antique shop for about 30 years. At left is a photograph of George M. Broughton from the late 1920s. (Both courtesy of Jim Broughton.)

Lil Tidmarsh, seated on the left in the carriage, and an unidentified woman, travel in style in 1908 on Wauconda's Main Street. The ice cream parlor was on the east side of the street just north of where Lindy's Landing is today. It was owned and operated by Eloise Jenks and later became a drugstore/ soda fountain run by Charles Buschick and Charles Haller. (Courtesy of the Lake County Discovery Museum.)

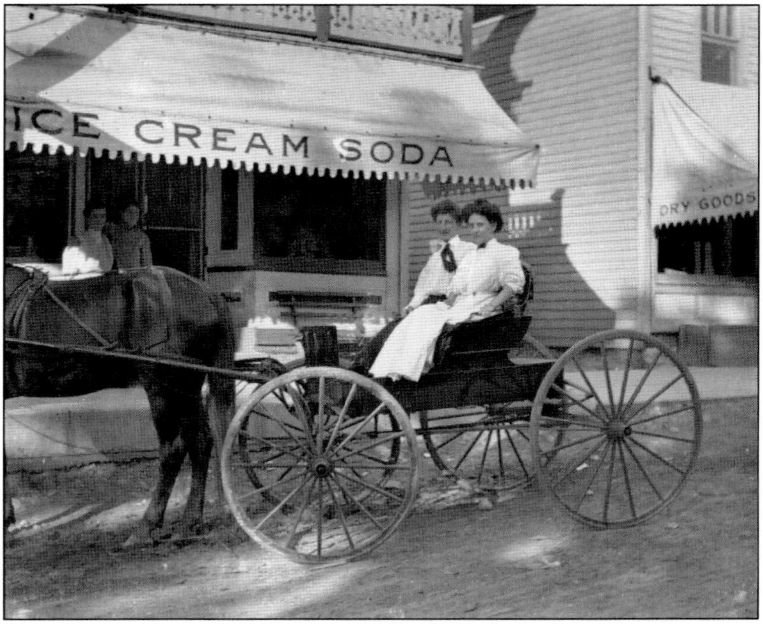

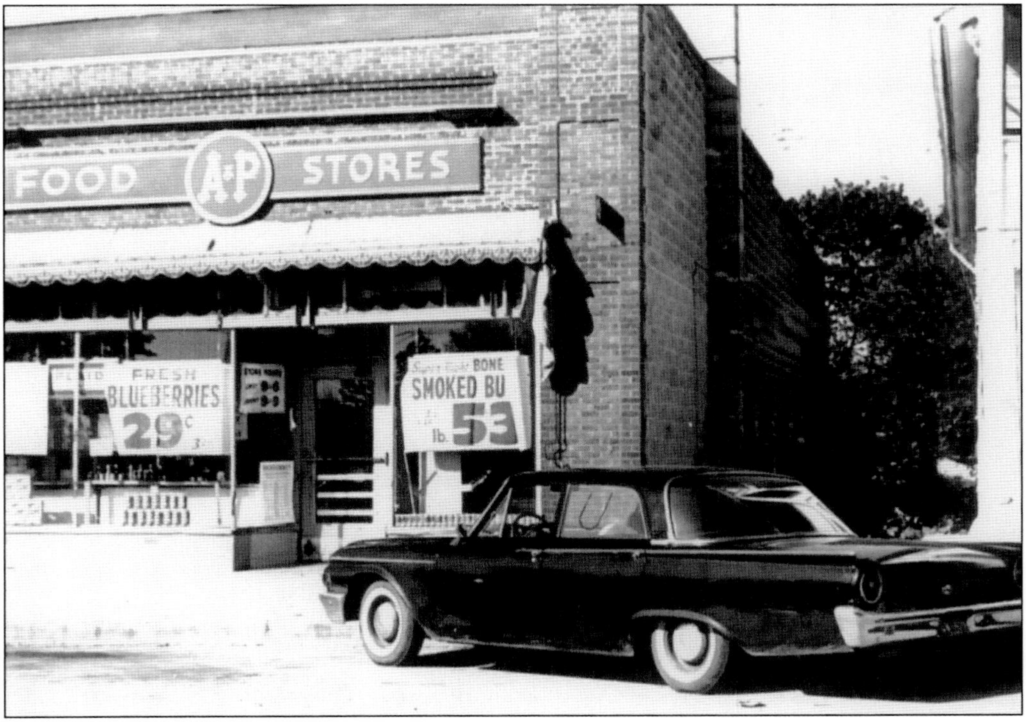

The aroma of A&P's famous Eight O'Clock coffee greeted shoppers as they entered 104 South Main Street until the mid-1960s. The store, part of the first national grocery chain, moved to Liberty Street to be closer to the Liberty Shopping Center, which had a National Tea, another national chain store. Before it was a grocery store, the building housed The Palace, a silent movie theater Dennis Murphy built in 1915. The storefront has had several lives, including a pool hall and carpet store, and has been Wauconda Paint & Glass since John and Betty Tarpinian opened the business in 1979. (Photograph taken by James Mantzoros.)

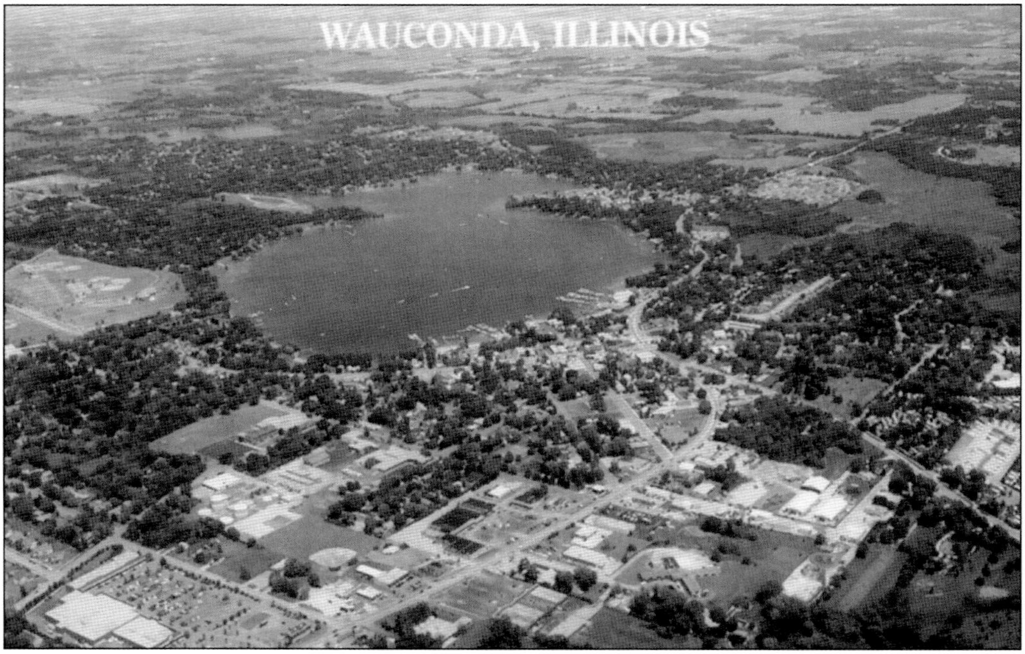

This 1970s postcard captures scenic Wauconda with the original downtown area (upper right) and newly developed shopping areas (lower left). Several boats are out on Bangs Lake in the background. (Courtesy of Kelly Lincoln.)

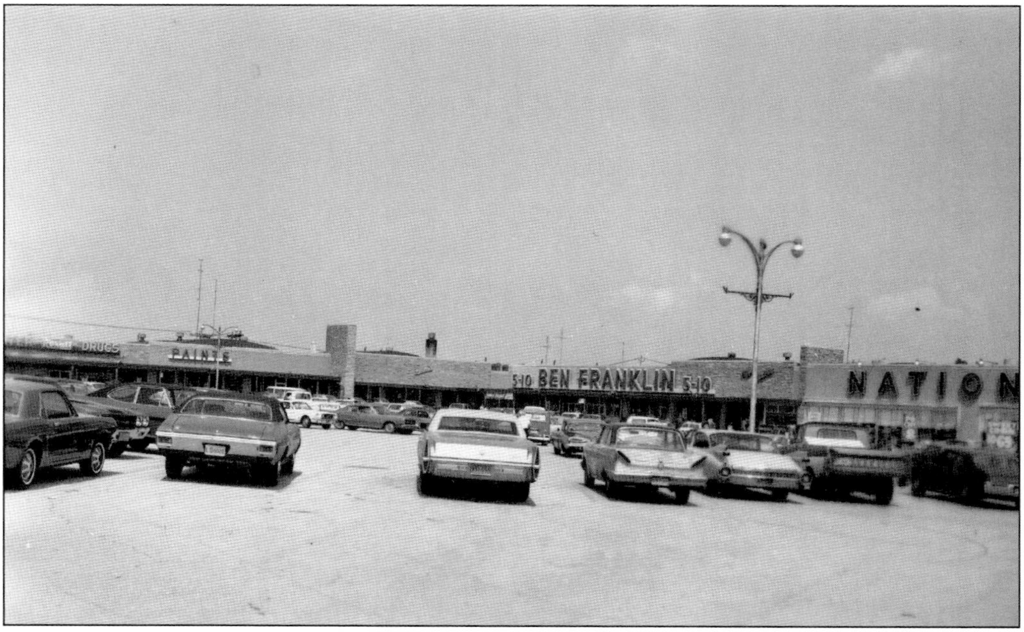

Wauconda's business district expanded from Main Street to a new shopping center on Liberty Street that boasted a number of stores, including National Tea, Ben Franklin's 5 and 10, and Painter's Rexall drug store. This photograph was taken around 1970. (Courtesy of Lake County Discovery Museum.)

Clyde Peck was born in 1910 in Wauconda. He moved to Chicago and married a city girl named Florence. Their daughter Barbara was born in 1941. The family moved to Wauconda in 1946 and owned the Greyhound bus depot and lunchroom for several years. Clyde was known for his chili and vegetable soup. Florence was the pie baker; while they owned the business, she baked more than 10,000 pies. (Courtesy of Barbara Peck Pawlak.)

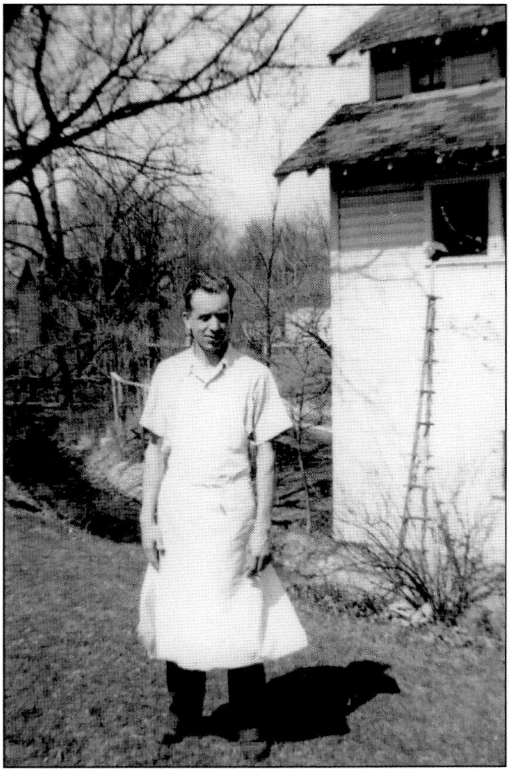

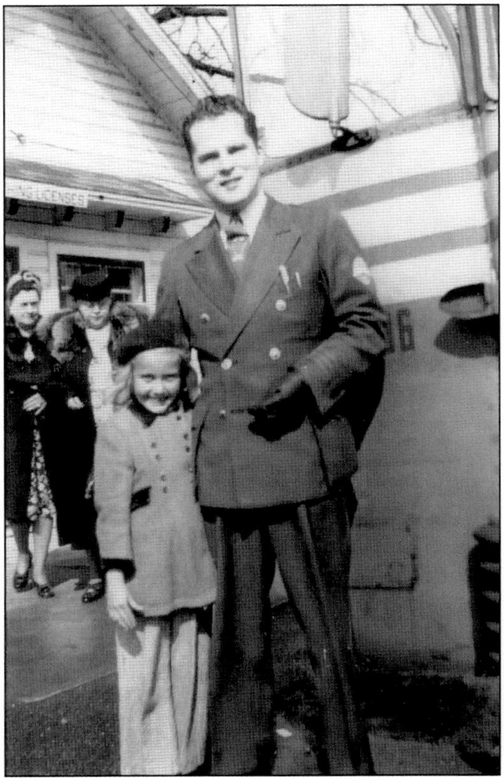

Barbara Peck Pawlak loved spending time at the depot and lunchroom with her parents. She is pictured here in the late 1940s with Jerry, her favorite Greyhound bus driver. (Courtesy of Barbara Peck Pawlak.)

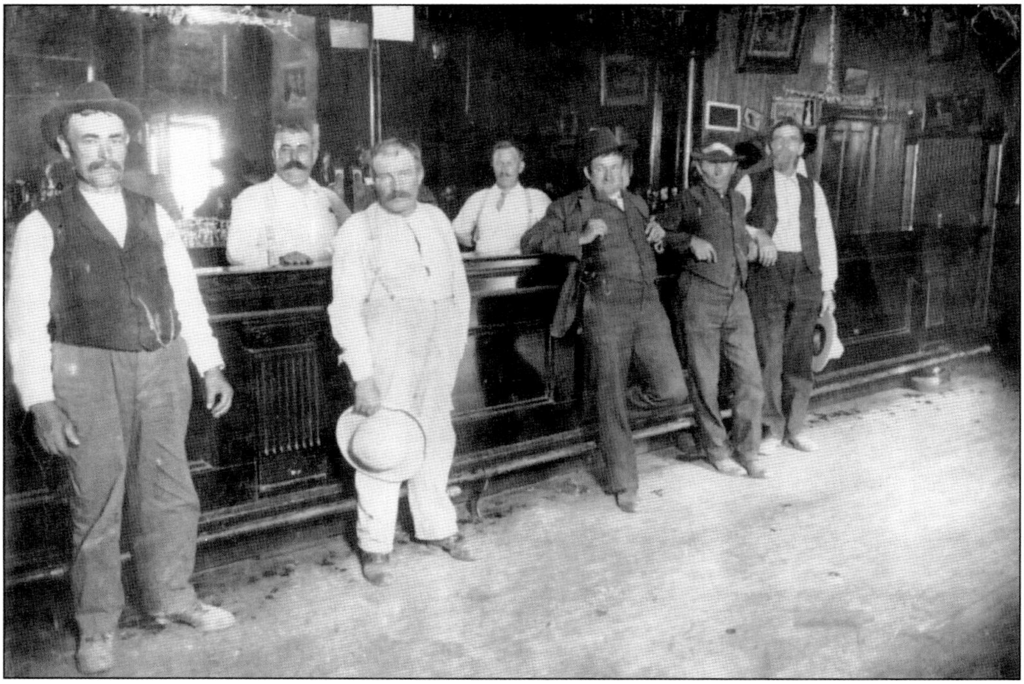

Some of Kirwan's earliest customers pose for this c. 1894 photograph. Arthur Kirwan bought a saloon at 108 East Mill Street from George Forbes in 1894. Six years later, Kirwan's moved to 202 South Main Street, where it operated until 1988. It survived an April 21, 1914, vote in which Wauconda residents were asked whether the village should become anti-saloon territory. Ten people voted yes, but an overwhelming 108 voted no. It did not matter much, as Prohibition became the law of the land from 1920 to 1933. During that time, Kirwan's became a place to gather and talk, more of a community center than a tavern, and a place to get results on election night. (Courtesy of Ira Bliss.)

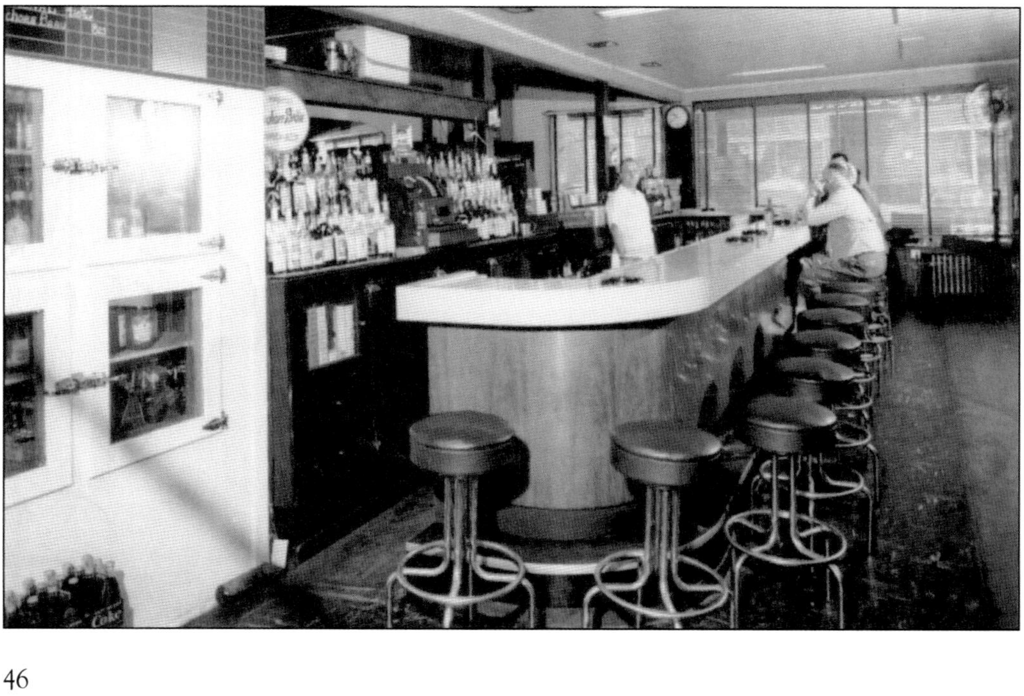

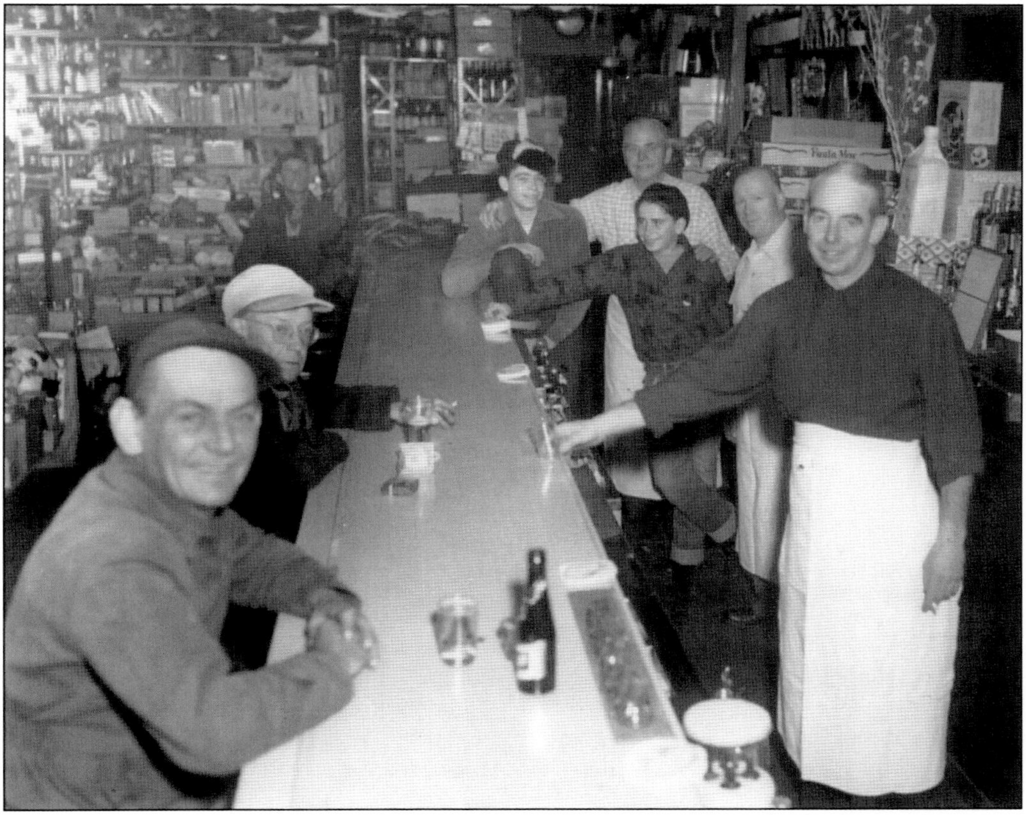

On the right is Willard Galusha, a longtime bartender at Kirwan's. In the background is Harry Kirwan, with his arms around Bill (left) and Doug Fuller (right). Their father was a bartender at the tavern, and an earlier generation of the Fuller and Kirwan families opened a blacksmith shop together in 1899. The men on the left are unidentified customers. Ira Bliss took over the family tavern business in 1963. His wife, Ann, cooked on Thursday nights and served soup, chicken, and sandwiches for free, creating a festive atmosphere. Kirwan's was known as a respectable business and a safe place for women to frequent. (Courtesy of Ira Bliss.)

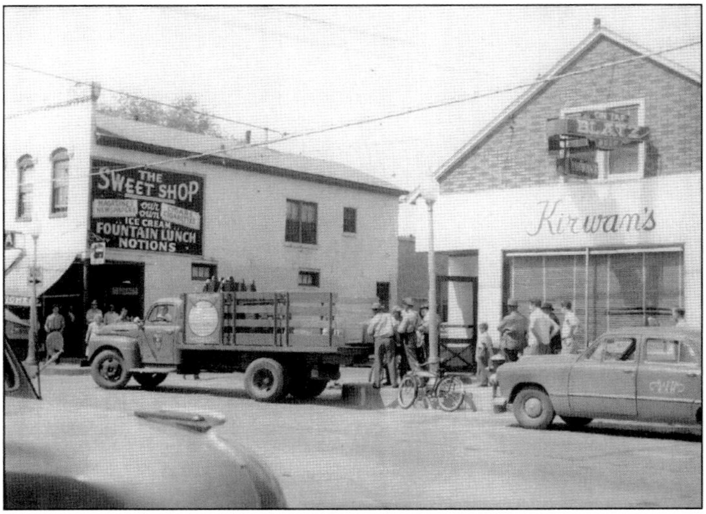

Businesses in Wauconda and throughout Lake Country had slot machines. They were fun, but not legal, so state inspectors often conducted raids to confiscate them. Here, slot machines taken from Kirwan's have been loaded onto a truck. Ira Bliss said that after a raid his father would call a supplier in Waukegan and more slot machines would be on their way. (Courtesy of Ira Bliss.)

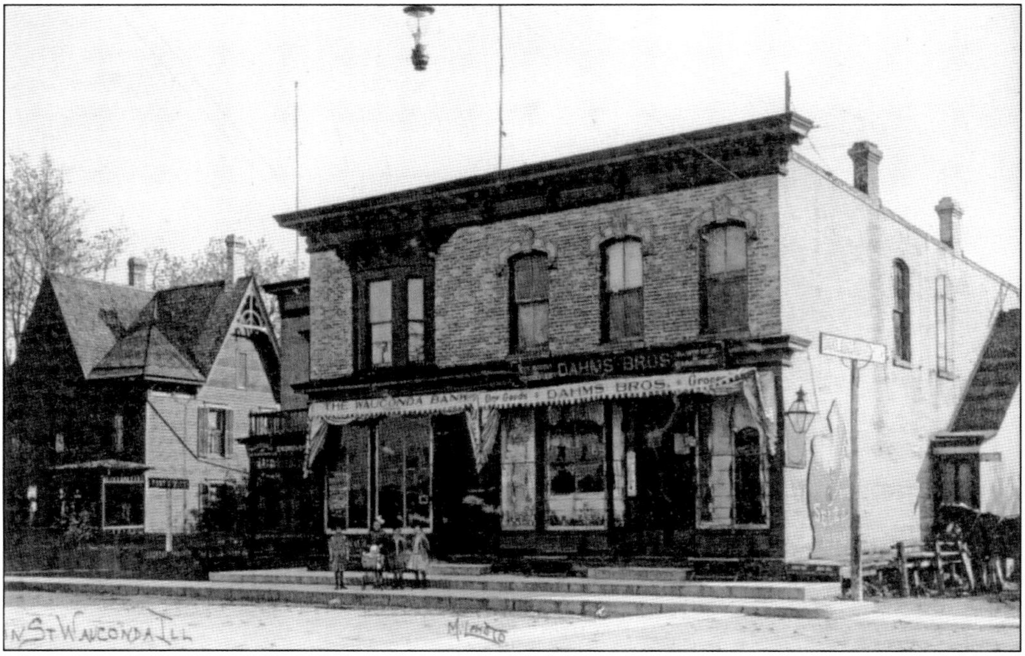

The Price Building, on the southwest corner of Main and Mill Streets, housed Wauconda's first bank (storefront on the left) and Dahm's Brothers dry goods and grocery store; the post office also was in the building. The bank opened in the late 1920s, and George Stroker served as president. The Depression took its toll on the bank, which closed at 3:00 p.m. October 15, 1931, and never reopened. (Courtesy of Kelly Lincoln.)

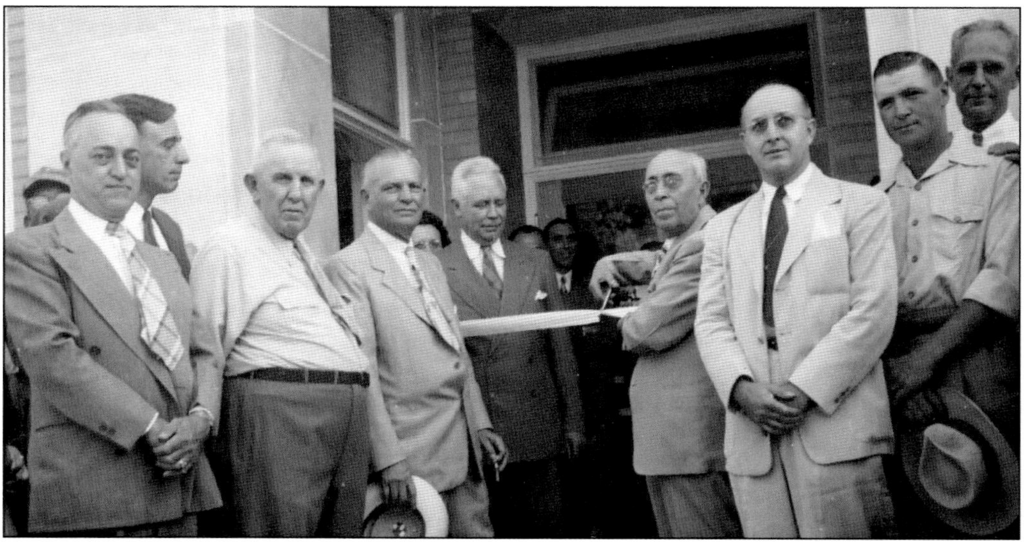

On September 30, 1947, local businessmen submitted a petition to federal authorities requesting approval to organize and operate a nationally chartered bank. Less than one year later, the bank became a reality. This photograph shows the July 1948 celebration of the opening of the Wauconda National Bank. Pictured from left to right are Frank M. McCartney; Roland Lueder; Homer Cook; Harvey Owens, president; Walter Payne, cashier; Dr. John A. Ross, mayor, cutting the ribbon; James F. Carr; Ronald Paddock; and Frank Dickson. (Courtesy of Jacque Ross Peterson.)

Homer "Abe" Lincoln (right) and his son Harmon "George" Lincoln (below) gave countless haircuts during their 70 years at 208 South Main Street. Abe came to Illinois to be educated at Illinois Teacher College. He taught in Tower Lakes in 1925. He changed careers and learned the barber trade before bringing his wife, Ethel, and nine children to Wauconda. The Lincoln Barber Shop building, erected in 1928 by Otis "Ode" Potter, became a popular place where men could freshen up, shoot the breeze and a game of pool, or even surreptitiously gamble with the back-room bookie—with nary an illegal incident but several myths. Ethel died in 1935, leaving Abe to raise the children. George took over the barbershop in 1941, served in World War II, and returned to marry Margot and start a family. Abe died in 1951 after seeing 32 descendents born and many local relations created through family marriages. A family legacy is the Lincoln Community Room donated to the Wauconda Area Public Library. (Both courtesy of the Lincoln family.)

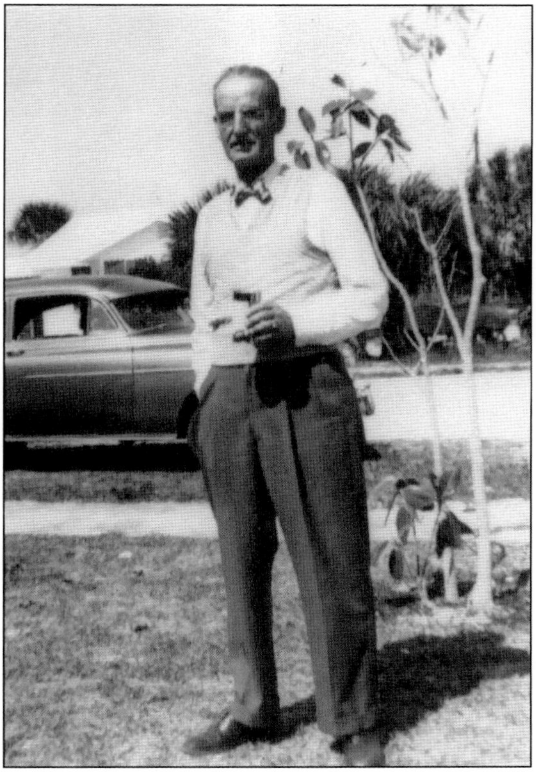

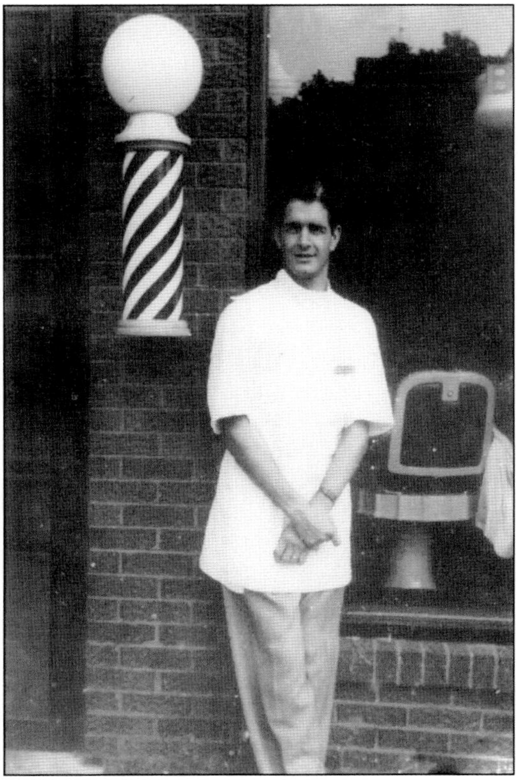

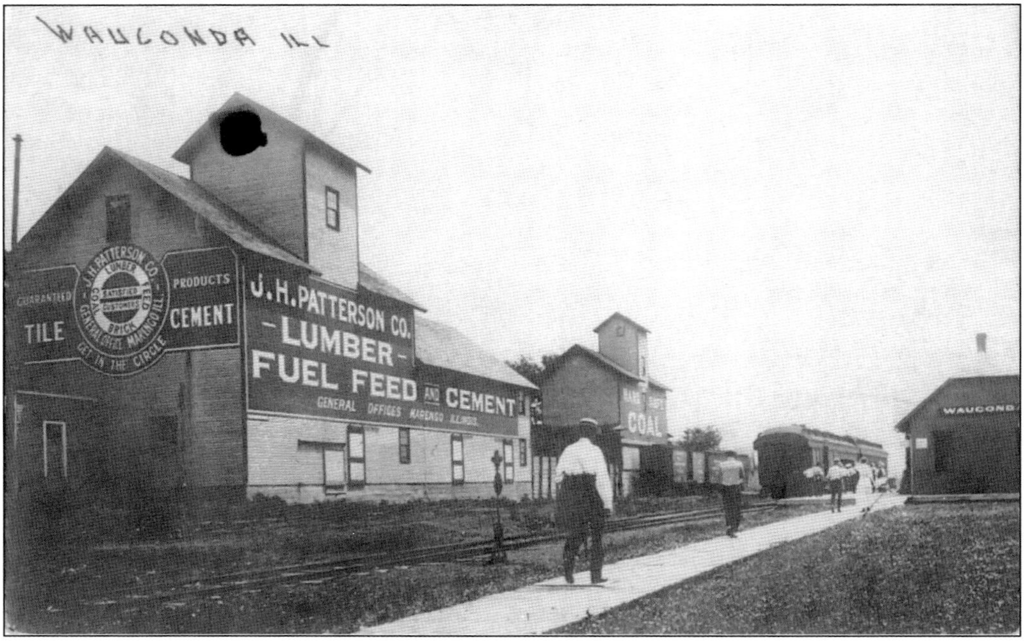

In 1913, J.H. Patterson of Marengo, Illinois, purchased the Gilbert and Kirwan properties, which adjoined the railroad right-of-way in Wauconda, and announced he would begin construction of a coal, lumber, and feed yard. In 1932, George Perkins bought the business and renamed it Perkins Lumber Yard. Much of the lumber and materials used during Wauconda's 1950s housing boom were purchased there. The business was later known as Wauconda Lumber. It eventually closed, and the building was torn down in 1987. (Above, courtesy of Kelly Lincoln; below, Angela Catrambone.)

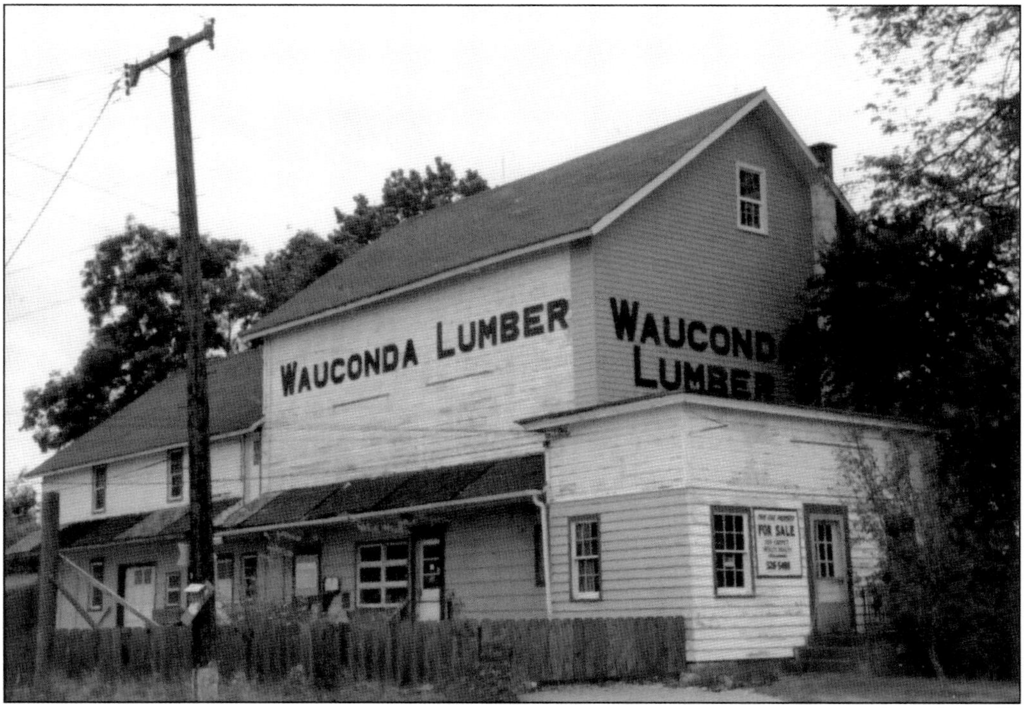

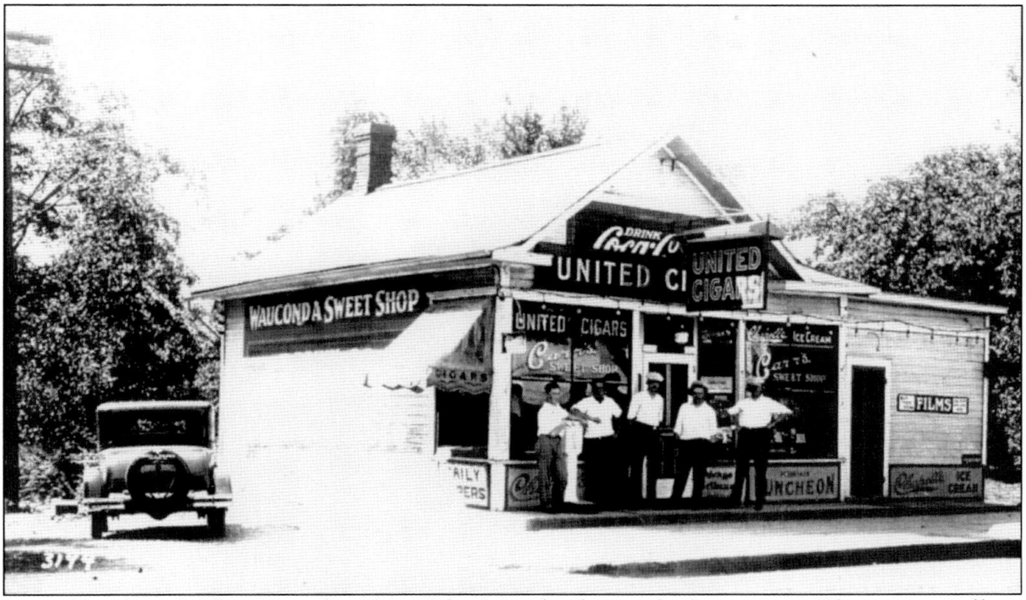

James Carr bought this sweet shop from John Murphy during the Depression. The current village hall is on the site now. Carr moved the business down the street to the corner of Main and Mill Streets, where he operated a lunchroom and ice cream parlor and sold newspapers and magazines. The building originally housed one of the village's early grocery stores owned and operated by the Harrison family. Ray Prior followed the Harrisons, and he sold the operation to Carr. Doug Crooks bought the business in the 1940s, and it continued as Wauconda Sweet Shop. He later opened Crooks Restaurant on Main and Liberty Streets. (Courtesy of Neville Carr.)

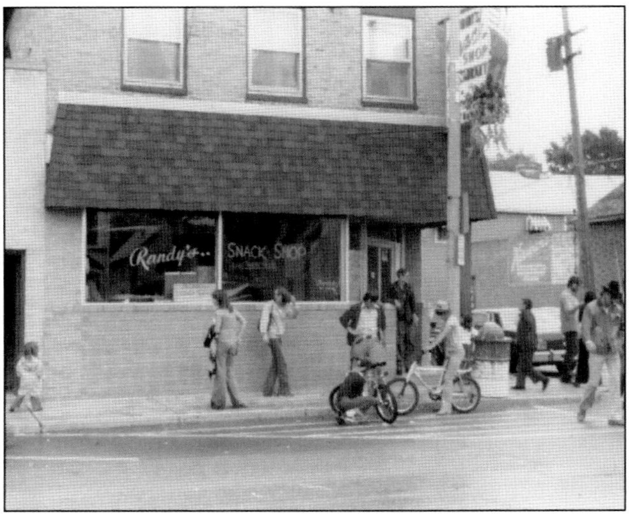

Randy Pfursich continued the tradition on the corner of Main and Mills Streets with Randy's Snack Shop, a favorite hangout for all ages in the 1950s into the 1970s. A person could get lunch or a milk shake or the latest comic book there. Inside the entrance were racks with magazines and comic books, a scale, and gumball machine. After different ownerships and names, the spot is now Bulldogs Grill, which still has the soda fountain counter. Pfursich's wife, Ellen, had a beauty shop in town for many years. (Courtesy of Doris Aimers-Voss.)

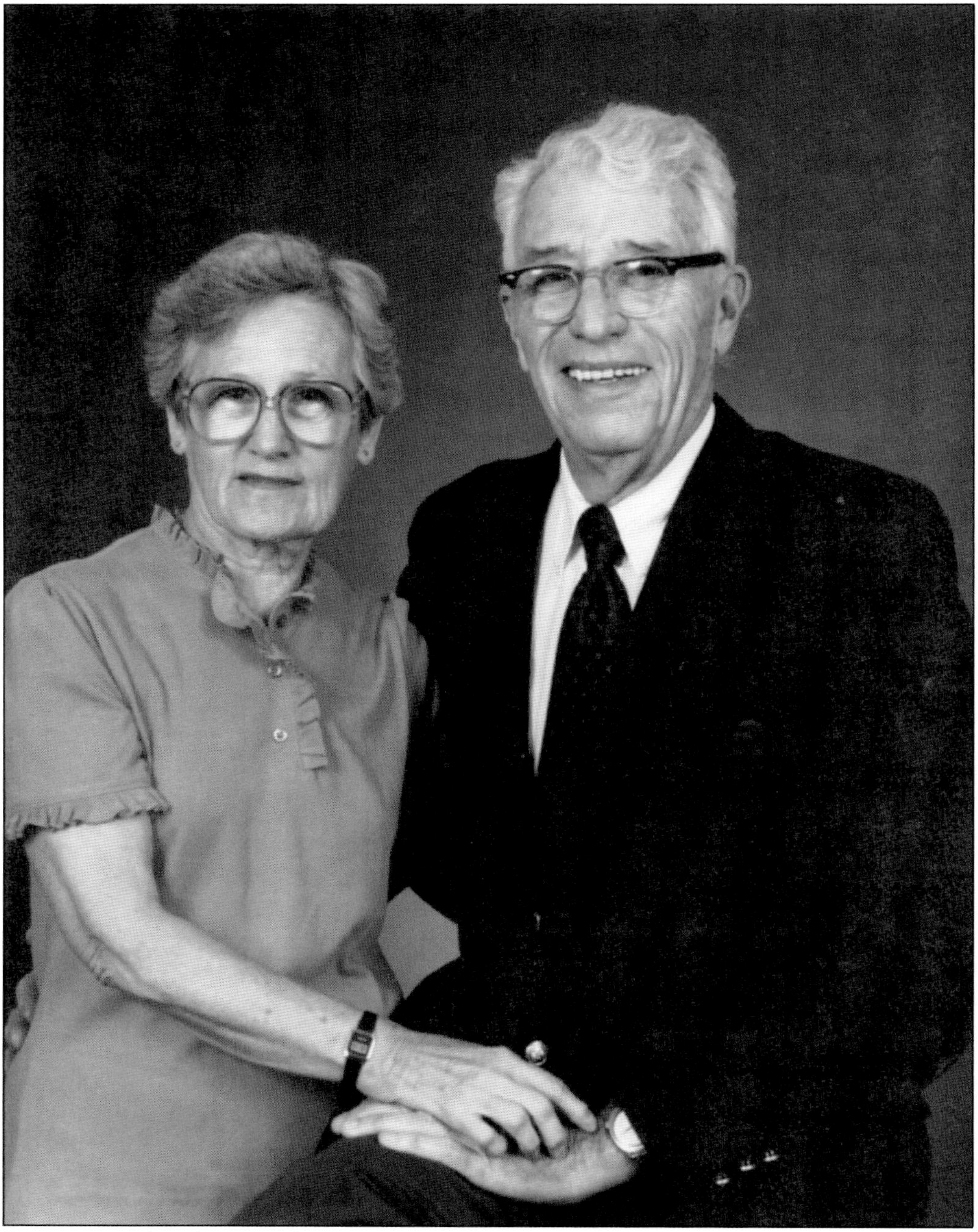

Rosemarie and Walter Broughton moved their family from Oak Park to Wauconda in 1949. They purchased Peterson's Department Store on Main Street. In the 1950s, they opened Peterson's Shoe Store in the then-new shopping center. Broughton was one of the founders of the Wauconda Park District and the chamber of commerce. He was a member and later president of the Lions Club. They had three children: Kathie, Walter, and John. (Courtesy of Kathie Broughton Carr.)

Ethel Newberg opened the successful Ethel's Apparel in 1953 on Main Street. Her paternal great-grandparents, Jonathan and Agnes Richardson, came to Wauconda Township from England in 1849. Her mother's family, the Dowells, had a farm in Volo. Ethel had three sisters and one brother. She was 11 when her father died and went to live with Dr. Ross's family. In 1941, she married Robert (Bob) Newberg. Active in the American Legion Auxiliary, she was a past president. (Courtesy of Jacque Ross Peterson.)

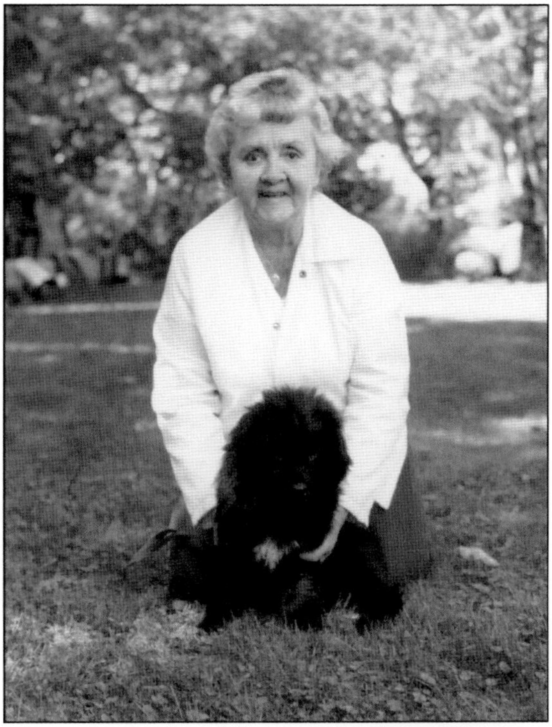

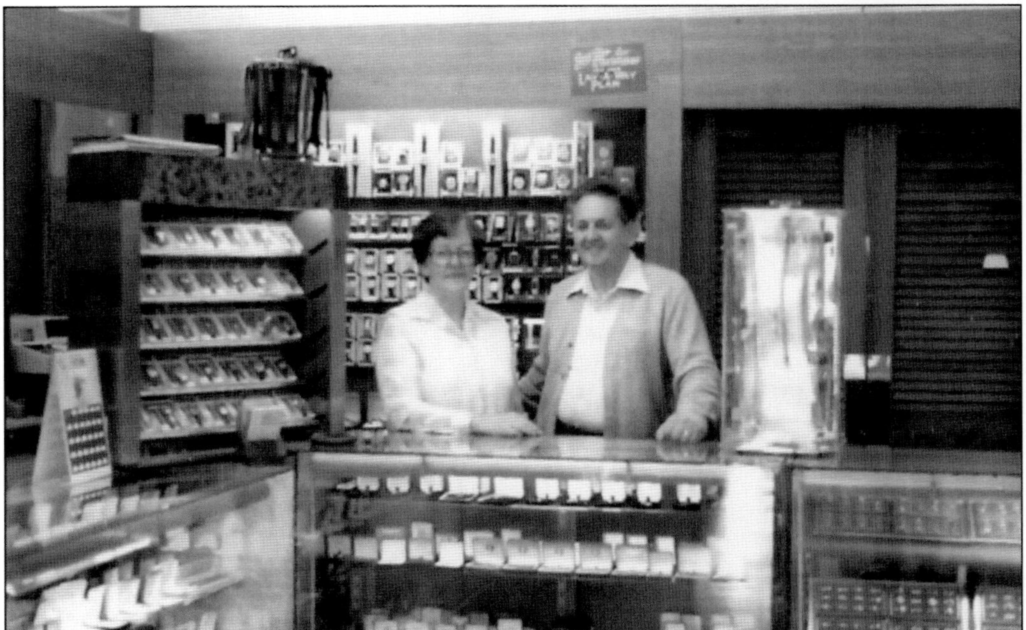

Ethel and Leonard Manyluk are behind the counter of the business he founded in 1954. Leonard's Jewelry opened on Main Street, when Clarence Gerber moved his jewelry shop to the Liberty Street shopping center. At first, to make ends meet, Manyluk drove a school bus. Many students recall bus sing-a-longs and fun and became loyal customers. Leonard's also moved to the shopping center in 1960, and it is now at 215 West Liberty Street and run by daughter Katie Manyluk Wolter. (Courtesy of Katie Manyluk Wolter.)

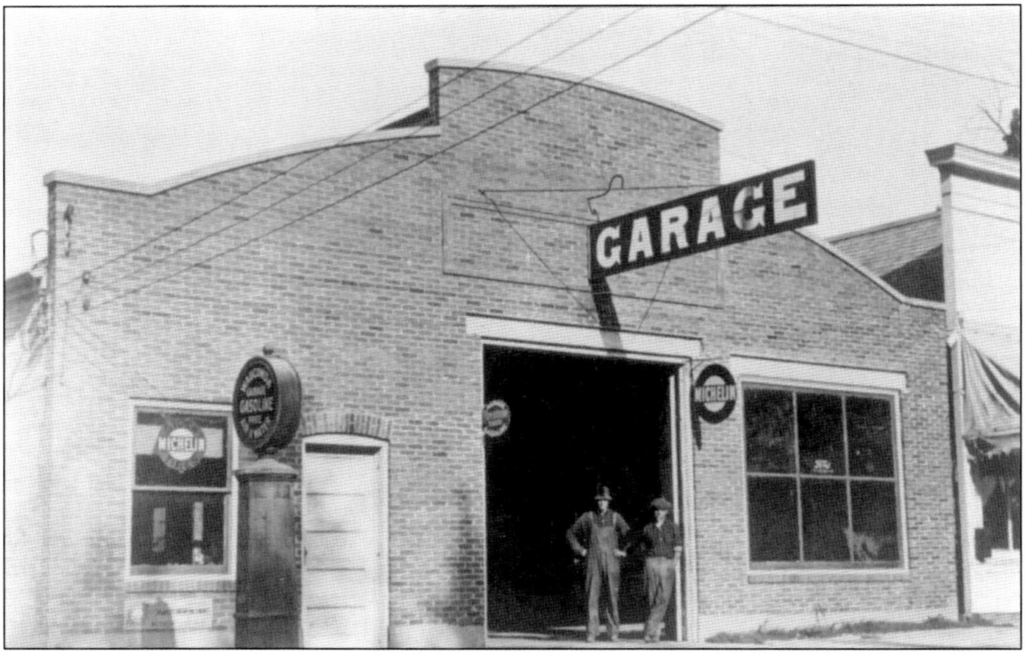

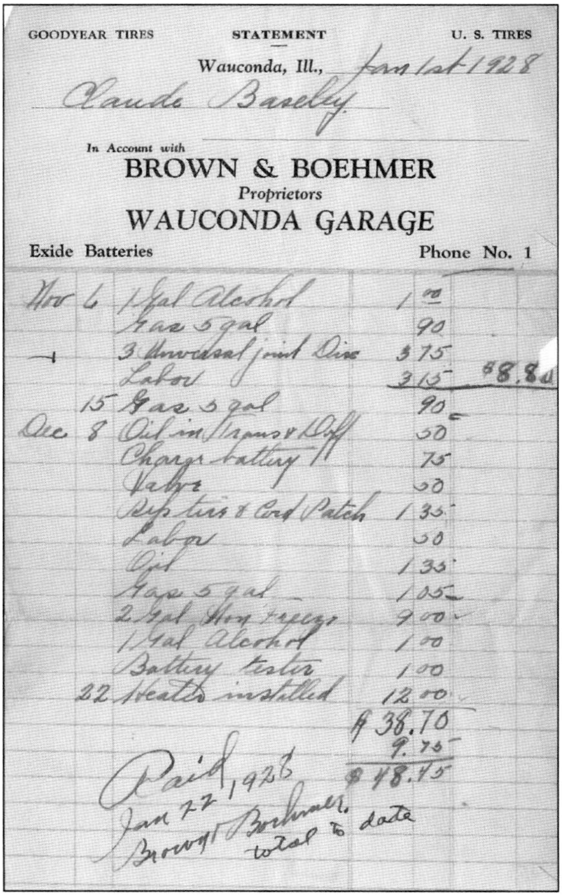
GOODYEAR TIRES STATEMENT U. S. TIRES

Wauconda, Ill., Jan 1st 1928

Claude Baseley

In Account with

BROWN & BOEHMER

Proprietors

WAUCONDA GARAGE

Exide Batteries Phone No. 1

Nov	6	1 Gal Alcohol	1 00	
		Gas 5 gal	90	
		3 Universal joint Disc	3 75	
		Labor	3 15	$8.80
	15	Gas 5 gal	90	
Dec	8	Oil in Trans & Diff	50	
		Charge battery	75	
		Valve	50	
		Rep tire & Cord Patch	1 35	
		Labor	50	
		Oil	1 35	
		Gas 5 gal	1 05	
		2 Gal Non freeze	9 00	
		1 Gal Alcohol	1 00	
		Battery tester	1 00	
	22	Heater installed	12.00	
			$38.70	
			9.75	
			$48.45	

Paid, 1928
Jan 27
Brown & Boehmer.
total to date

Arthur Henry Boehmer and Darwin Lee Brown opened Wauconda Garage, an auto repair business, on Main Street in 1913. It sold the first available gas north of Des Plaines from a hand-operated gas pump; gas was cranked out one gallon at a time. In 1914, Brown & Boehmer started selling cars, and 10 years later it expanded to include a one-car showroom. (Courtesy of Steve Boehmer.)

Claude Baseley paid this January 1928 bill for work done in November and December 1927. On this statement, the Wauconda Garage telephone number is 1. (Courtesy of Steve Boehmer.)

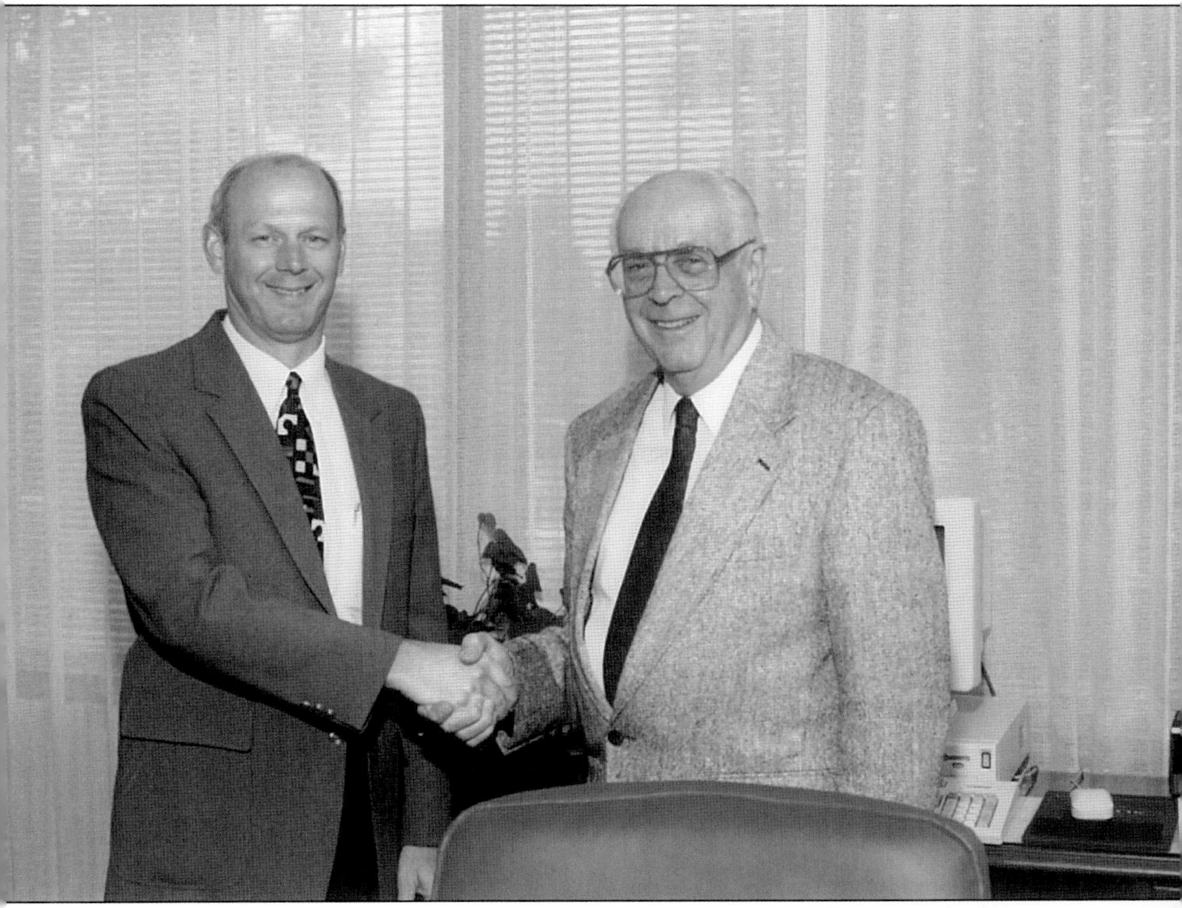

The Boehmer family represents three generations in the auto business. Arthur Henry Boehmer was the grandfather of Steve Boehmer (left), and father of Ken Boehmer (right). The eldest Boehmer and his partner, Darwin Lee Brown, obtained a Chevrolet franchise in 1929. During World War II, cars were hard to get when manufacturing focused on the war effort, so the company primarily did car and truck repairs. Ken started working for his father when he returned from World War II. They bought out Brown in 1952 and changed the name to Boehmer Chevrolet Sales. In 1960, they built a showroom at 416 West Liberty Street. (Courtesy of Steve Boehmer.)

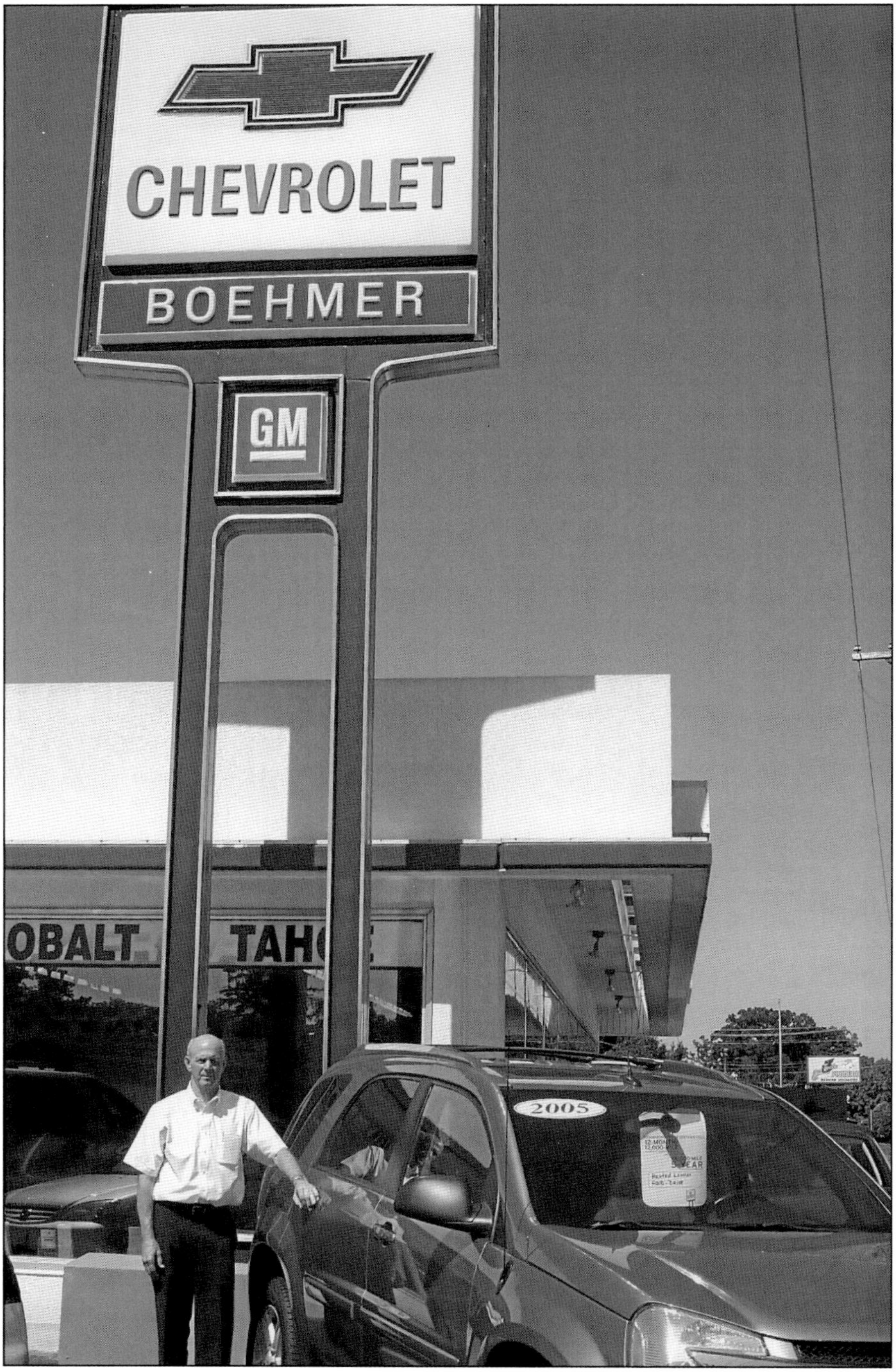

Steve Boehmer began working for his father as shop foreman in June 1969 after college and Army duty, and he became a salesman. His father died in 2006. The dealership supported local groups and events and played a prominent role in community life. The changing auto industry and economy caused Boehmer to lose its dealership in 2010. It is now Boehmer Automotive, focusing on service and used-car sales, another chapter in the story of the 97-year-old family business. (Courtesy of Marianne Folise.)

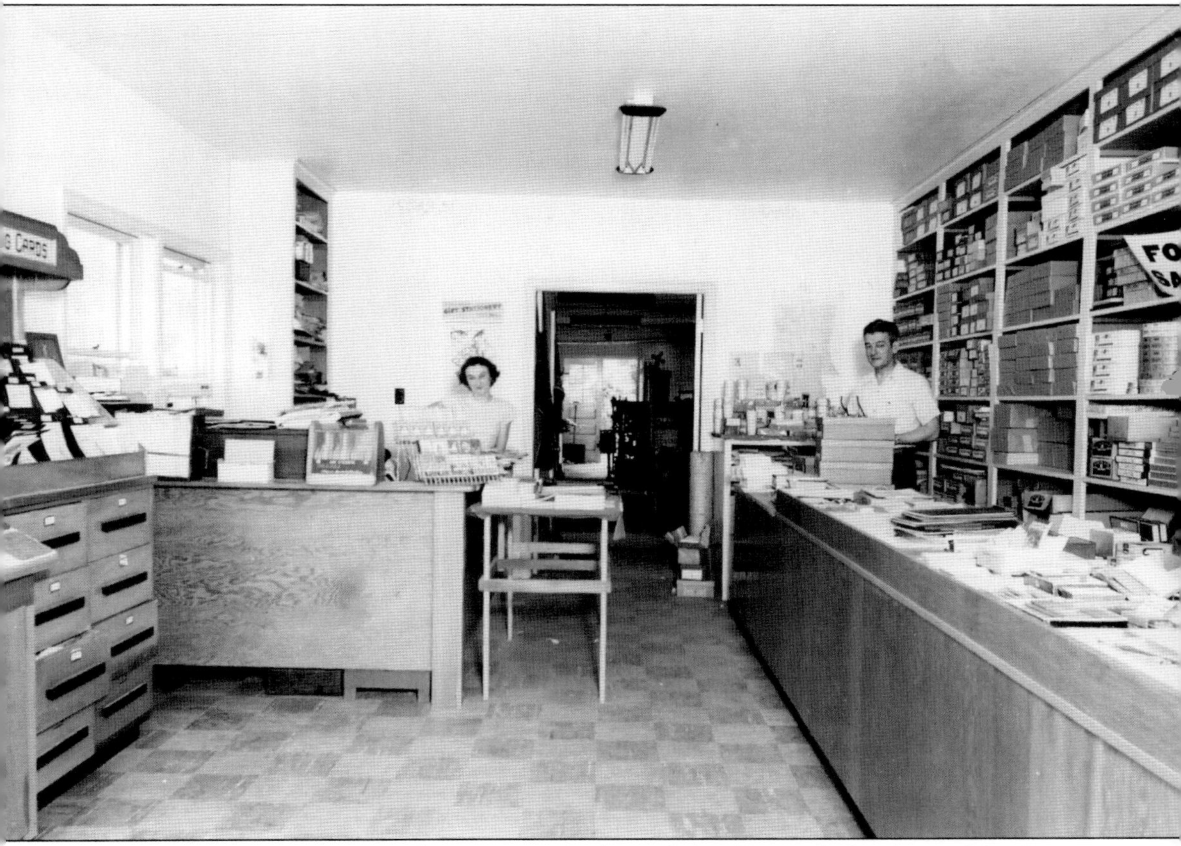

Pictured in 1948 are Walter Banks, owner and editor of the *Wauconda Leader*, and Jan Prior Hironimus, an employee, in the office on Bangs Street. The paper was printed in the back room of the store, which also sold cards and stationery supplies. A newspaper, the *Star*, was established in 1888. Frank Carr purchased the paper in 1908 and renamed it the *Wauconda Leader*. In 1914, he sold it to John P. and Della Blanck, who continued printing the paper until Mr. Blanck was found dead at his desk on October 21, 1923. Della sold the paper to P.E. Schlettleman, who sold it to Banks, the owner for the next 40 years. The paper had other owners and ceased publication in the 2000s when tough times hit the newspaper industry. Banks held the position of village clerk for 15 years. (Courtesy of Deanne Wiemuth Rogers.)

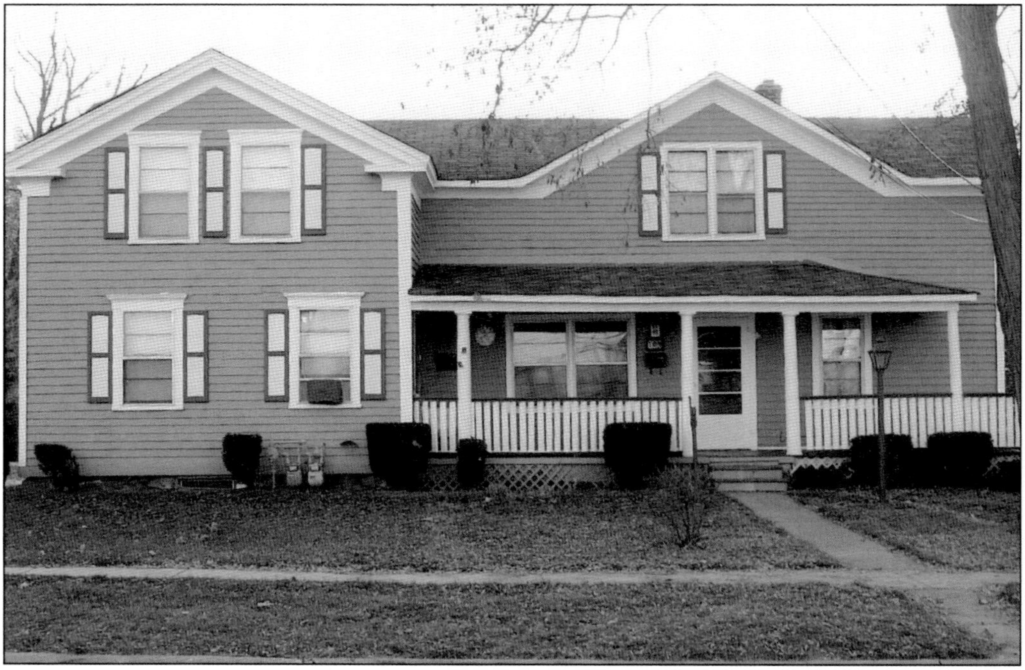

Beatrice and Walter Banks purchased and renovated this house at 109 Maple Avenue. The original structure was built by Justus Bangs after his marriage to Caroline Cone, his second wife, in 1852. (Courtesy of Marianne Folise.)

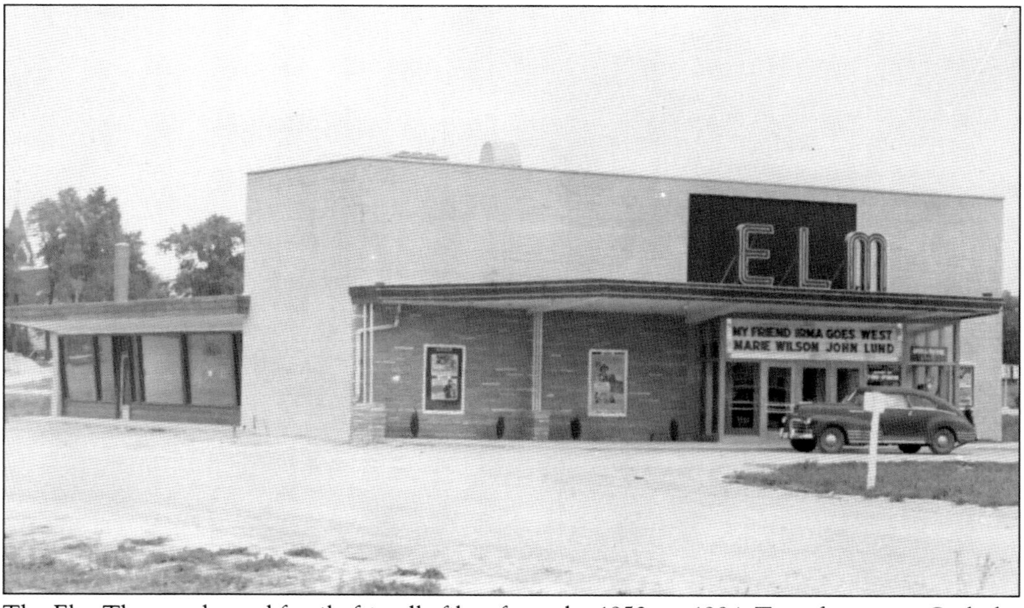

The Elm Theater showed family-friendly films from the 1950s to 1984. Transfiguration Catholic Church owned it and leased it to Leonard Deasey for 15 years. In the 1970s and 1980s, Deasey's five children and their friends worked the concessions and ticket booth. Because Transfiguration owned it, movies had to pass the Catholic Church's code for acceptable movies—the theater would be packed for Disney movies. It was razed to make room for a new church building. (Courtesy of the Lake County Discovery Museum.)

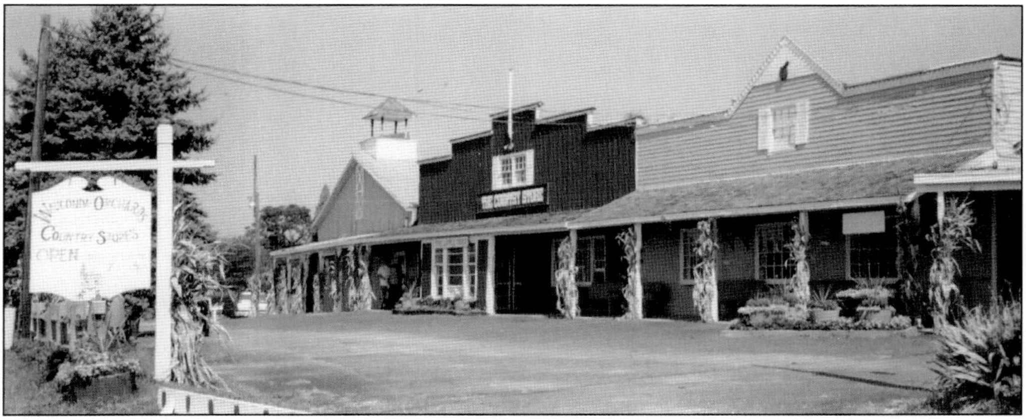

In 1951, Richard and Margaret Breeden purchased 75 acres, and later an additional 25, and began Wauconda Orchards modestly with 500 apple trees. It grew to more than 10,000 acres, making it one of the largest orchards in Illinois. The Breedens converted the milk house to a cider mill and the smokehouse to the apple kitchen. In the spring of 1976, the 116-year-old barn was converted to an antiques and collectibles store. For many years, from apple-picking season through Halloween, Wauconda Orchards was a wonderful place to wander back in time. Legions of Chicago-area residents have treasured memories of picking apples and berries, taking tractor rides, and enjoying apple cider and other apple treats. In 1962, the Breedens purchased the Cheese Factory and property at 1201 Fairfield Road. Acquisition of the farmland near the Cheese Factory was begun by Michael Synnett in 1841. On this site, the Breedens envisioned Old Wauconda, which would capture the flavor of rural pioneer life. In 1968, the Wauconda Village Board denied their request for annexation of the land needed for the project. (Courtesy of Angela Catrambone.)

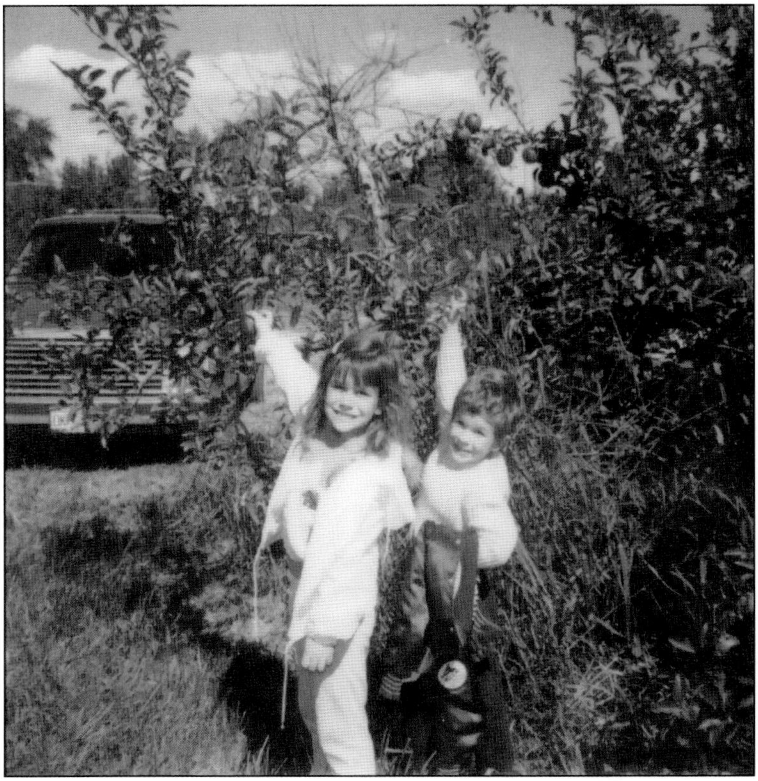

Gina and Phillip Serratore are pictured picking apples at the Wauconda Orchards in 1990. (Courtesy of Sue Serratore.)

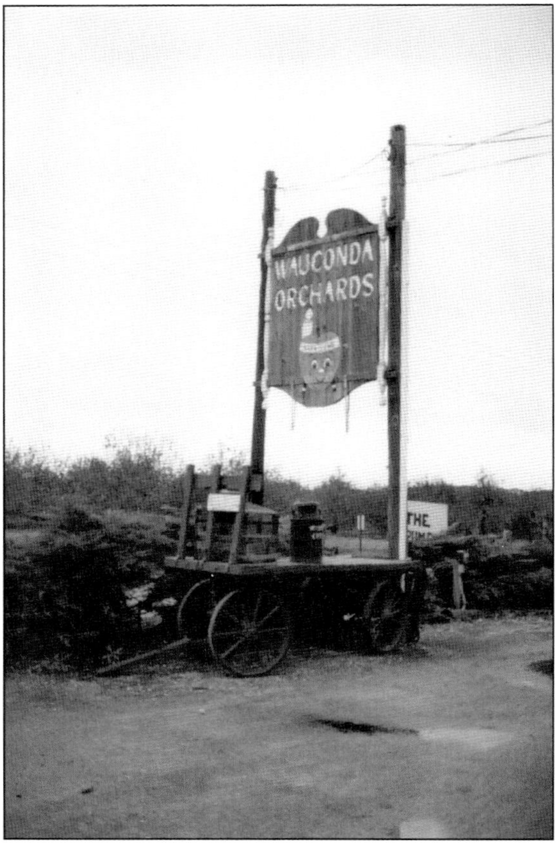

The orchard closed after picking season 2001, and it became a housing development. (Courtesy of Angela Catrambone.)

Tony Victor moved Victor Implement Co. from Libertyville to the new Route 12 in Wauconda in 1954. He supplemented the farm-implement business in 1956 with a Ford dealership. In 1955, he married Jackie Murphy Victor, and they had four children: Jeff, Vicki, Rod, and Connie. All of the children worked in the business. Upon his death in 1994, son Jeff became manager; Rod was more involved in the snowmobile and boat aspects of the business. (Courtesy of Victor Ford.)

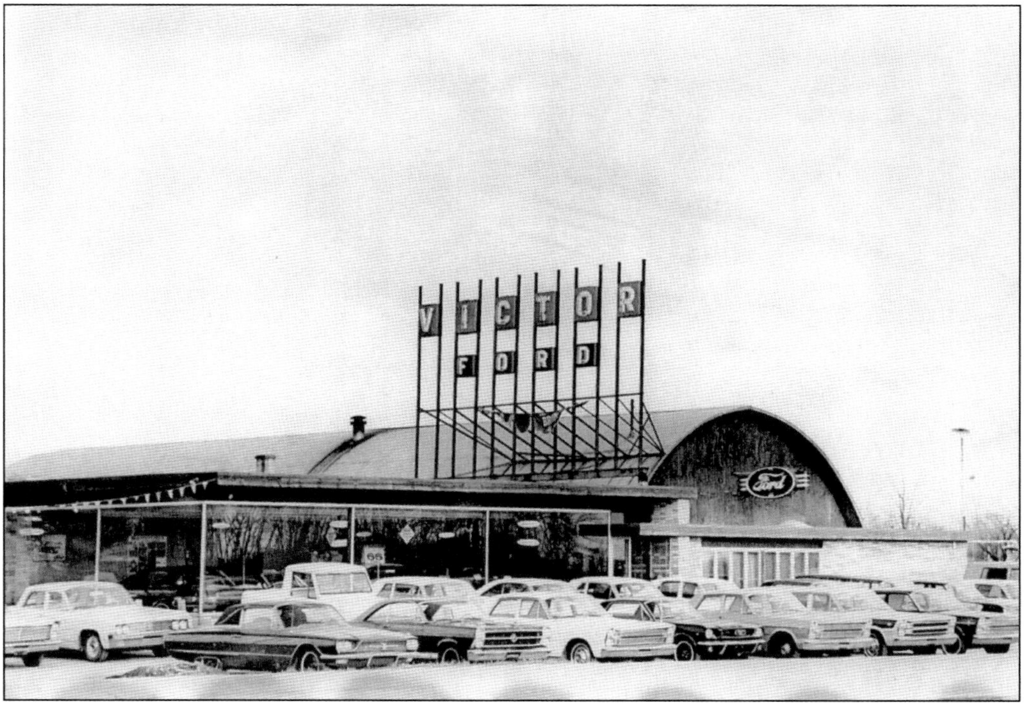

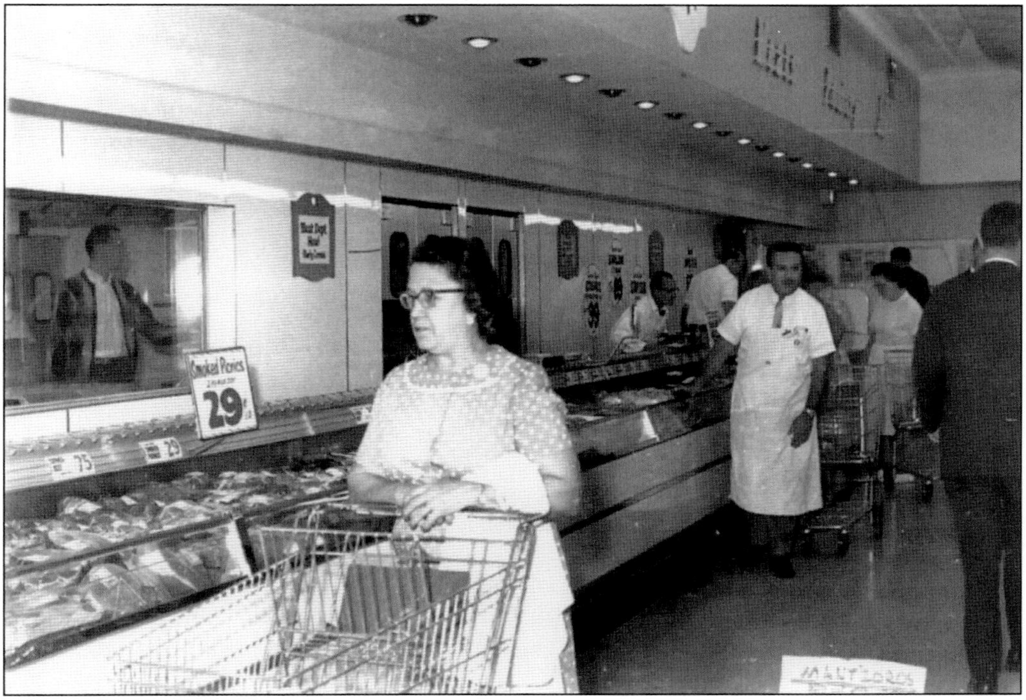

The National Tea Company grocery store opened at the new Wauconda Shopping Center on Liberty Street in 1956. Pictured doing her shopping is Mabel Stone, wife of then-mayor Melvin Stone. Gone are the days when smoked ham was 29¢ per pound. (Courtesy of Cindy Francisco Bilisko.)

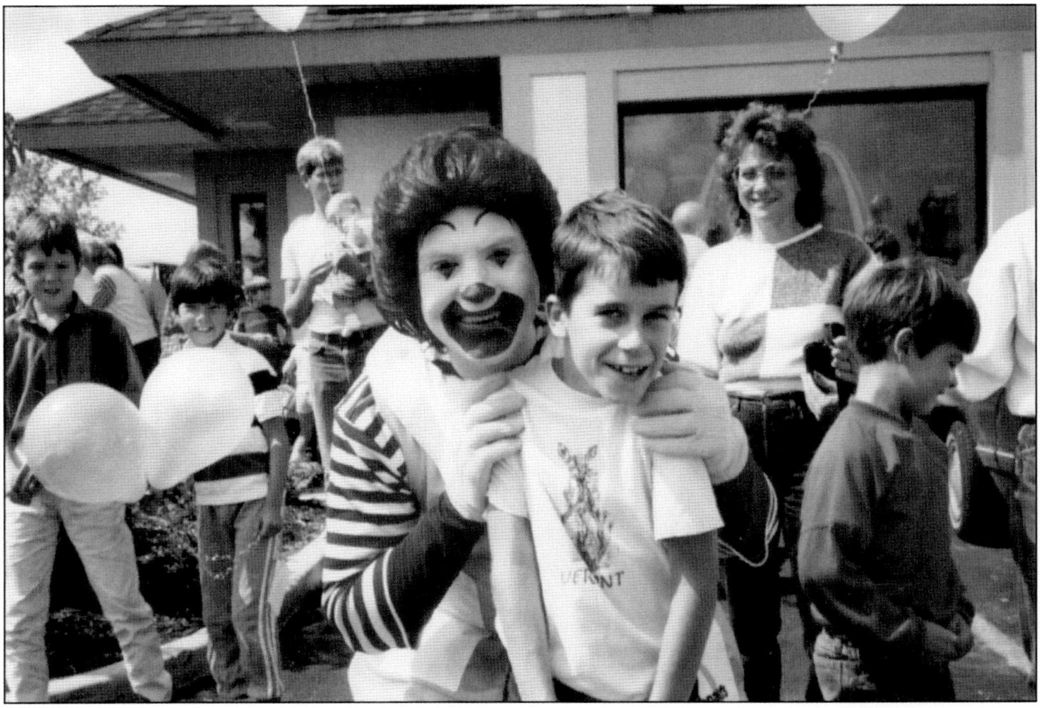

Ronald McDonald poses with Ron K. Vaughn Jr. of Wauconda during the 1986 grand-opening festivities for the new McDonald's at 511 West Liberty Street. (Courtesy of Ron K. Vaughn Sr.)

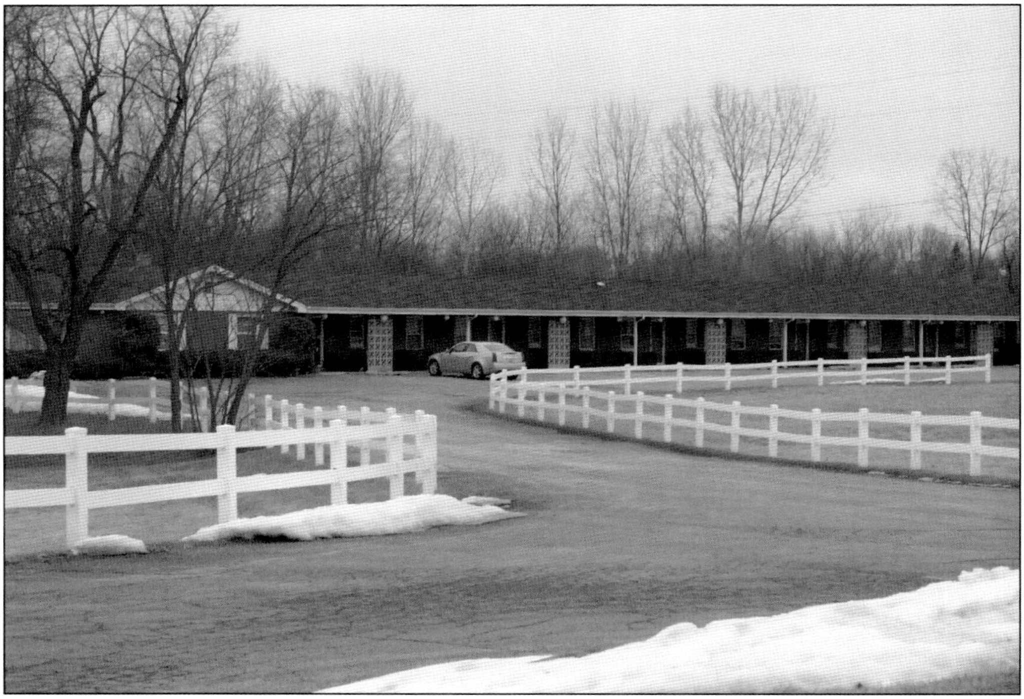

The Wauconda Motel is a fixture on Route 12. William Slowik built it in 1954 during the post–World War II boom that saw Americans traveling by car farther from home for vacation. He and his wife, Emily, have been the only owners. Emily continues to run the 10-unit motel since her husband's 2002 death. Below is the motel's sign around 1970. (Above, courtesy of Marianne Folise; below, Lake County Discovery Museum.)

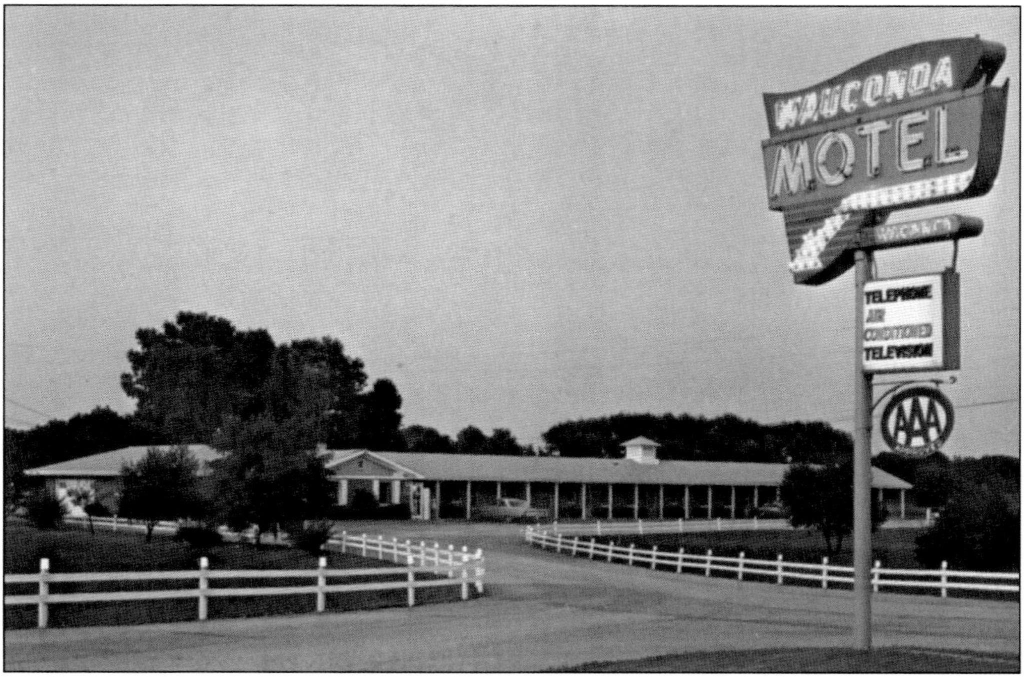

William M. Kisselburg and his son Bertram are seen in 1925 outside their funeral parlor on Madison Street in Chicago. The business opened in 1890. (Courtesy of the Kisselburg family.)

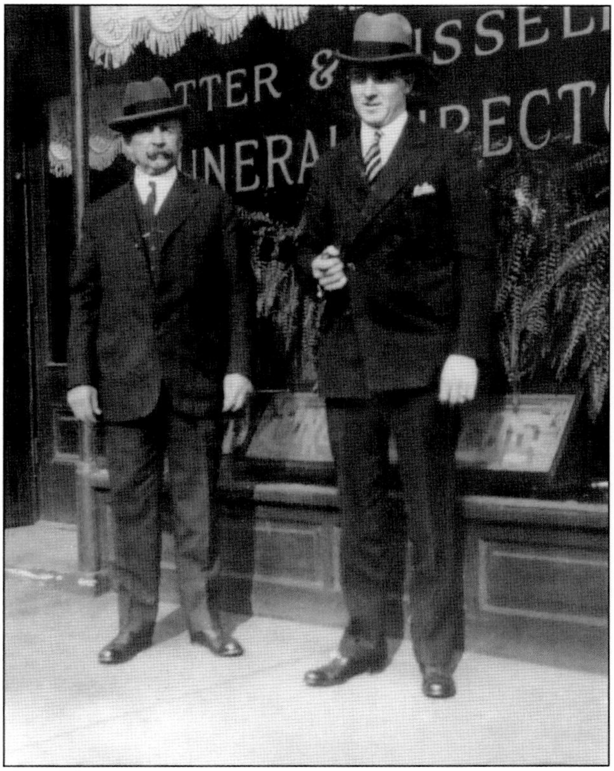

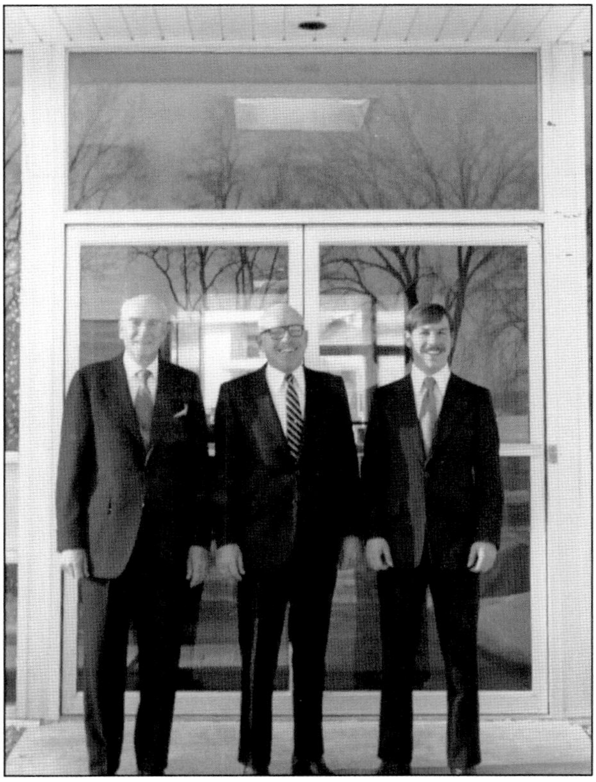

The family business moved to Wauconda in 1949. Outside of the Kisselburg Funeral Home on 235 North Main Street are, from left to right, Bertram, William C., and Craig Kisselburg. Craig's son Mark (not pictured) is the fifth generation in the business. (Courtesy of the Kisselburg family.)

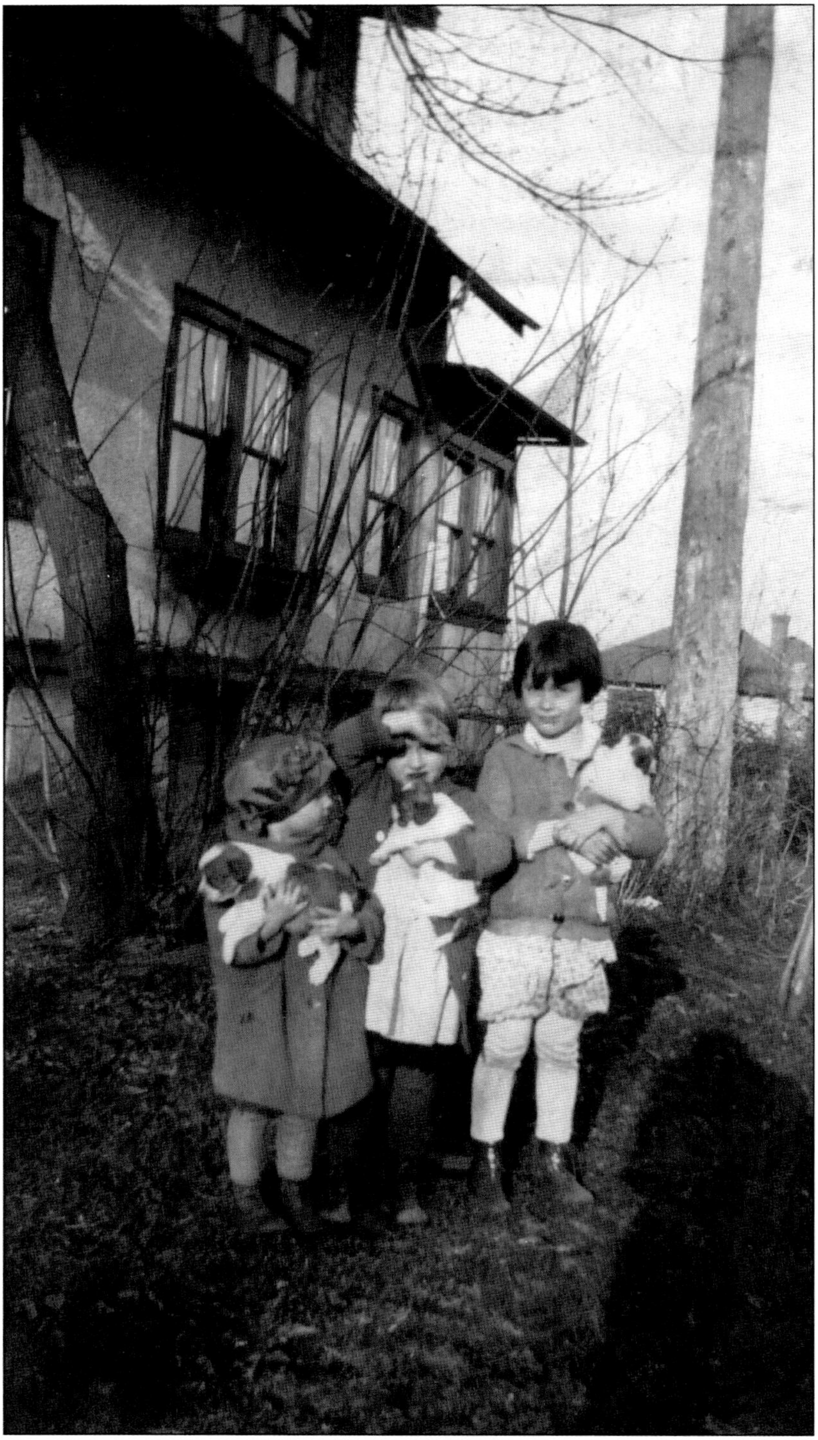

Pictured from left to right are Jan Prior, her sister Ethel, and their friend Gerry Kirk. They are pausing here in the 1920s with a group of puppies next to the Prior family home at 402 North Main Street. The Priors owned and rented out six cottages along the lake. (Courtesy of Jan Prior Hironimus.)

Five

BEACHES AND RESORTS

Wauconda's beautiful lake, beaches, and resorts were places to relax and have fun away from the stress of everyday life. For many, Wauconda was an escape from the hot, crowded city. Whether swimming, boating, fishing, picnicking, or just lying in the sun on a lazy afternoon, Wauconda offered all of this and more.

The beaches surrounding Bangs Lake were built up from wilderness in the early 1900s. The lake had to be dredged and filled with sand before it could accommodate swimmers. Visitors came by rail and car, and their numbers increased as road conditions improved.

One of the first beach owners was August Kuebker, who purchased 66 acres in 1915, part of which was called Kuebker's Landing. He dredged the beach, added sand, and operated the beach and picnic grove until 1924, when his daughter Mertie Cook and her husband, Homer, inherited the property upon his death and renamed it Cook's Boathouse. Part of the acreage on the southeast shore of the lake became another popular beach known as Cook's Grove. After 40 years, the Cooks sold to Tony Barnas and Mike Barnas, who enlarged the beach and improved the facilities. They changed a cornfield into a baseball diamond and added sewer and water to accommodate the large crowds. They now had four slides, two rafts, a diving board, a floating horse, 500 picnic tables, and 20 acres of playing fields.

Some of the other beaches, cottages, and resorts that attracted visitors included Farman's, Honey Hill, Wauconda Beach Hotel, Bartell's Villas, the Best Rest Cottages, Villa Beach Club, and, perhaps the most famous, Phil's Beach. In the 1940s and 1950s, several beaches and rental cottages posted signs declaring "Gentiles Only," "No Colored," and "Restricted." The Council Camp, established by the Chicago Section of the National Council of Jewish Women, offered summer vacations yearly to almost 700 tired mothers and children who needed the out-of-doors and who otherwise would enjoy no vacation of any type.

While Bangs Lake was enjoyed in the summer by locals and visitors alike, local residents used it for fun and business in the winter. The lake provided winter sports, including ice-fishing, skating, and boating, as well as the occasional sulky racing.

Employees of Grantham Ice House would cut ice from the lake, keep it in the icehouse, and sell it to local residents and summer visitors. The Bowman Dairy would ship local farmers' milk to Chicago, cooled by ice from the lake.

As years went on, most of the summer cottages were converted to year-round homes. High insurance rates forced the public beaches out of business by 1990.

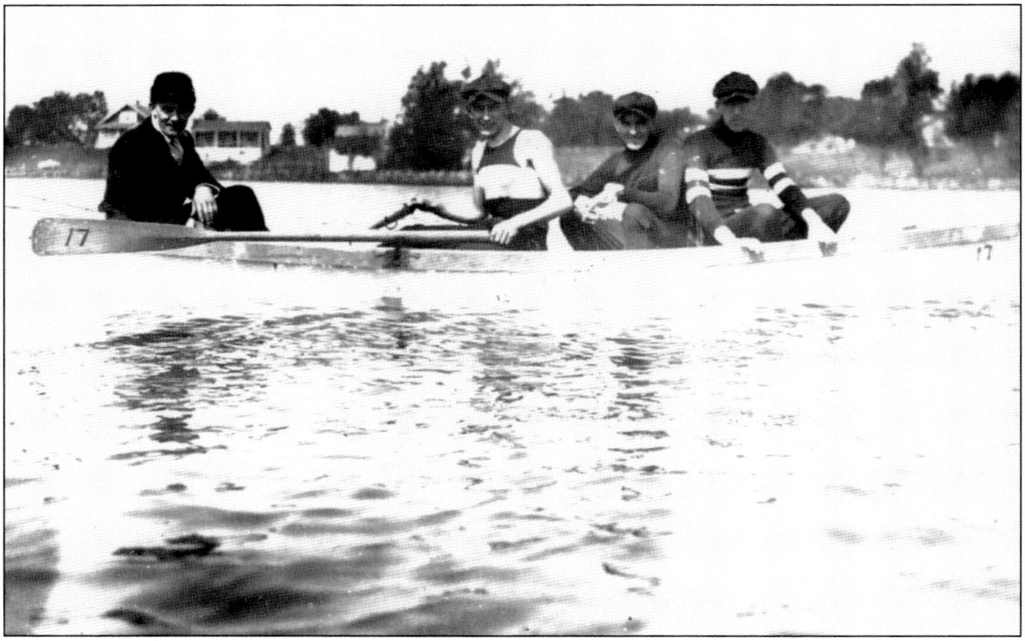

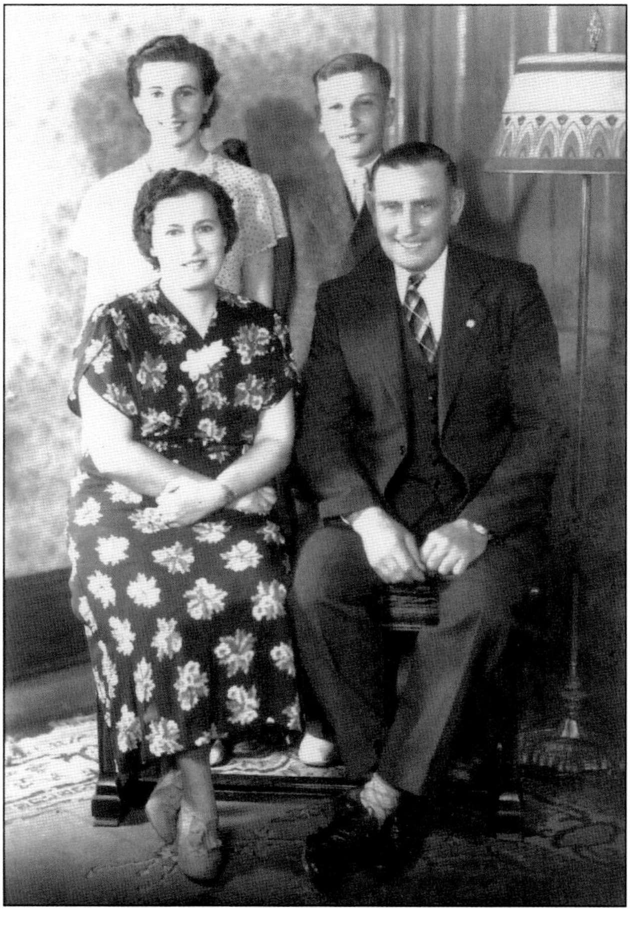

In this c. 1915 photograph, Phillip Froehlke is second from left. He began coming to Wauconda from Chicago with his brothers and friends for swimming, boating, fishing, and fun. They would stay at Kuebker's Landing. In 1922, he moved to Wauconda to operate Kuebker's Landing and, in 1926, he purchased property on Bangs Lake and developed Phil's Beach. (Courtesy of the Reilly family.)

Wanda and Phillip Froehlke pose with their children, Lorraine and Bud, for this late-1930s photograph. A former Chicago fireman, Phillip was Wauconda's fire chief for 25 years. Lorraine and Bud attended Wauconda schools. Lorraine went on to Rosary College and Illinois State University. Bud, a basketball star at Wauconda High School in 1941, attended the University of Notre Dame (see chapter nine for more). (Courtesy of the Reilly family.)

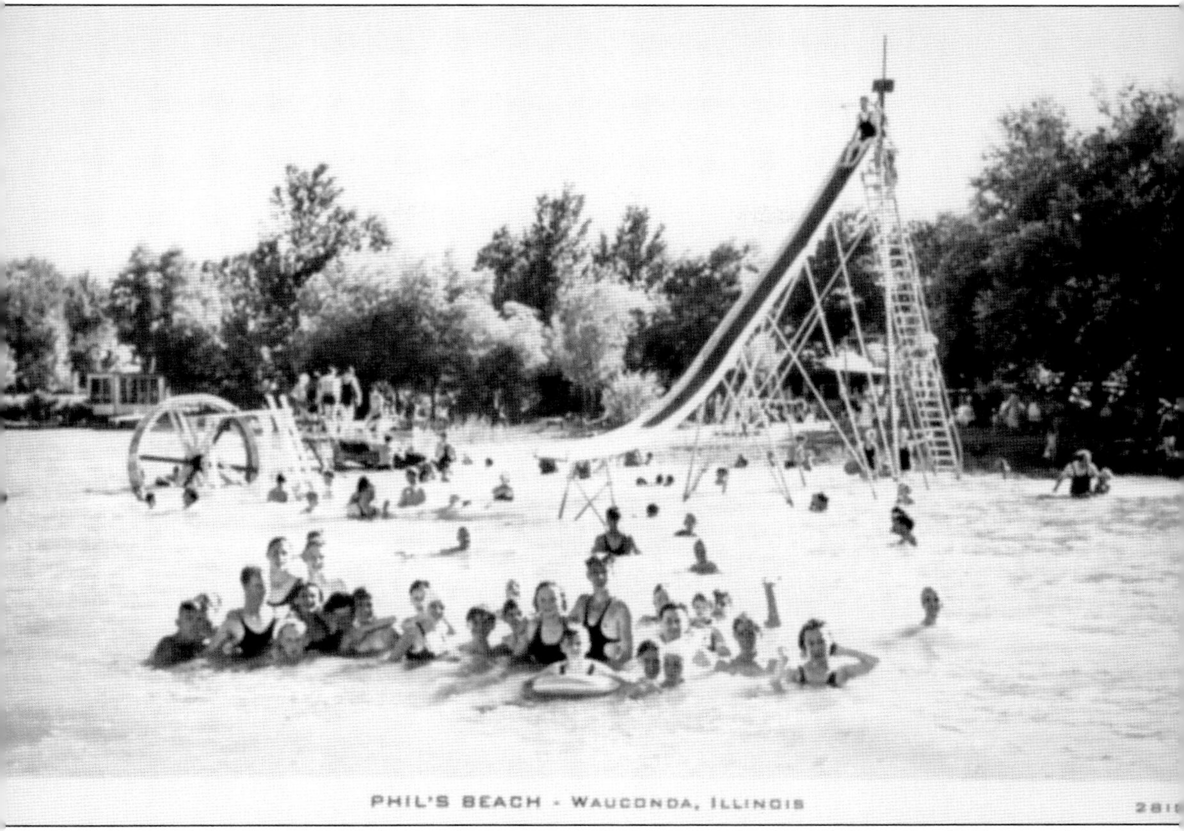

Bathers are having fun at Phil's Beach in 1938, with its iconic 36-foot slide in the background. Phillip Froehlke and his wife, Wanda, purchased the property at 336 North Main Street in 1926. Admission was 50¢ per car, regardless of how many people were crammed into it. The lake had to be dredged with a team of horses and a device known as a slip scraper, with a man who walked behind picking up mud and gravel. This material was used to fill a cattail swamp to make a parking lot, and the lake was filled in with three feet of sand. In 1948, Tom Reilly, who married the Froehlkes' daughter, Lorraine, started working at the beach. Phil's Beach rented rowboats, paddleboats, canoes, and sailboats. The beach opened as early as 4:00 a.m. for fisherman and closed as late as 11:00 p.m.; hours were shortened when the beach switched to swimming only. Reilly attributed the change from fishing camp to swimming beach as one of the main contributors in making Wauconda a tourist town. (Courtesy of the Lake County Discovery Museum.)

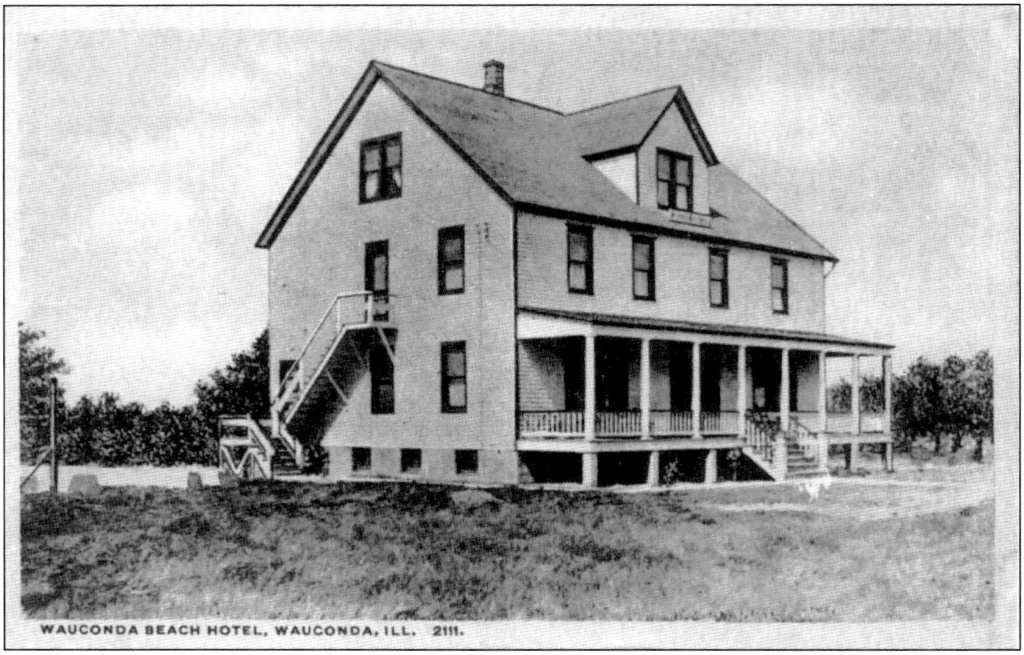

The Wauconda Beach Hotel, dating back to 1909, was a boardinghouse and coach stop. In 1941, Ed Tudor purchased the hotel and immediately improved and modernized it, attracting a guest list that included racetrack executives, jockeys, movie star Hedy Lamarr, and prominent people from political, legal, and entertainment circles. After Tudor's death in 1958, the Mers family—Bob Sr., his wife Dorothy, Bob Jr., and Bob's wife Rosemary—bought the business. (Courtesy of Doris Aimers-Voss.)

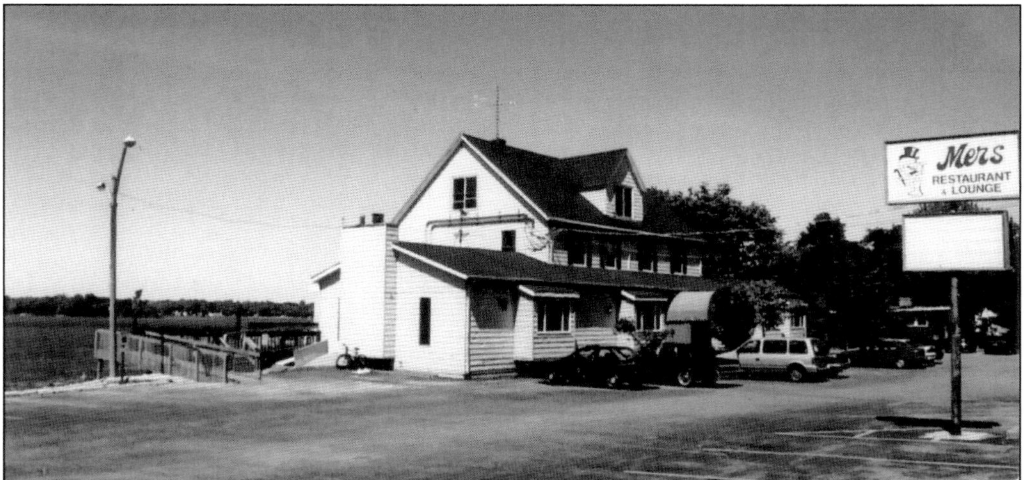

As Mers, Bob Jr. was the main chef and hired many local young people, many who went on into the culinary field and restaurant management. Bob Jr. also taught wrestling at Wauconda High School. He delighted in the political fundraisers held at the restaurant. He and Rosemary had three children. After her husband's 1987 death, she and her son ran the business until 1996, when after 38 years they decided to retire and sell the property. The building is no longer used as a hotel. It has had various owners and now is Docks, which has a popular outside bar and deck. (Courtesy of Marianne Folise.)

The Mers family had been customers when the Tudors owned the business. Although coming from varied work backgrounds, they decided to venture into the restaurant and hotel business. Bob Mers Sr. (at right with wife Dorothy) remained a businessman and was the silent partner and financial backer. He helped by grocery shopping and banking. Because he was such a good-hearted man, he bought customers more drinks in a day than were sold, so he was not often asked to help in the daily operation. Dorothy was a secretary. She tended bar and kept customers captivated with her jokes and stories. Bob Jr. (below, with Rosemary) was an insurance agent. He and Rosemary were married in 1954 and moved to Wauconda in 1958 when they bought the business. Rosemary had been a registered nurse. At Mers, she was bartender, hostess, and chambermaid. (Both courtesy of Rosemary Mers.)

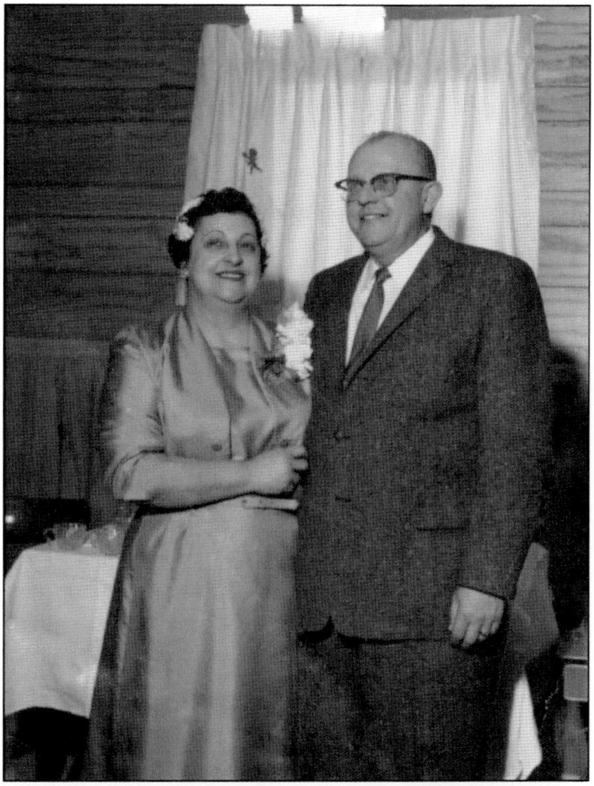

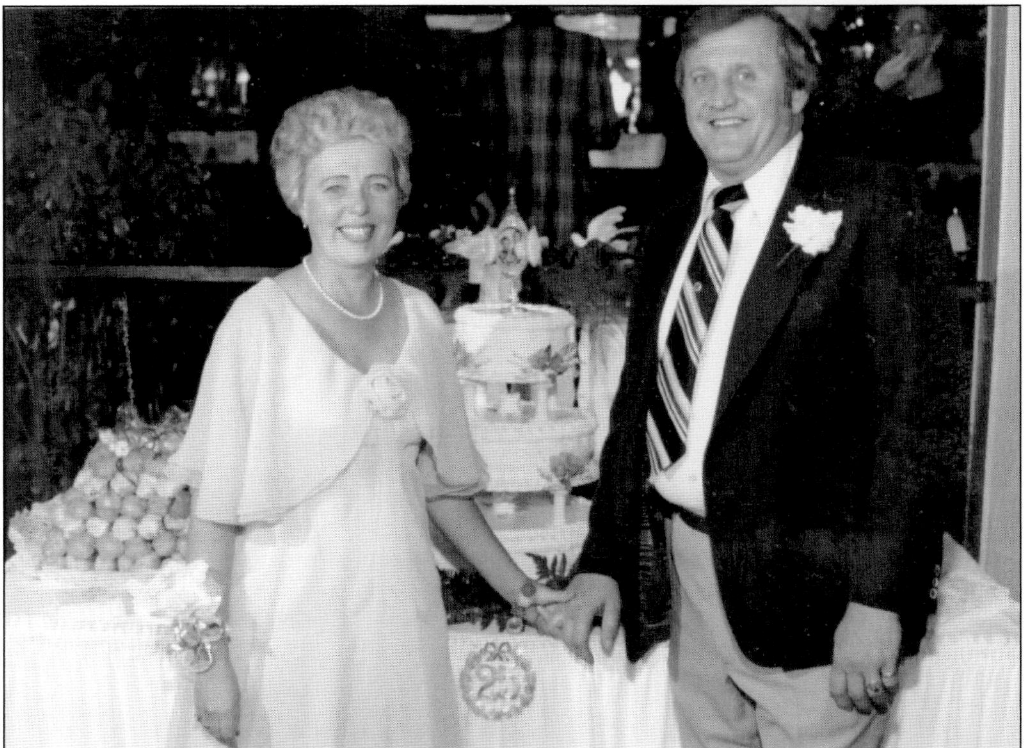

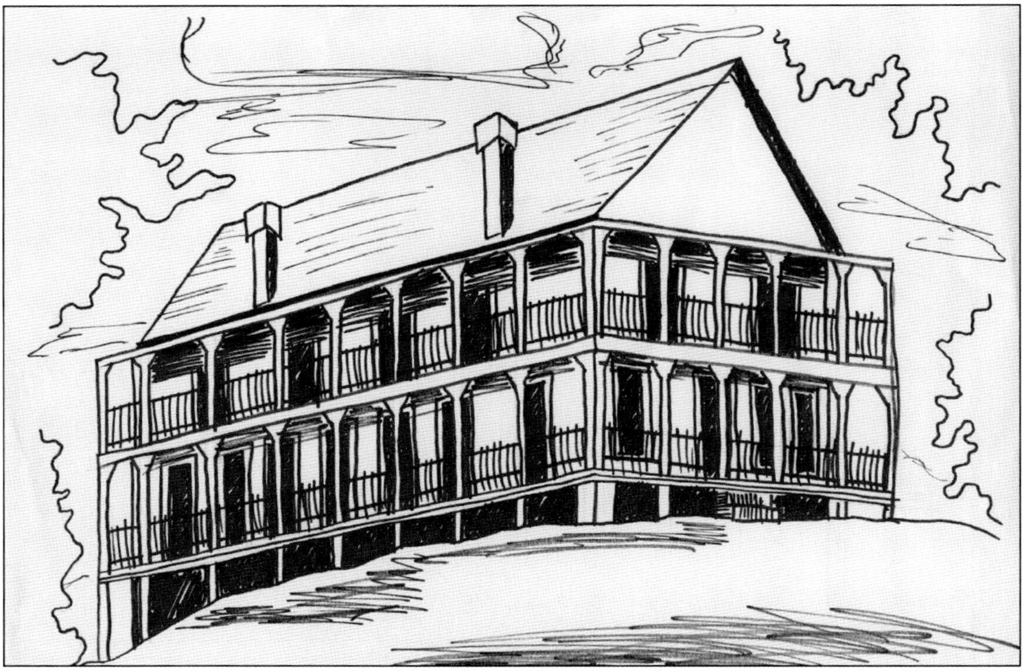

The Oakland Hotel was built in 1876 at the corner of Maple Avenue and Mill Street. In the early 1900s, residents and guests danced to the music of Kimball or Hapke's orchestras. On special occasions, there was an all-night dance with a delicious supper served at midnight. Crowds came in all kinds of weather to dance at the Oakland. With the passing of time, a state inspector declared it unsafe. For several years it stood empty, a monument of memories to the old-timers, but it was an eyesore to the younger generation. It was a sad day in 1928 when the historic landmark was torn down. The old "Oakland," the pride of Wauconda, passed into oblivion. (Courtesy of Liz Rondone.)

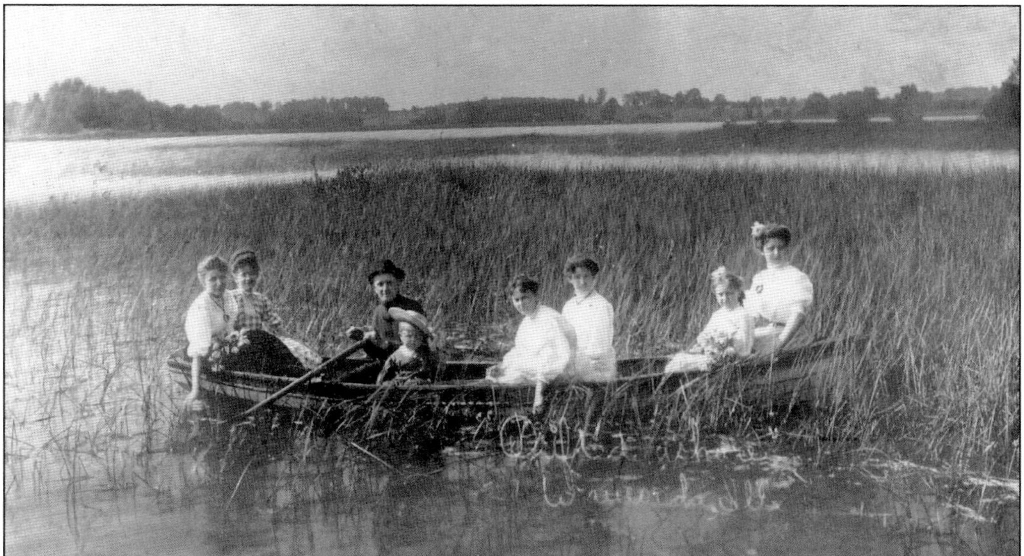

These ladies are enjoying a boat ride in this c. 1900 photograph. Iza Platt, third from the right, was the great-niece of Justus Bangs. (Courtesy of Kathy Reilly.)

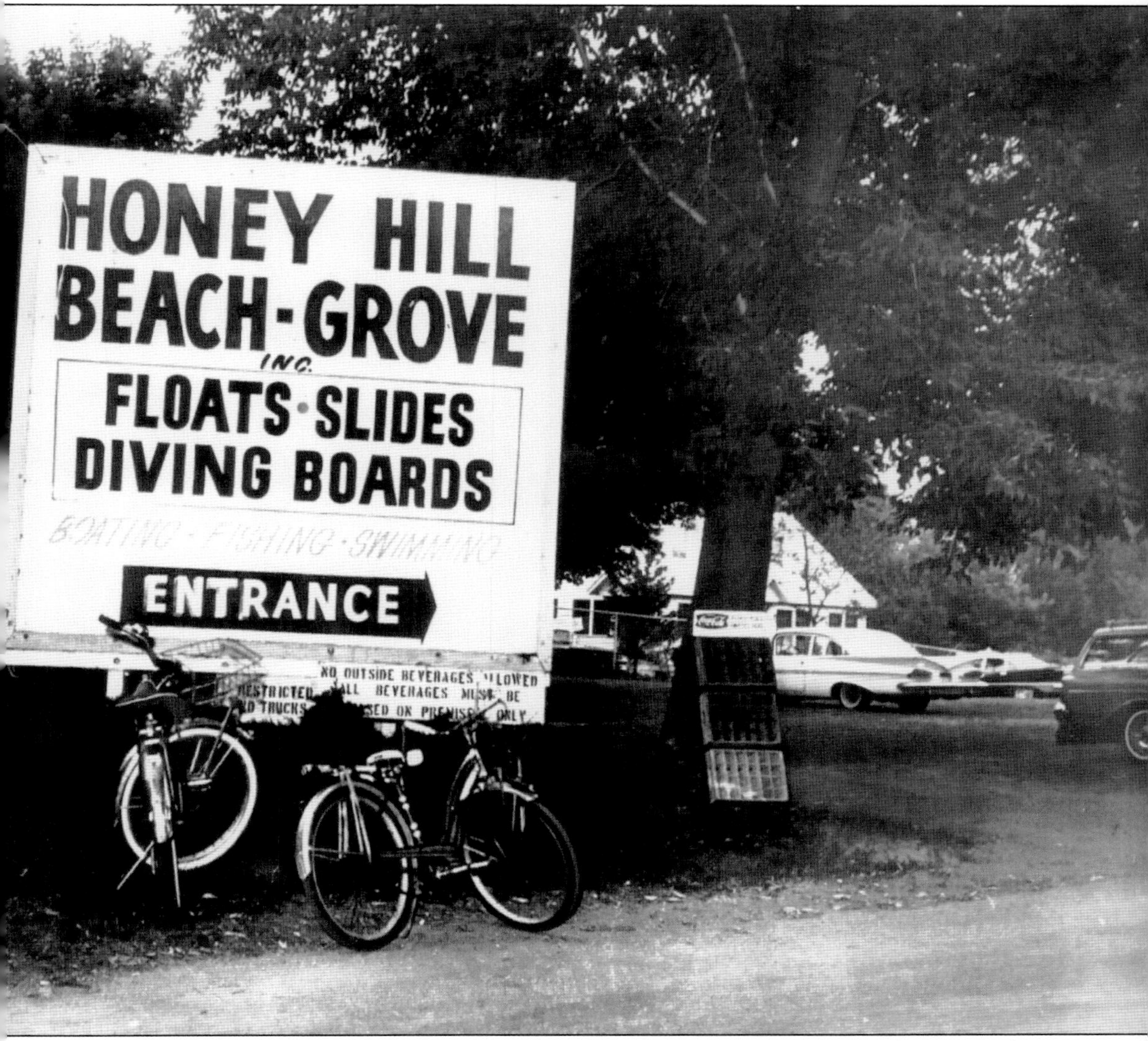

The sign points the way to Honey Hill Beach at 354 North Main Street. It opened in 1945, when the Jachec family, including brothers Ed, Tony, and Hank, bought 3.5 acres on the lake. It took many man-hours to develop the beach and turn it into a beautiful resort. One of the highlights of the beach was the J-slide, which was one of the highest in the country at the time. It had a 40- to 50-foot-long chute. Accommodations for tourists included 150 picnic tables, rowboats, paddleboats, and canoe rentals. They also had a game room, four diving boards, a waterwheel, two rafts, and a staff of seven lifeguards. (Courtesy of Cindy Francisco Bilisko.)

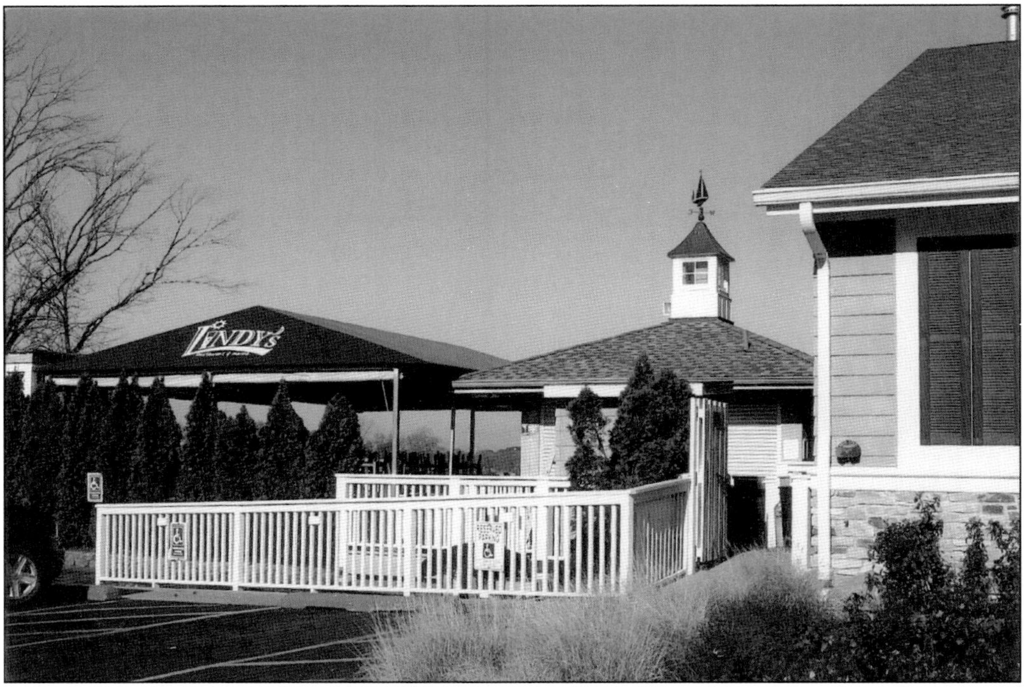

In 1965, Bob "Lindy" Lindstrom bought Farman's rickety old boathouse and realized the dream of owning his own lakeside bar/marina. He called it Lindy's Landing. During the next few years, it underwent multiple building upgrades and renovations. The original structure was built in 1908. Lindy loved life and lived it to the fullest until February 2000, when he passed away. Wanting to keep the legacy going, his three daughters, Laurie, Cheryl, and Bonnie, along with the help of family and friends, did just that. There were two additional major renovations in 2003 and 2006. These photographs show Lindy's Landing today. Now, more than 45 years and three generations later, his daughters and five grandchildren continue to keep his dream alive. (Both courtesy of Marianne Folise.)

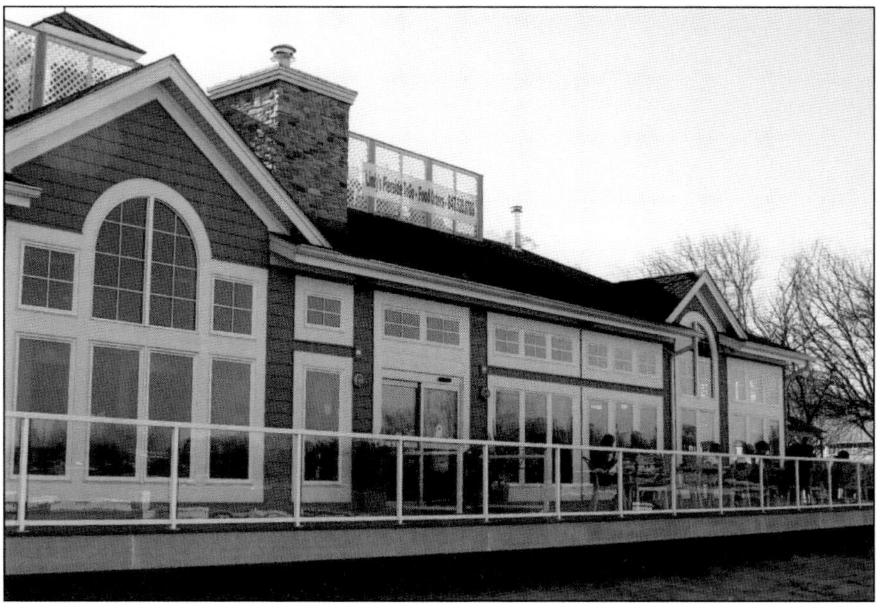

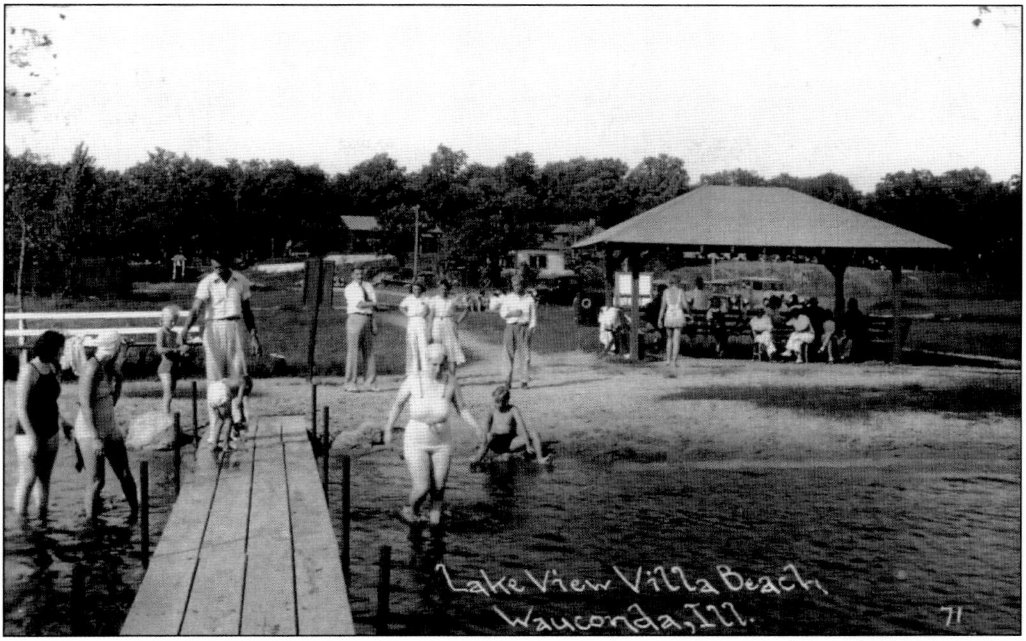

Lake View Villa was founded by Ed Turk on the north shore of Bangs Lake and was platted in 1926. It became a mixture of year-round homes and summer cottages. Pictured here in the 1930s are residents and summer renters enjoying a day at the Lake View Villa beach. (Courtesy of Ron K. Vaughn Sr.)

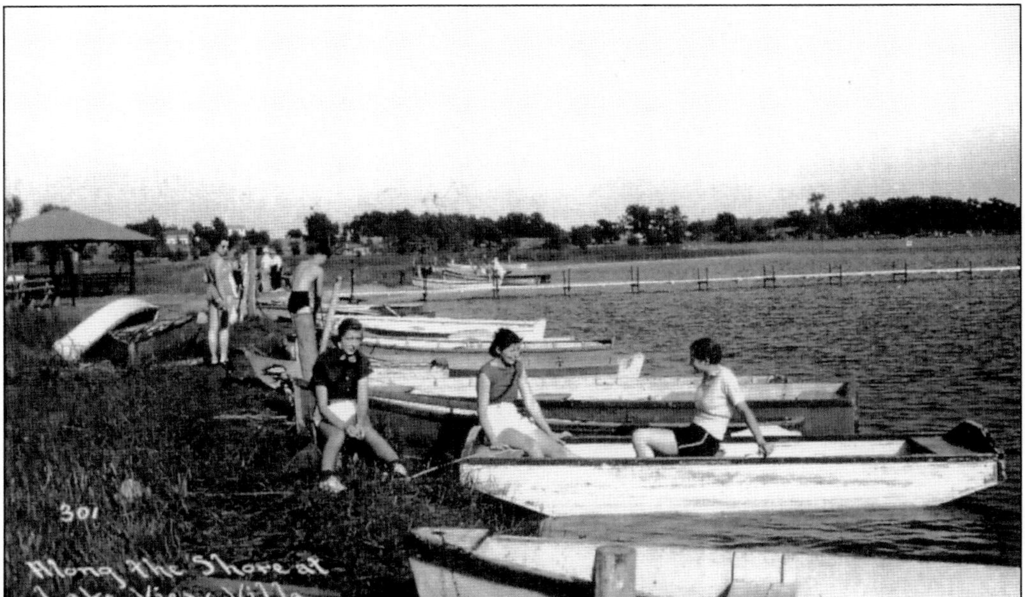

Summer is a time for boating, and these people are enjoying a leisurely day on the boats docked at the Lake View Villa Beach in the 1950s. (Courtesy of Ron K. Vaughn Sr.)

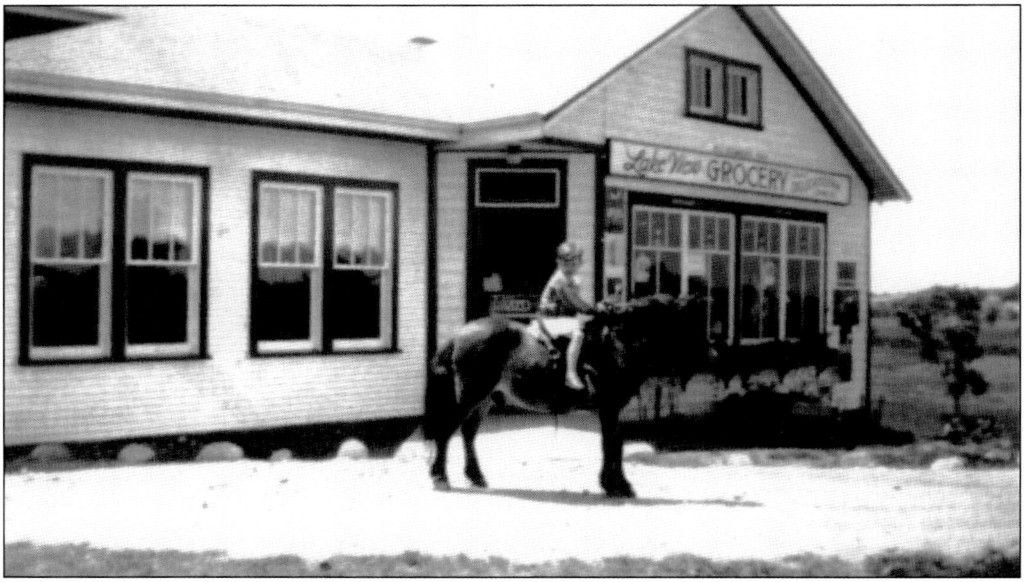

A boy and his pony are pictured in front of Somers's Lake View Villa Store in 1928. The store sold groceries, candy, ice cream, soft drinks, cigarettes and cigars, and beer on tap. (Courtesy of Ron K. Vaughn Sr.)

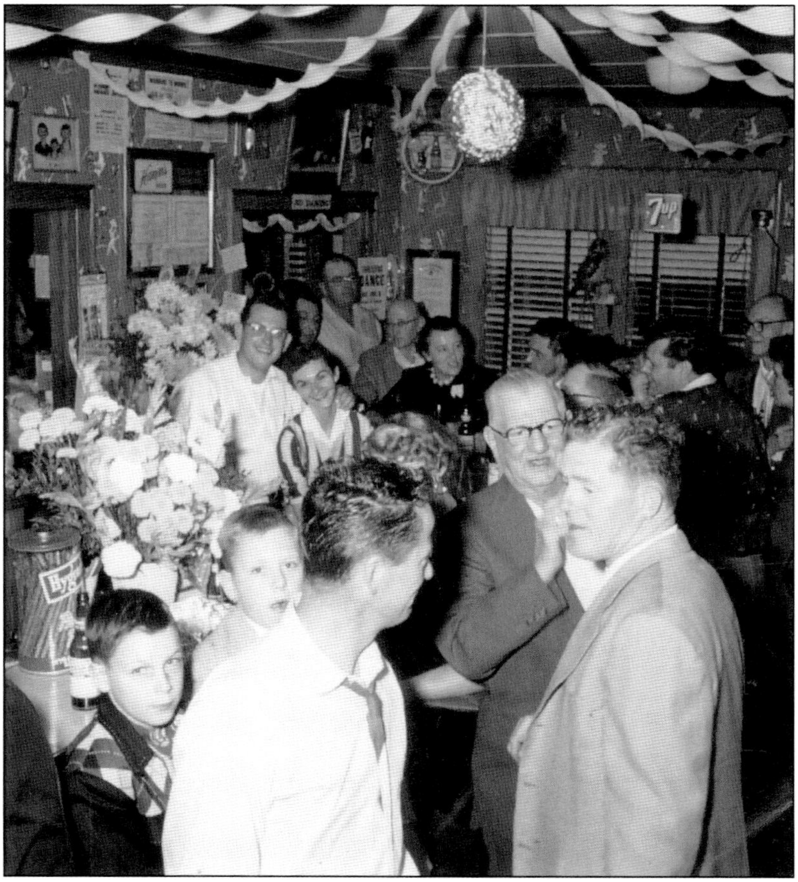

Mr. And Mrs. C. Somers sold their grocery store and tavern in Lake View Villa to Frank and Virgie Eglinas. This picture was taken at the Eglinas's grand-opening celebration in 1956. (Courtesy of Ron K. Vaughn Sr.)

Every corner had a community pump where people got their water, which was carried in crocks and pails. This pump, at the corner of Woodland Avenue and Grand Boulevard in the Maiman Lakeside subdivision, stands as a testament to earlier days. (Courtesy of Marianne Folise.)

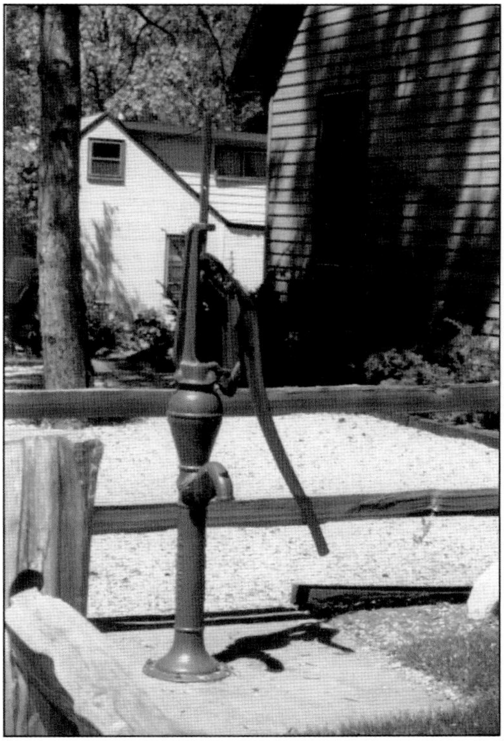

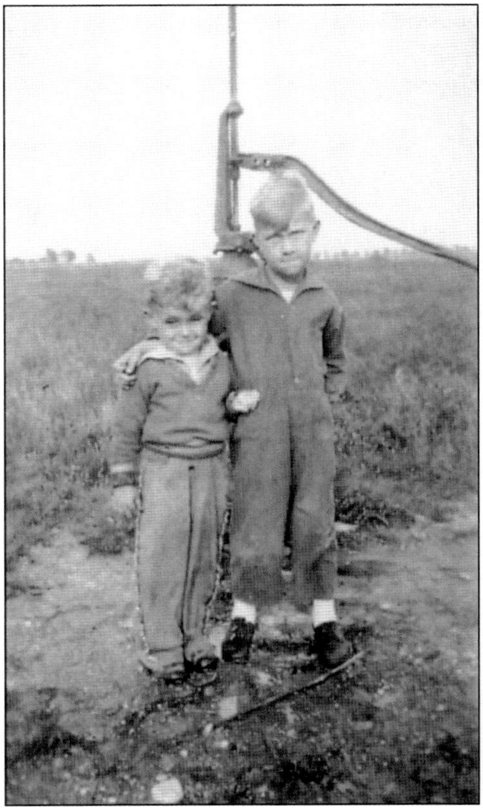

Pictured at a pump in this 1930 photograph are Jim Turk (left), son of Lake View Villa founder Ed Turk, and Norman Somers. Children often felt proud when they could do their part to get water and carry it home. In school, if children had finished their lessons, they might be appointed to carry the water. (Courtesy of Ron K. Vaughn Sr.)

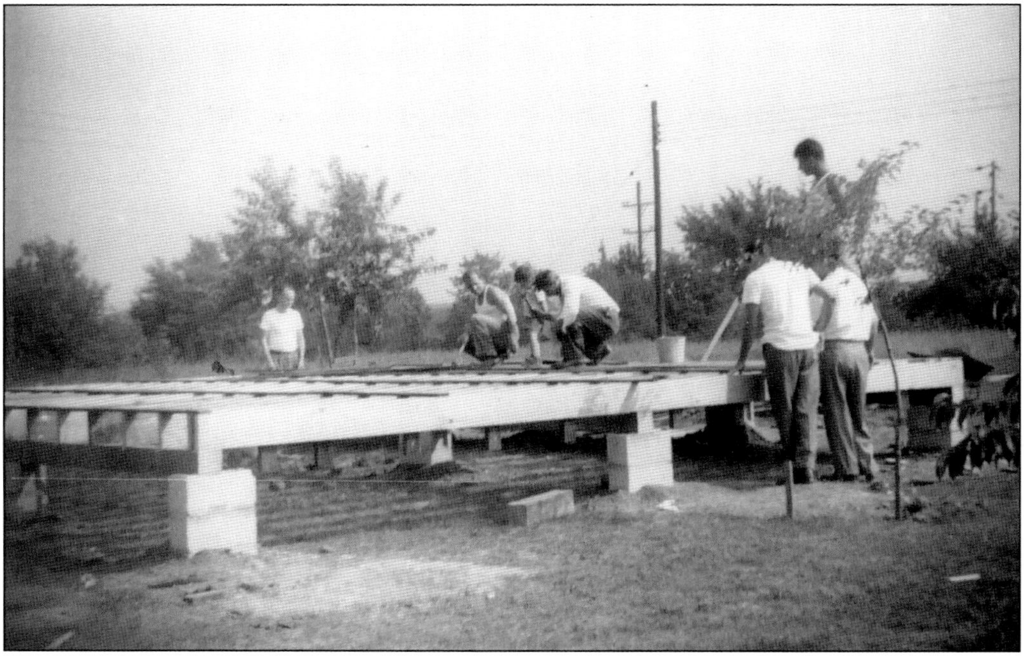

In the 1949 photograph seen above, brothers-in-law John Danza, Jim Folise, and Anthony Provenzano and other family members look on as the foundation is laid for one of three cottages they built next door to one another in Maiman's Lakeside subdivision. The end of World War II sparked expansive growth in Wauconda. One of the main factors was the movement of veterans by automobiles to the area. Many of the new residents buying property from the old-timers were ex-soldiers primarily from Chicago's west and northwest sides. Both Jim Folise and Anthony Provenzano, World War II veterans, transformed their summer cottages to year-round residences in the 1950s. John Danza was a World War I veteran. Below, after shampooing her hair with rainwater caught in a barrel, Connie Folise (left) looks on as family and neighborhood children pose in front of the cottage under construction on Highland Avenue in 1949. (Both courtesy of Marianne Folise.)

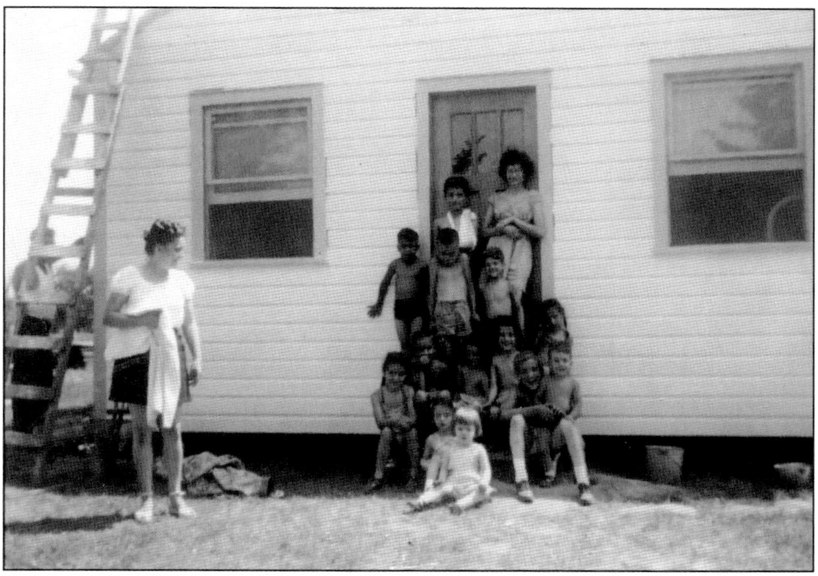

Six

Life on the Farm

The men and women who first moved to the region in the 1830s and 1840s found the fertile land ripe for farming. They were industrious, self-sufficient, and of rugged stock, but life on the Illinois prairie was difficult. They depended on each other, usually working sunrise to sunset making just about everything needed to survive and buying or trading goods with country peddlers who occasionally came through selling goods that could not be made locally. Through hard work and ingenuity, many prospered.

While the farm was a family's main source of food, successful settlers found other ways to make or grow goods for trading. One of the biggest challenges they faced was the changing of the seasons. They had to be completely prepared before the onset of freezing-cold temperatures, biting winds, and fierce snowstorms that would keep most settlers trapped in their homes during winter. Because they were cut off from Chicago and other neighboring communities at the time, this isolation forced them to form a community of their own.

In addition to raising grain, many farmers also raised stock such as cattle, horses, pigs, and sheep. When it was time to take crops and stock to market, they gathered together as a group and went to Chicago, the nearest market. Farmers found hunting a rewarding sideline. Deer, birds, and small animals were plentiful.

The dairy industry became important in Wauconda in later years. Three different creameries, among them the Bowman Dairy, were established in the community where farmers would bring their milk to have it processed.

In 1916, the dairies, which were under the authority and influence of the Chicago Board of Health, were having differences with local farmers over milk prices and regulations. The farmers in Wauconda went on strike and refused to deliver their milk to the Borden plant.

Agriculture became responsible for the growth of Wauconda in those early days. Every member of the family played a role in farm life. There was a great sense of community and the desire to help each other, especially at planting and harvesting time. Sharing Sunday dinners and socializing at each other's homes was a favorite pastime.

Some of the early farm families included Bacon, Case, Crown, Darrell, Fisher, Kimball, Matthews, Paddock, Pearson, Potter, Roney, Smith, and Vasey.

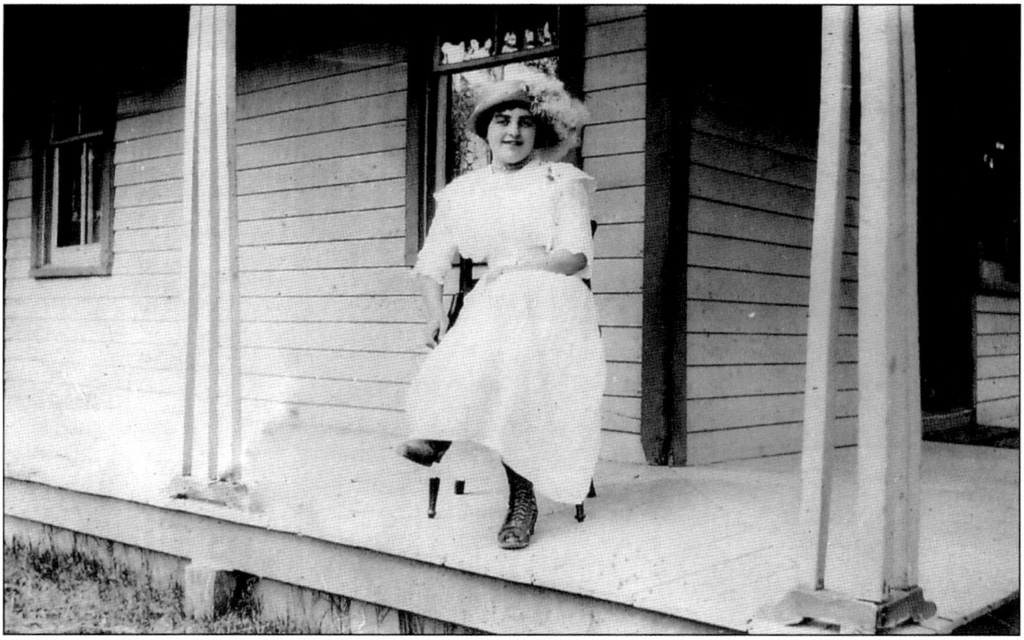

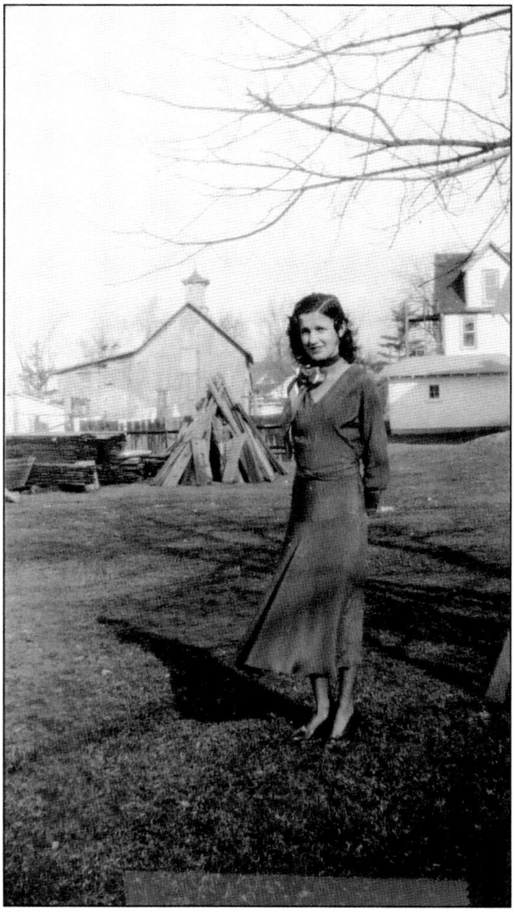

Beatrice A. Kimball, born in February 1898 as a daughter of Vernon Kimball, sits on the front porch of the family farmhouse on the corner of Main Street and Route 176 in 1914. She married Walter Banks on July 12, 1915, the future owner of the *Wauconda Leader*. (Courtesy of Deanna Wiemuth Rogers.)

In this 1933 photograph, Irma May Banks Wiemuth, poses on her grandfather Vernon Kimball's farm. Her mother is pictured at the top of the page. (Courtesy of Deanna Wiemuth Rogers.)

Here is Vernon Kimball in the 1930s on his farm at Main Street and Route 176. He also had a butcher shop on Main Street, which later became Peterson's. (Courtesy of Deanna Wiemuth Rogers.)

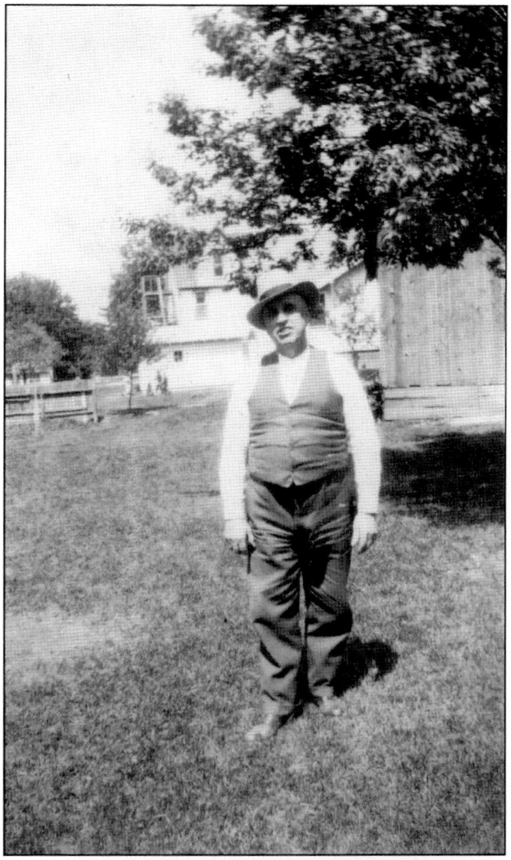

Paul Smith stands next to a Farmall M-D tractor purchased by R.C. Raven in 1941 at Blackburn and Broughton Hardware Store, also an International Harvester dealer. Raven drove the tractor to his Darrell Road farm from the Wisconsin State Fair where it was displayed. Its unique feature was a German Bosch diesel-injection pump. German engineers came to the United Stated in 1941 specifically to build the pump, but World War II hostilities forced them to return home. (Courtesy of Paul Smith.)

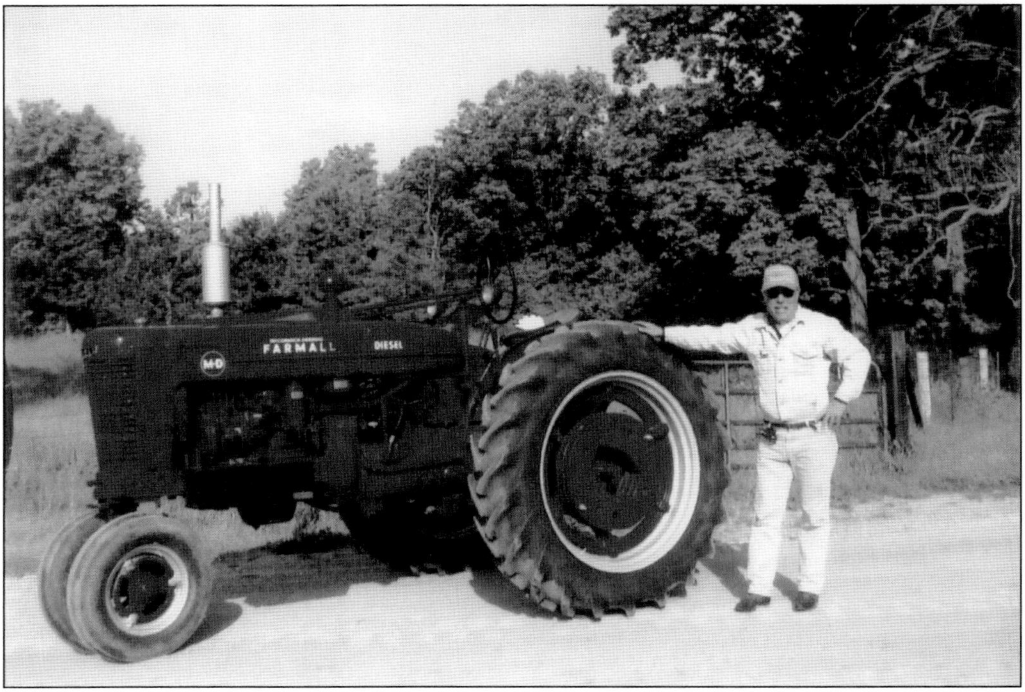

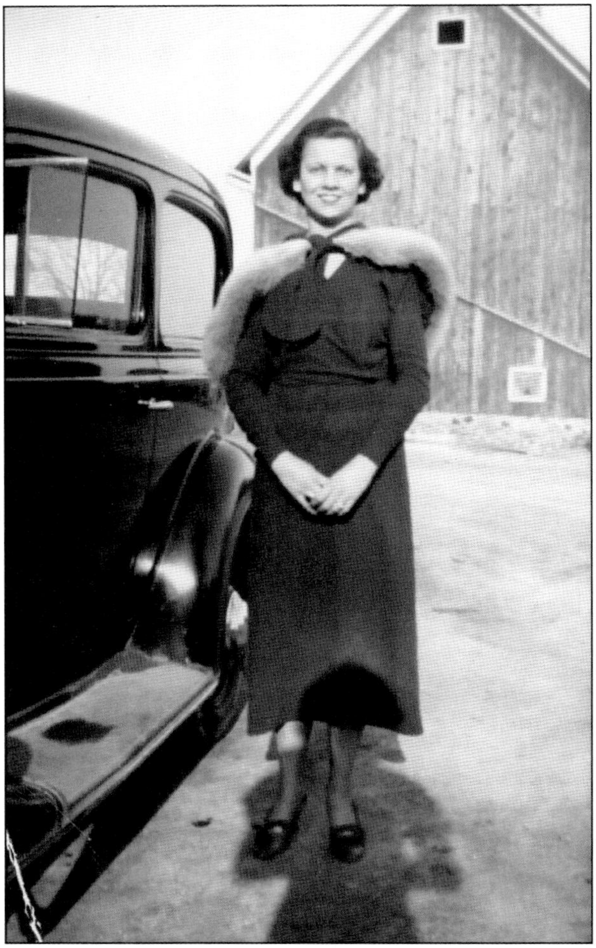

Pictured is 16-year-old Mary Etta Nicholls Freund on the family farm on Case Road in 1937. (Courtesy of Steve Freund.)

This 1950s photograph shows the Nicholls sisters and their mother on the family farm on Case Road. With their married names, they are, from left to right, (first row) Jane Kennebeck, Mary Etta Freund, and Toni Steiskal Kuester; (second row) mother Myrtie, Francis Willoughby, Fern Stoffel, Grace Flary, and Mert Lincoln. (Courtesy of Steve Freund.)

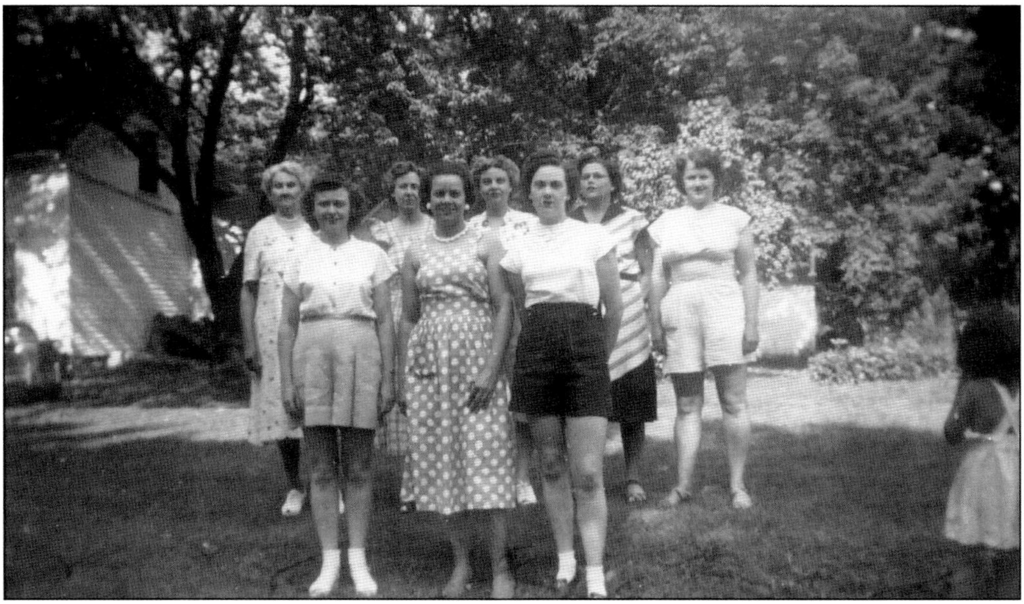

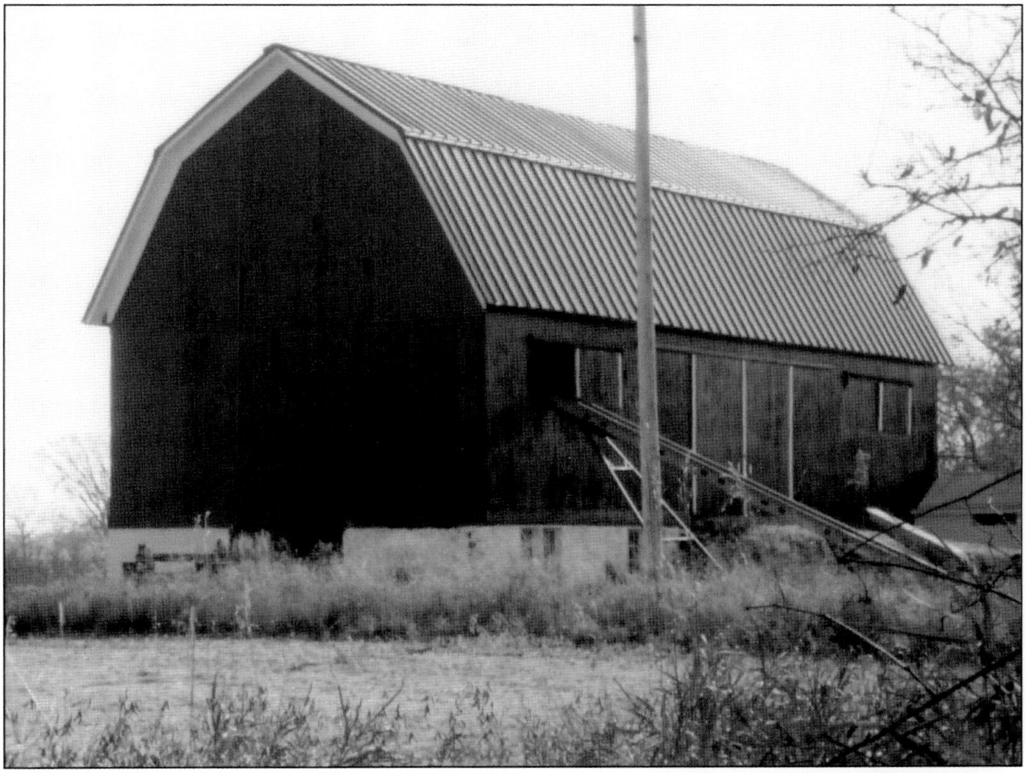

Arvilla "Annie" Fisher Peterson loved life on the Fisher farm. Among the most memorable highlights was the barn dance held in the loft of the barn (above) her junior year of high school. Her great-grandfather Thomas Fisher came to America from Yorkshire, England, in 1844. In July 1845, he received a land grant from Pres. James Polk to buy 100 acres at $1.25 an acre. After purchasing the land, he built a log cabin and then wrote his bride-to-be in Yorkshire, Elizabeth Fairweather, that the house was ready and waiting for her arrival. She came to America on December 1, 1845, and they were married. To this union eight children were born, five of whom died of black fever. The farm remained in the family until 1966, when Arvilla's father's health failed and the farm was sold to Leo and Germaine Henningfield. (Above, courtesy of Kathie Broughton Carr; at right, Marianne Folise.)

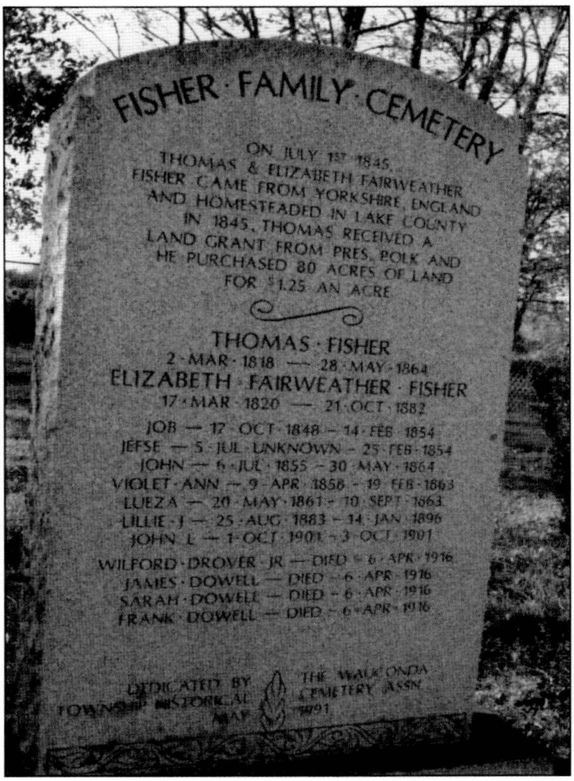

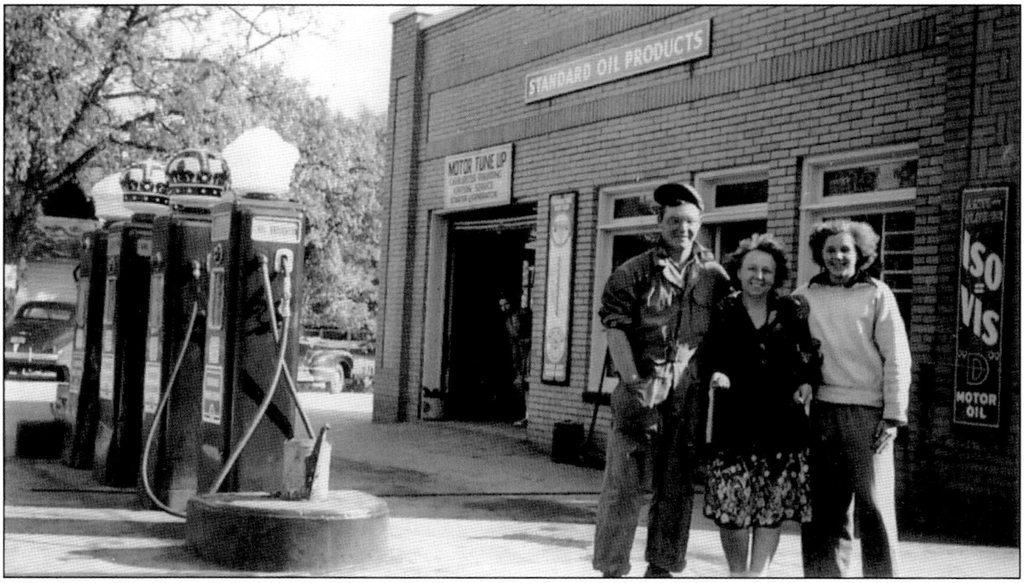

In January 1925, Emma Quastoff Fish (center) married Ben W. Fish, who owned and operated Fish's Standard Gas Service Station on Main Street across from the beaches from 1946 to 1953. They had three children, 10 grandchildren, and numerous great-grandchildren and great-great grandchildren. Two of her children, Ben Fish Jr. and Louise Fish Matthews, are in this 1948 photograph at the gas station. (Courtesy of Louise Fish Matthews.)

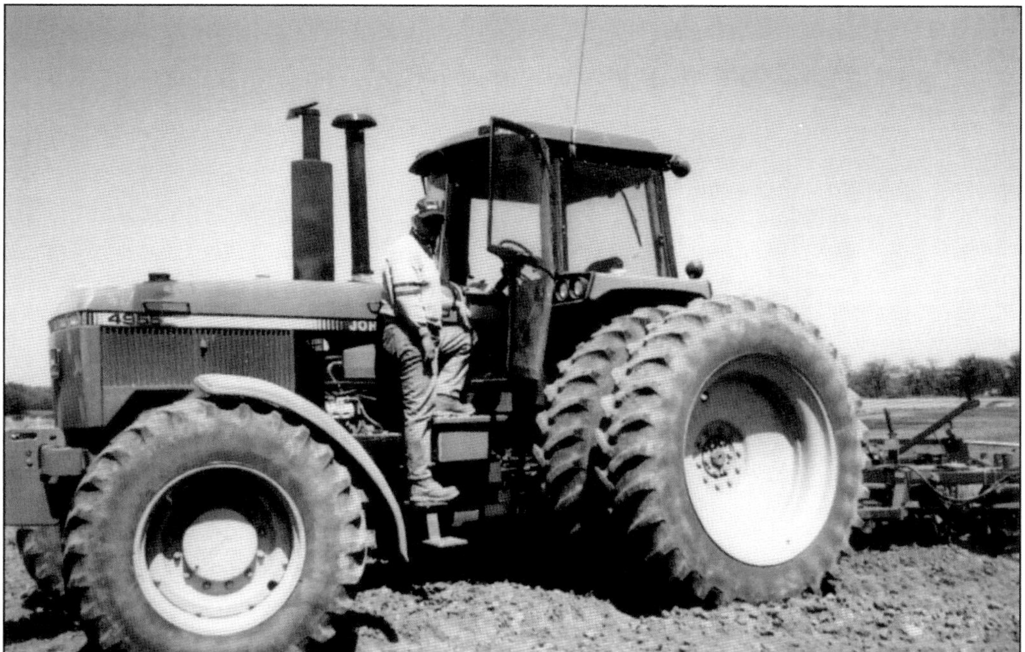

Lyle Matthews takes a break from working at the Golden Oaks Farm in May 2000. Although retired after 32 years as a dairy farmer, he just could not give up the farm life. (Courtesy of Louise Fish Matthews.)

The Old Oak Glen Barn

It was new then this barn, built to last and to
Serve, of sturdy woods and pegged.
Its roof and sides kept safe inside its owner's
Goods, its owner's pride!
The team and harnesses, cattle and feeds, the
Milking tools every dairyman needs.
From far and near, neighbors had helped with the
Building.
It was 1906 in the time of "barn raising."
And for all who had worked since it was begun,
There was dancing and food, now that it was done!

At his Daddy's side little Lyle learned each day
About cows and horses and feed and hay.
And as he grew strong he helped his Dad
In the high old barn; and their hearts were glad!
More cows were raised, and tractors soon
Replaced the teams; and they added more room.
Lyle was, as his Dad had hoped he'd be,
His "right-hand" man.
Then on year he brought a "sweet city girl"
Out to come and see their barn, and the place,
And to meet his Dad.

With this first visit our Louise had lost her heart,
And knew right then she would want to visit again
And again!
She had noticed Lyle for quite awhile,
Loved his blue eyes and reticent smile.
And she liked Lyle's Dad, the cows, the Big Barn,
She found herself liking the whole busy farm!

Very soon Lyle knew he'd found the "ONE"
With whom his farming was sure to be fun!
And Louise, tho used to city life, would
Be happy to be a farmer's wife!

Emma Quastoff Fish loved to write poetry. Born in Chicago on September 6, 1904, she grew up on a farm in Tinley Park, Illinois, which was owned by sports magnate Keith Spaulding. Her father managed the farm before opening Quastoff Flowers in Chicago and River Grove. Here is a touching poem about one of her daughters, Louise, who married Lyle Matthews. (Courtesy of Louise Matthews Bundy.)

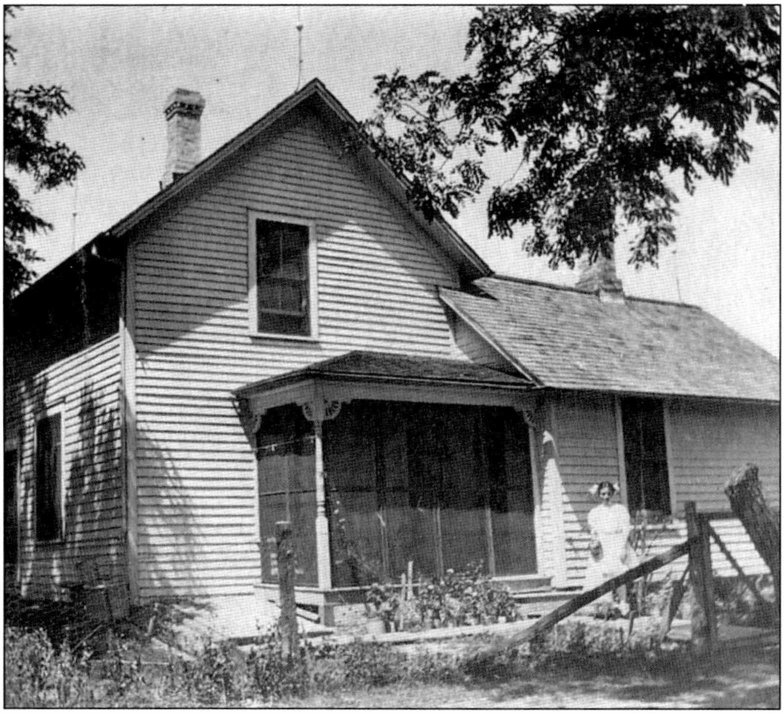

This farmhouse, originally built in 1842, became the Darrell family home when George F. Darrell purchased the farmland in October 1884. The land was then passed down to Willard Darrell in 1923, to Harry and Mabel Darrell Matthews in 1942, and then to the Matthews brothers, Robert and Lyle, and Lyle's wife, Louise, in 1965. (Courtesy of Louise Fish Matthews.)

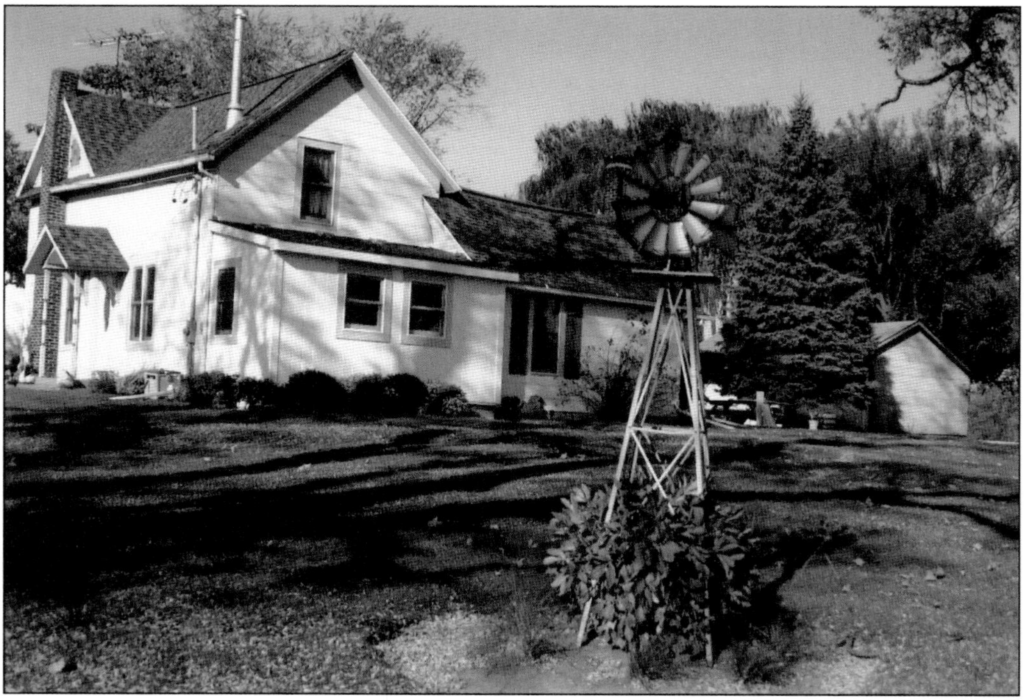

Leanne Matthews Roseman, her husband Russ, and their son Jeremy restored the main farmhouse. (Courtesy of Marianne Folise.)

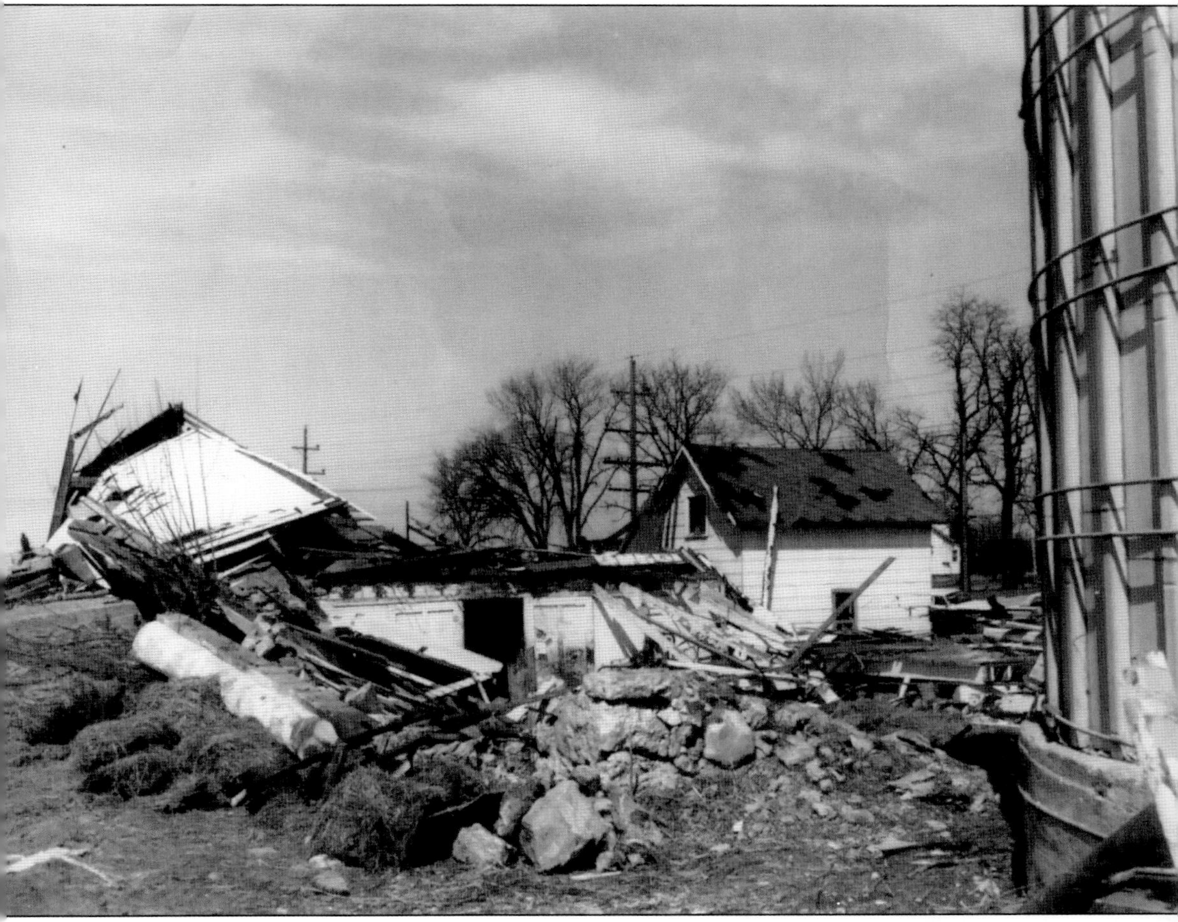

A tornado struck the Matthews farm on Palm Sunday, April 11, 1965. Ten cows were lost that day and five died later of injuries. The barn and some of the farm buildings were destroyed, and the roof was torn from the house. With the help of a legion of family and friends, the barn was rebuilt before the end of the year. (Courtesy of Louise Fish Matthews.)

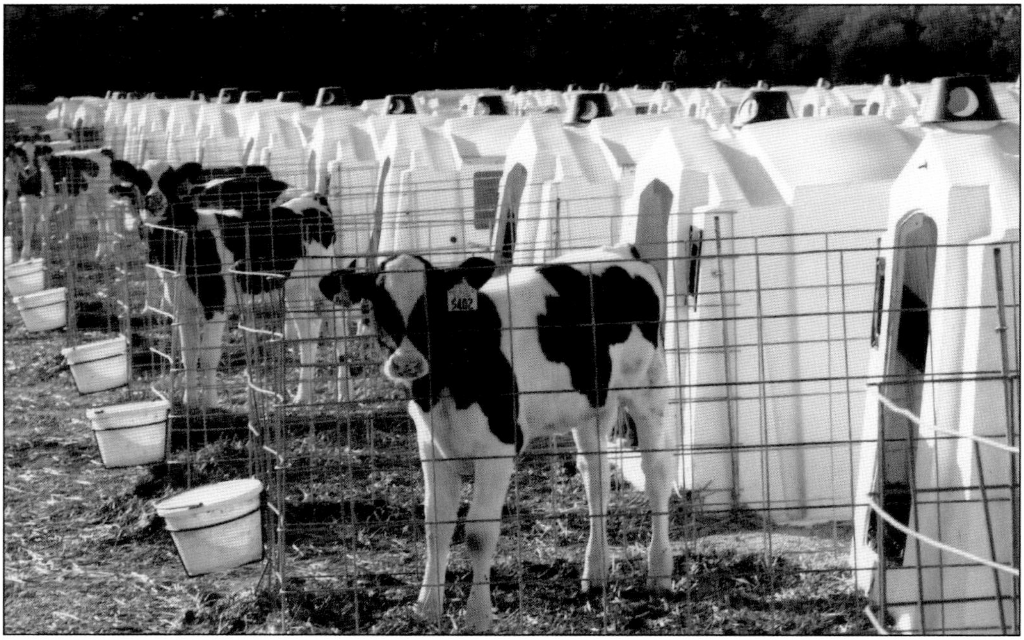

One of Wauconda's last surviving dairy farms is Golden Oaks Farm, at 27730 Bonner Road, which was established by the Crown family in 1948. It is known worldwide within the dairy industry because of the farm's advances in the breeding and development of superior Black and White and Red and White Holsteins. The herd consists of 650 young stock (above) and 700 milking females (below). The farm's goal is to produce 18.2 million pounds of milk per year with solid components. Cows are milked twice a day, and most of the cows' feed is grown on the farm. Each year the farm hosts numerous dairy enthusiasts, as well as several hundred local students eager to learn about the dairy industry. The farm employs 14 full-time and several part-time employees. It also has an internship program for college students. (Both courtesy of Marianne Folise.)

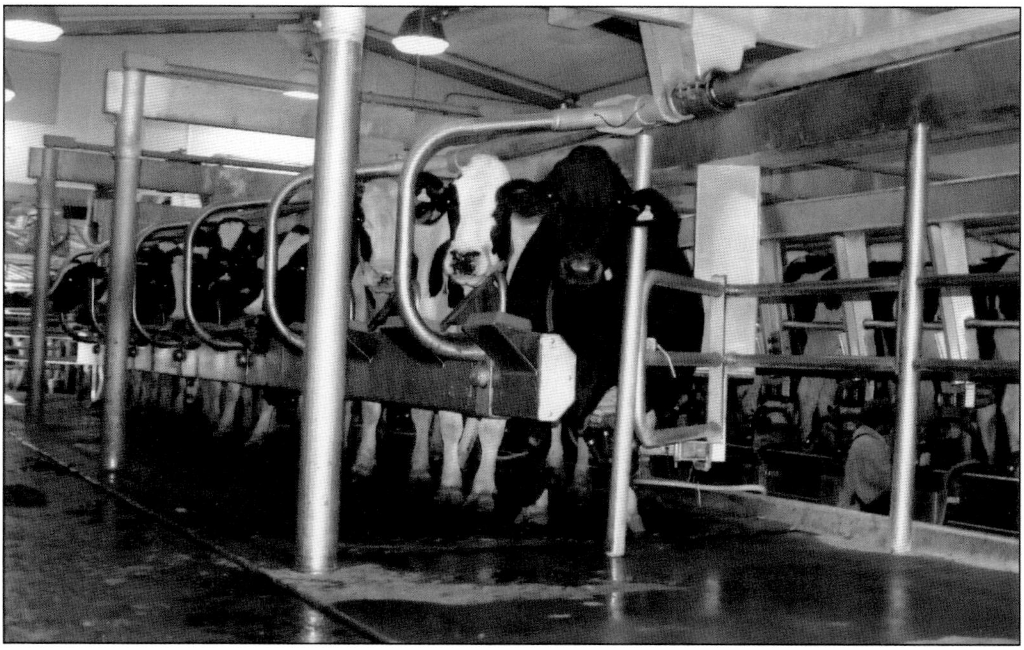

Seven

Churches

Religious faith was a moving force for the early pioneers as they forged a new life in a new town. In the fall of 1838, the Baptist Society of Wauconda was formed by Elder Wheeler of McHenry. Services were held in the homes of Mark Bangs and Zebina Ford and moved to the Little Red Schoolhouse a year later.

In 1853, the Rev. Charles French organized the First Methodist Episcopal Church. The Baptists and Methodists built a church together in 1856 on the corner of Route 176 and Maple Avenue that they would use on alternate Sundays. In 1870, the Methodists decided to use the church every Sunday, so the Baptists built their own across the street.

In 1915, the two churches came together again to form a federation—thus the Federated Church. Each group kept its denominational connections. Worship services and Sunday school classes were held at the Methodist church, and the Baptist church was used as a community center.

This arrangement worked well until the early 1930s, when, to accommodate the new Route 176, the land on which the Methodist church stood was needed. The congregations were already federated, so the Methodist church was moved across the street, the two buildings were remodeled into a single structure, and they were dedicated as the Federated Church in 1935.

Wauconda's first Catholics were Irish immigrants; John and Michael Murray, Hugh Davlin, and six others established Murray Settlement. They worshiped in homes until missionary Pere Jean Gueguen began coming once a month to say Mass, perform baptisms, and officiate at weddings. He agreed to come if they built a chapel, and in 1844 they built a log church on farmland the Murrays donated. The church was named St. John after its benefactor and placed under the jurisdiction of the new Diocese of Chicago. The land is now Transfiguration Cemetery on Route 176.

In 1876, under the leadership of the Rev. Patrick O'Neill, the congregation purchased land from Justus Bangs and built a white frame church, which still stands, and renamed it in honor of the Feast of the Transfiguration. The parish outgrew that building, and another church was constructed that today houses the parish's offices. Since 1985, Transfiguration Church has been at 315 West Mill Street.

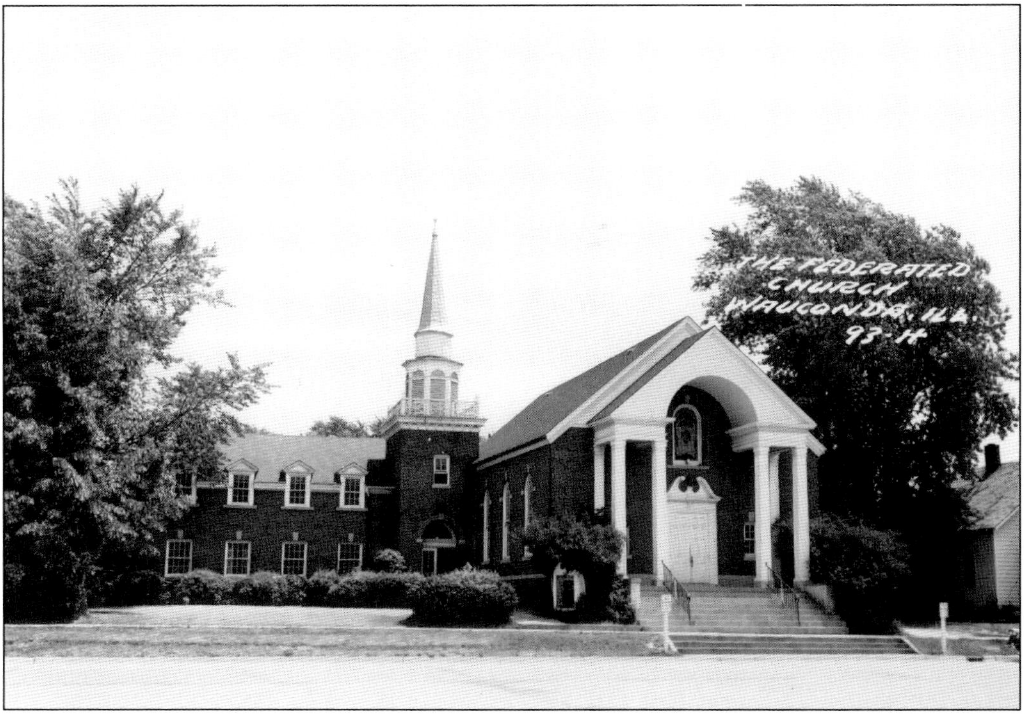

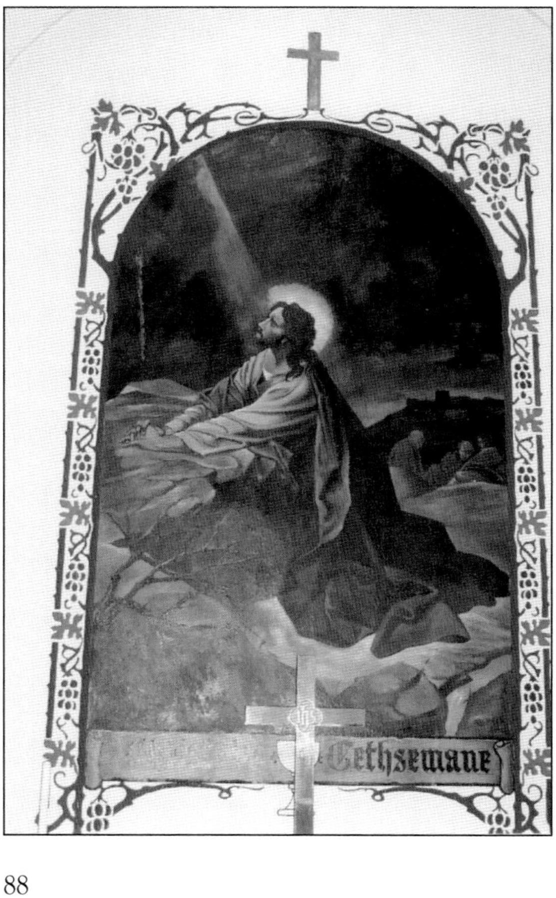

The Methodist church building was moved to join the Baptist church building, and they were remodeled into a single structure. In 1935, a brick veneer was added, the joint structure was dedicated, and the Federated Church had a new home. Worship continues in the original Baptist sanctuary; Sunday school, sacristy, and the lounge are in the former Methodist building. In September 1955, ground was broken for a two-story addition, with a dining room, kitchen, youth center, assembly rooms, and classrooms. (Courtesy of Marianne Folise.)

This 1935 oil painting, *Christ in the Garden of Gethsemane*, adorns the wall over the altar. It was painted by artist Oliver Croyden and his wife, Ruth. They and their son Fred were members of the congregation. Oliver died in 1949 at the age of 77, and Ruth at age 103. The Croydens are buried at the Wauconda Cemetery. Another artistic element is the tin ceiling in the sanctuary, installed by George M. Broughton. (Courtesy of Marianne Folise.)

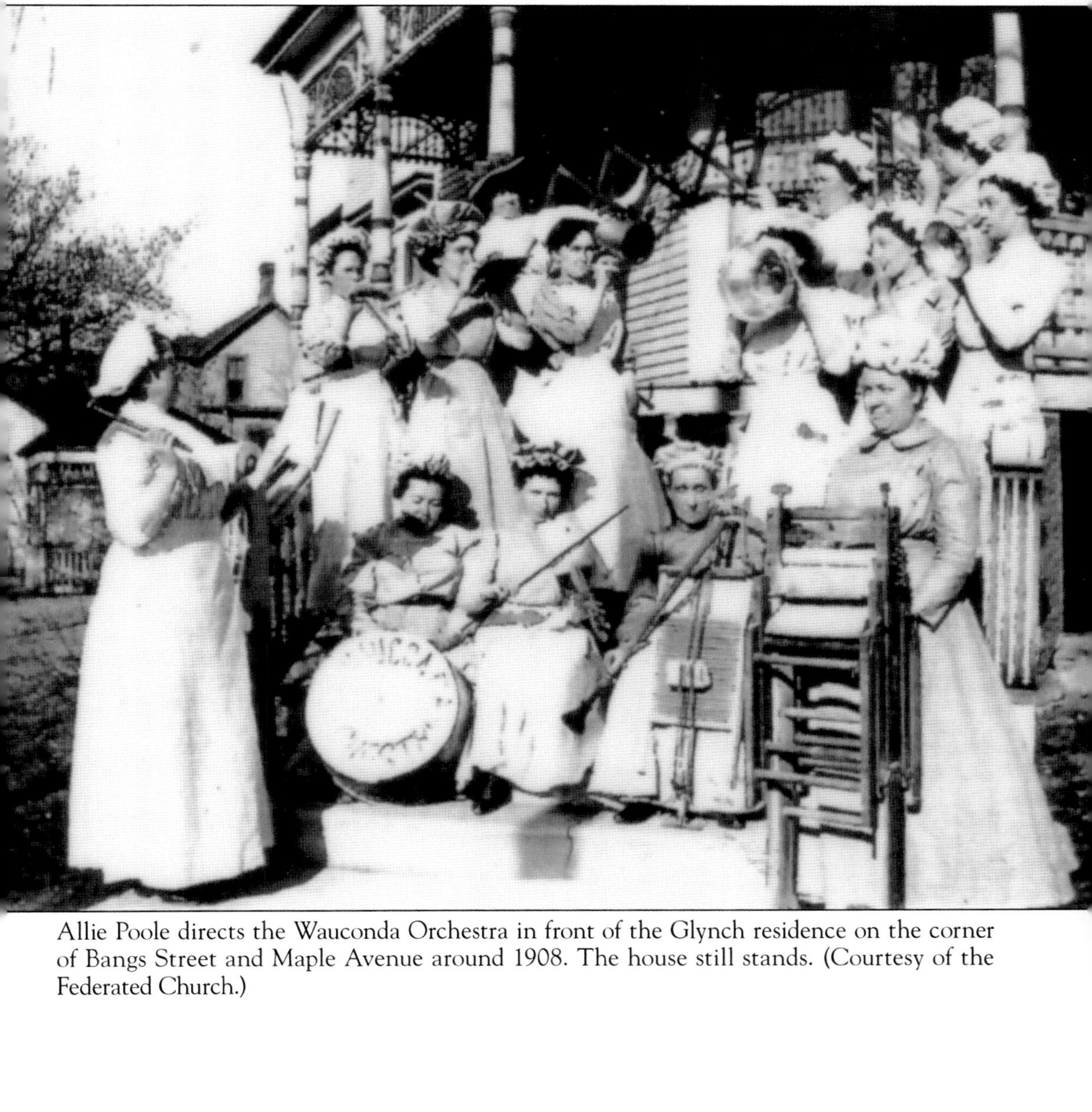

Allie Poole directs the Wauconda Orchestra in front of the Glynch residence on the corner of Bangs Street and Maple Avenue around 1908. The house still stands. (Courtesy of the Federated Church.)

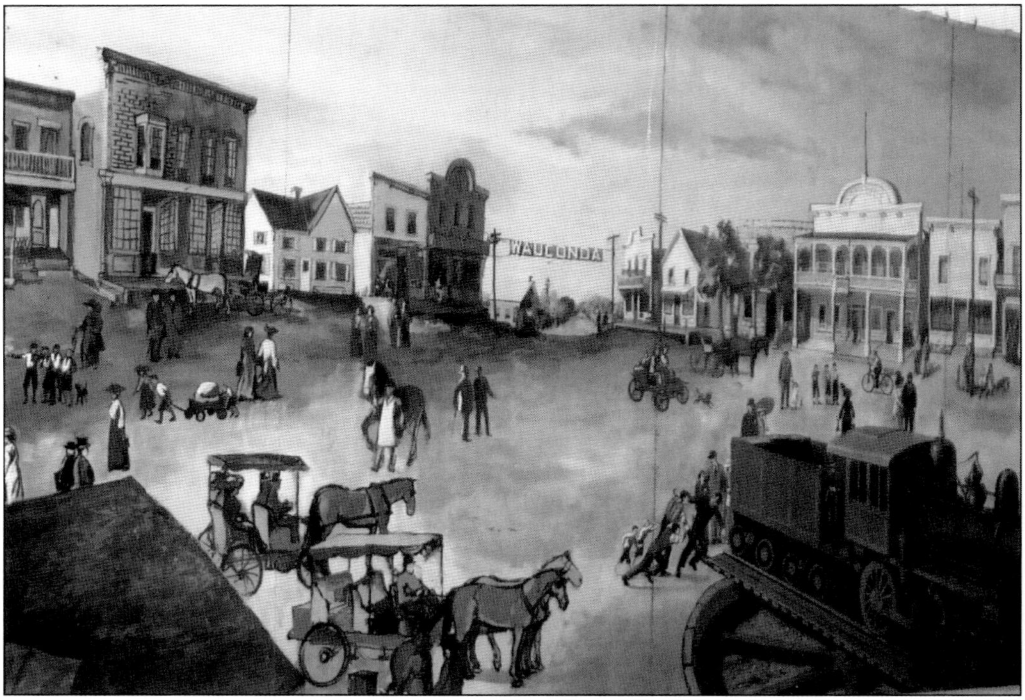

This section of the mural on the south wall of the dining room in the Federated Church depicts life on Main Street in the village in the early 20th century. Shown are some of the area buildings, as well as the PLZ&W Railroad. (Courtesy of Marianne Folise.)

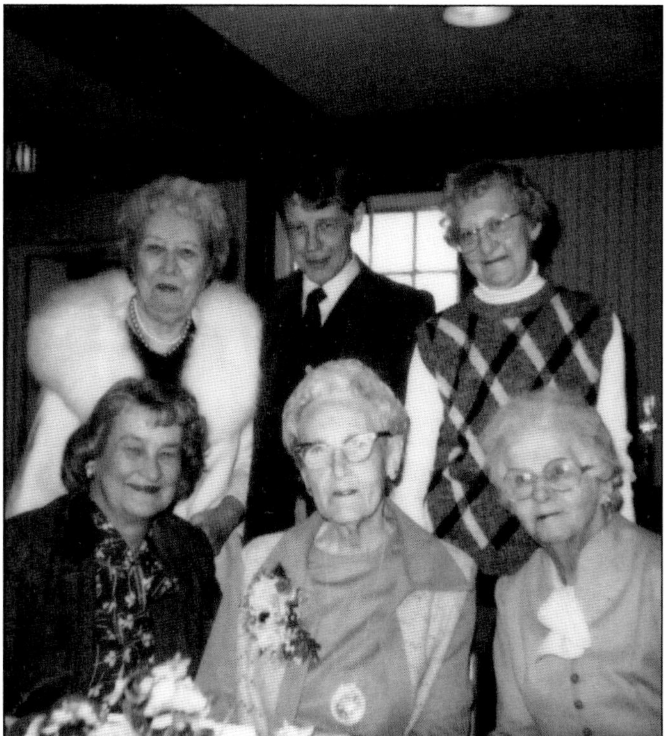

Rev. Ralph Smith and his wife, Evelyn, are pictured after returning to the Federated Church in March 1973 to attend Della Kirwan's 75th birthday celebration. Pictured, from left to right, are (first row) Evelyn Smith, Della Kirwan, and Edith Case; (second row) Gladys Meyer, Rev. Smith, and Velda Bittner. In May 1956, the church and community received nationwide recognition. *Look* magazine printed the article, "Many Lives of a Minister's Wife," depicting Evelyn Smith as a typical country minister's wife and mother of four active daughters. Many photographs of the Smith family and familiar sights of Wauconda accompanied the article. (Courtesy Jacque Ross Peterson.)

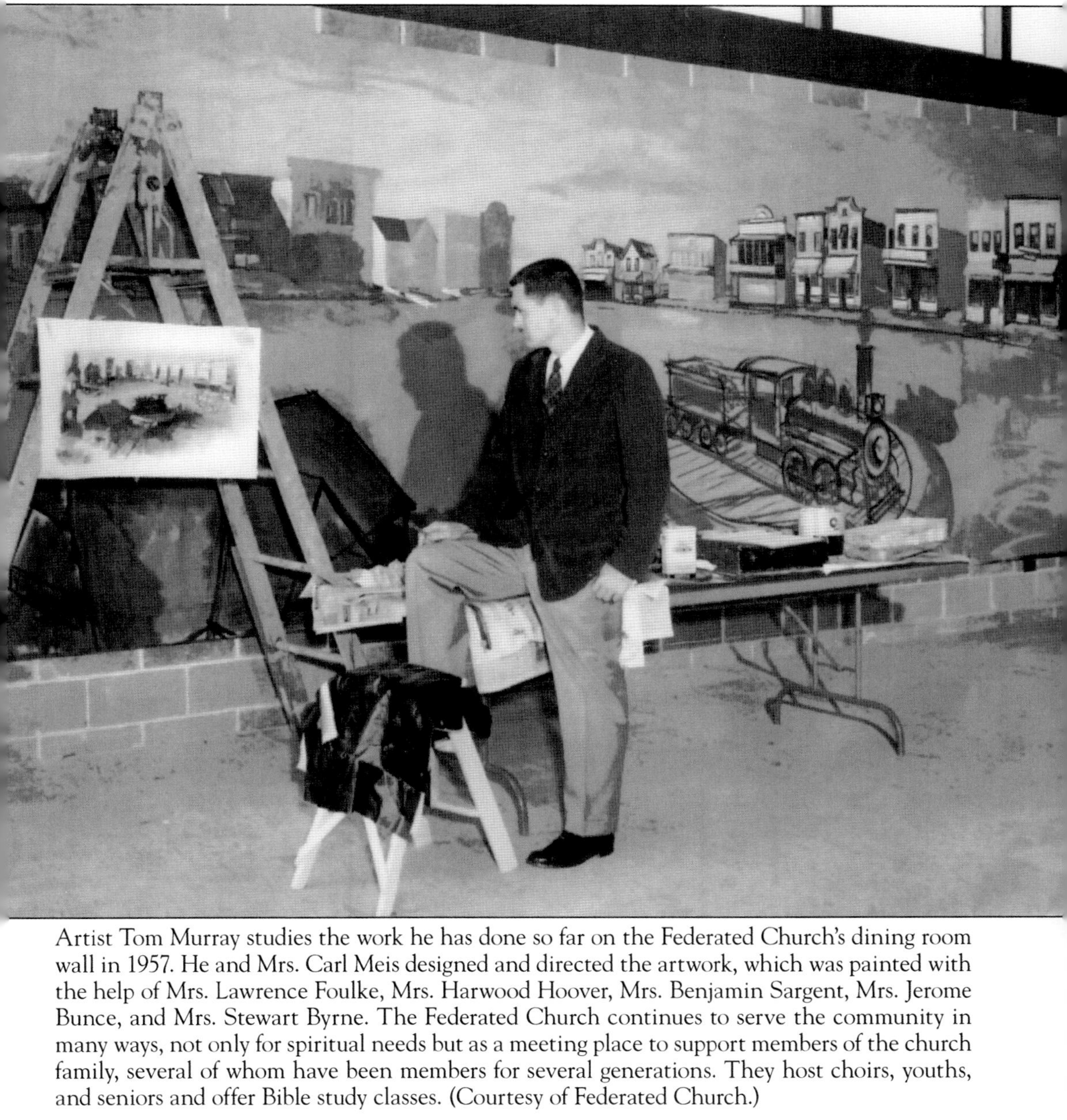

Artist Tom Murray studies the work he has done so far on the Federated Church's dining room wall in 1957. He and Mrs. Carl Meis designed and directed the artwork, which was painted with the help of Mrs. Lawrence Foulke, Mrs. Harwood Hoover, Mrs. Benjamin Sargent, Mrs. Jerome Bunce, and Mrs. Stewart Byrne. The Federated Church continues to serve the community in many ways, not only for spiritual needs but as a meeting place to support members of the church family, several of whom have been members for several generations. They host choirs, youths, and seniors and offer Bible study classes. (Courtesy of Federated Church.)

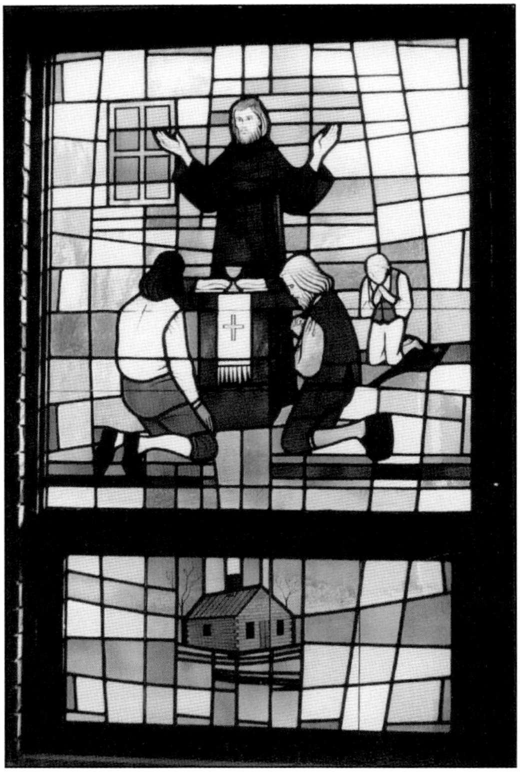

Eight stained-glass windows in the 1985 building for Transfiguration Church depict events in the church's history. At left, in Window 5, Pere Jean Gueguen offers Mass at St. John's log church at Murray Settlement, the first place of worship for what would become Transfiguration Parish; it is where Transfiguration Cemetery is now. Window 6, below, depicts celebrating Mass at the old white church, located on land purchased from Justus Bangs; the church still stands. (Both courtesy of Marianne Folise.)

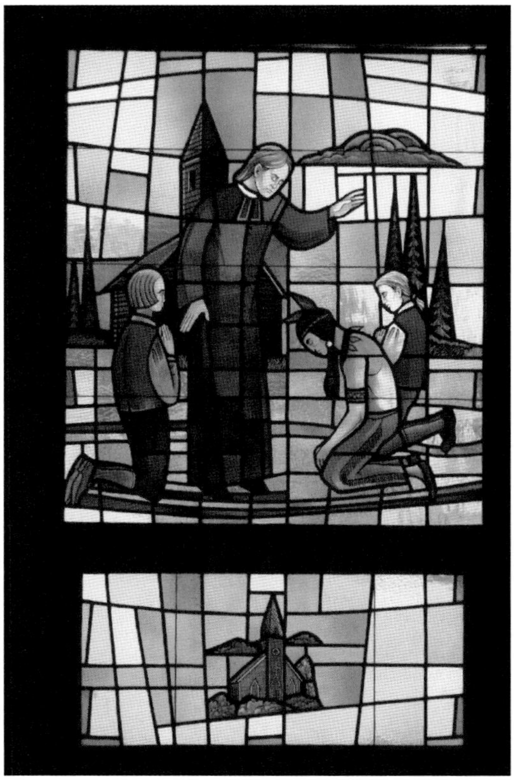

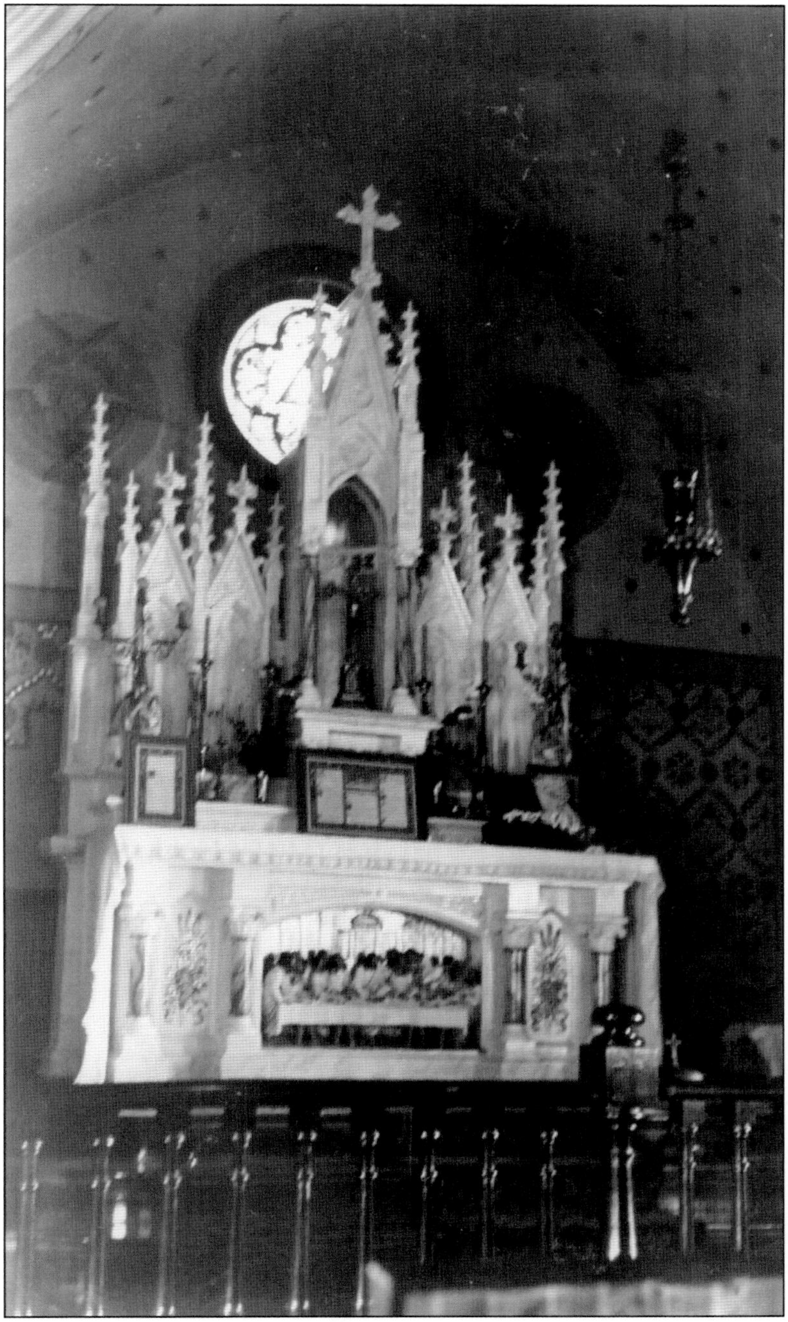

Under the leadership of the Rev. Patrick O'Neill, the Catholic congregation purchased land from Justus Bangs on the western edge of Wauconda. There, in 1877, they built a white frame church, which still stands. On August 6, 1877, Bishop Foley of Chicago blessed and dedicated the church and renamed it in honor of the Feast of the Transfiguration. Twelve days later, Wauconda was incorporated as a village. Pictured is the altar in the white church. The "summer people" would swell the numbers in the congregation so much that the church could not hold all the worshippers who wanted to attend Mass. The windows would be opened so the overflow crowd standing outside could hear the prayers and hymns. (Courtesy of Transfiguration Parish.)

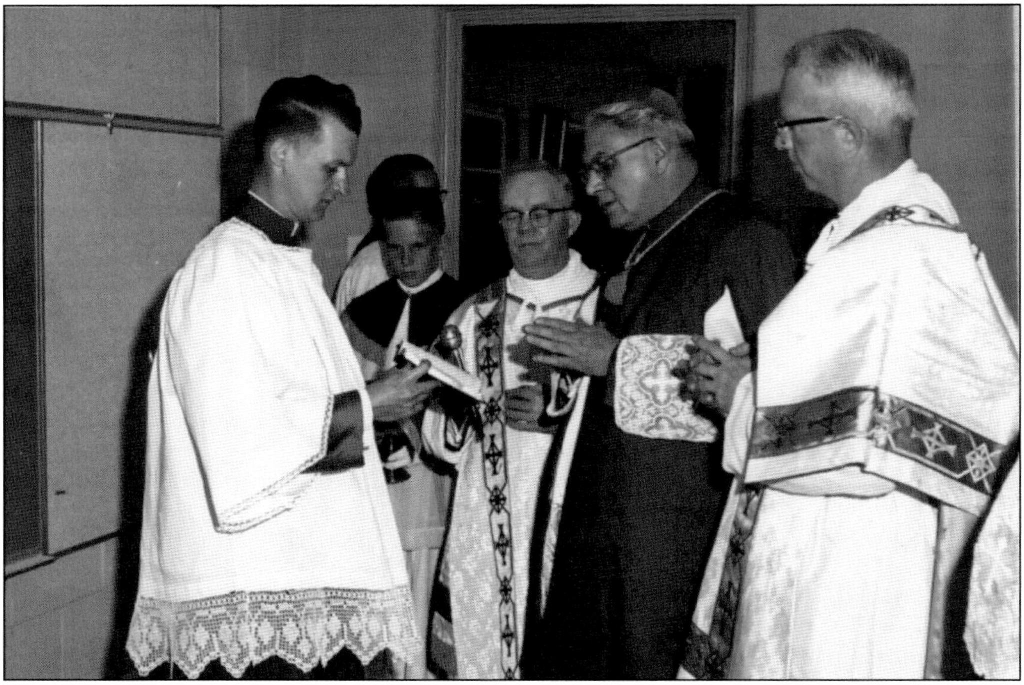

The Transfiguration Parish outgrew the white church and thus built a new one in 1955. Pausing before the dedication of the new building are Samuel Cardinal Stritch, the Archbishop of Chicago (second from right), and other members of the clergy, as well as an altar boy. The Cardinal blessed both the church and Transfiguration School on November 29, 1955, according to the ancient rites of the Catholic Church. A parish dinner, attended by 250 guests, followed. (Courtesy of Transfiguration Parish.)

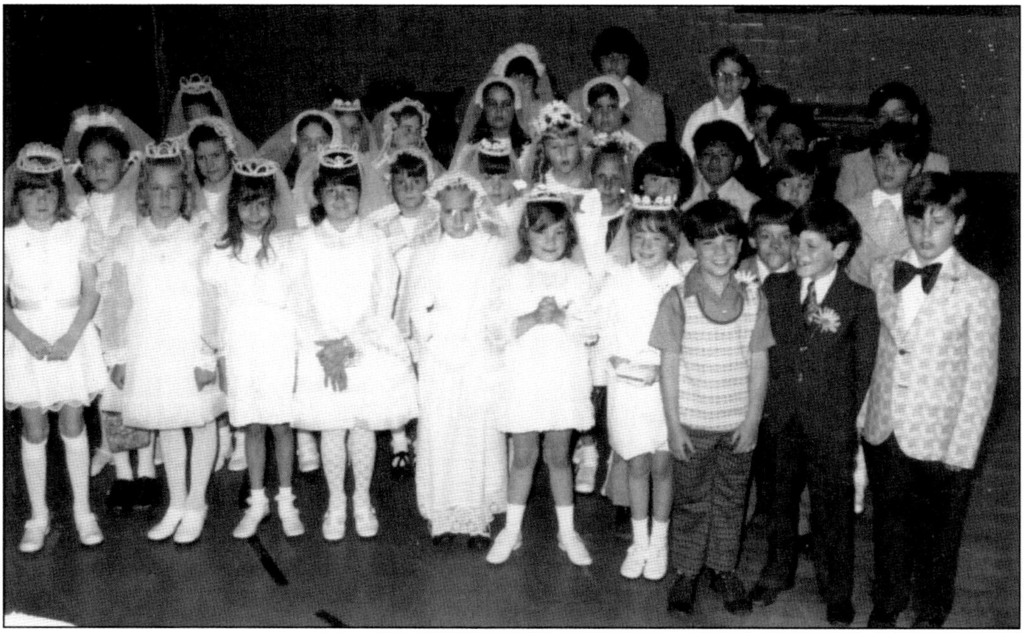

Looking like angels are members of Transfiguration Parish's in a c. 1970 Holy Communion class. (Courtesy of Transfiguration Parish.)

Rev. Thomas McMahon was named Transfiguration Church parish administrator on November 9, 1955, and pastor on July 7, 1956. During Father McMahon's pastorate, all the land bounded by Liberty, Church, and Mill Streets was acquired for the parish's future needs. He served as pastor until August 8, 1963. The Reverend Msgr. Thomas J. Fitzgerald succeeded him. (Courtesy of Transfiguration Parish.)

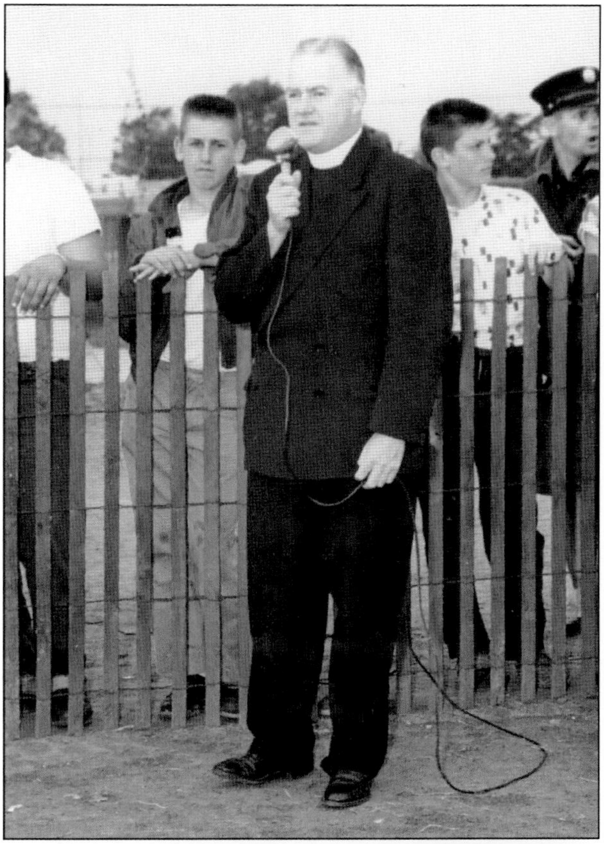

Seen on May 5, 1985, is Joseph Cardinal Bernardin of the Archdiocese of Chicago offering Mass for the dedication of the current church. (Courtesy of Transfiguration Parish.)

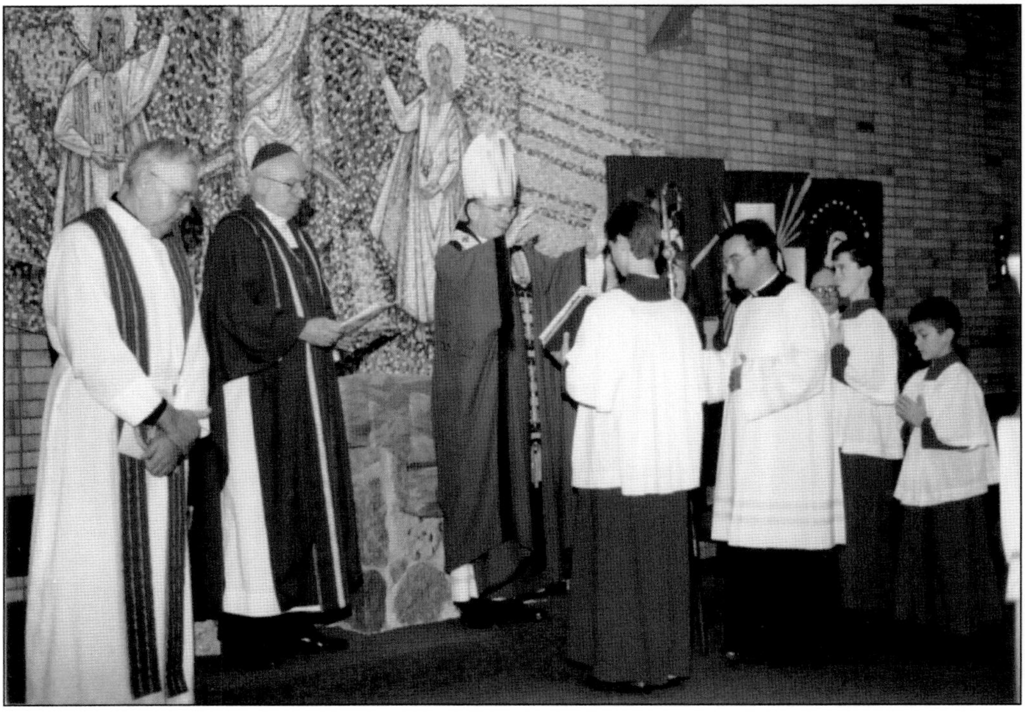

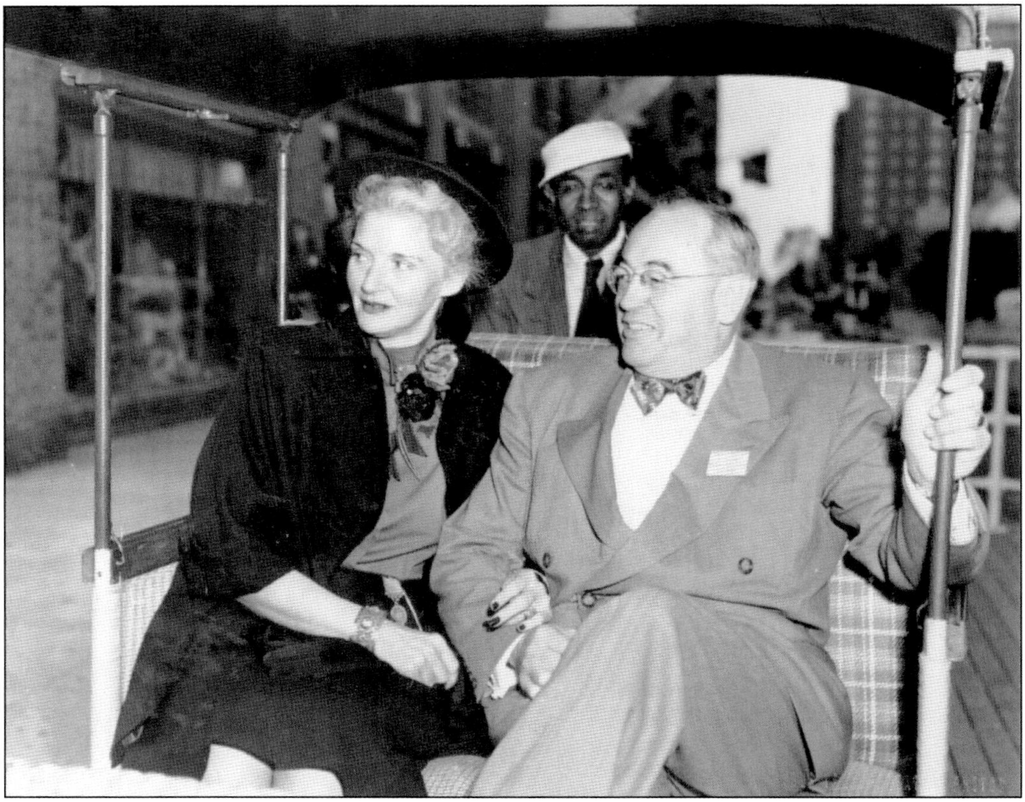

Pictured here are Mr. and Mrs. Charles P. Krupp. Although, not made public until 1983, Charlie Krupp donated $700,000 at the time of his death in 1981 for the purpose of building a new house of worship for Transfiguration Parish. The new church was dedicated in May 1985. (Courtesy of Transfiguration Parish.)

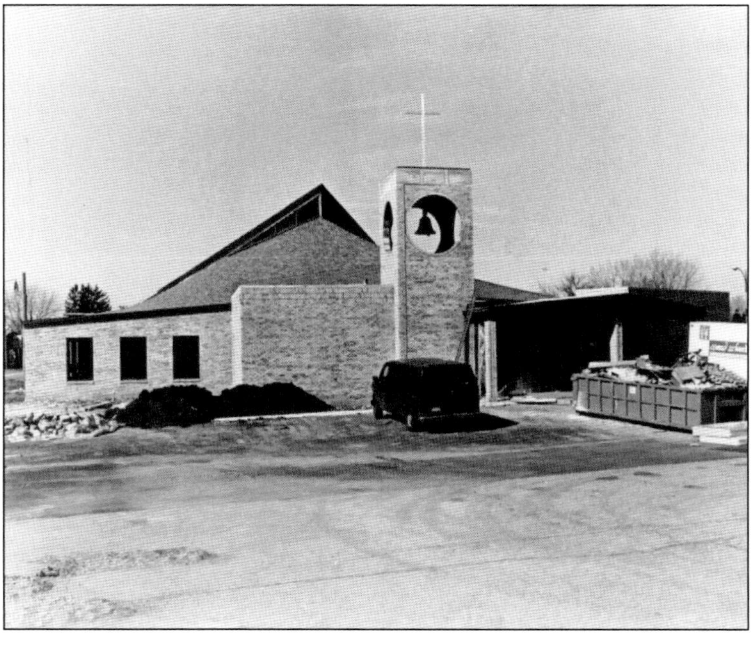

The current Transfiguration Church is shown under construction in March 1985, which is on the property that had been occupied by the Elm Theater. Since the early 1990s, in addition to English, Masses are offered in Spanish and Polish. (Courtesy of Transfiguration Parish.)

Eight

Schools

In 1839, a log schoolhouse was built with generosity; Justus Bangs donated land in the northeast part of town, and volunteers constructed it from logs gathered in the nearby woods. The first teacher was La Fayette Mills. Later, three Davis sisters succeeded each other as teachers. The school was named the Little Red Schoolhouse. Books were few, and the primary sources of learning were Cobb's speller, some readers, an arithmetic primer, and the Bible.

Recorded memories of one student recalled that in winter it took until noon for the stone fireplace to heat the building, and lunches were kept in the potbelly stove so they would not freeze. There were two outhouses: one for boys and one for girls. Early teachers were paid from money obtained by contributions and enforcement of game laws.

In 1856, the Wauconda Academy opened, putting Wauconda on the map, as the only other academies in Lake County were in Waukegan and Lake Forest. The academy's first teacher was Euphemia Valentine. Classrooms for the first three grades were on the ground floor, and classrooms for fourth through eighth grades were on the second. Later, freshman and sophomore classes were added to the eighth grade. The academy was a center for local activity, such as debates, spelling bees, plays, religious services, and meetings. The Wauconda Fire Department now sits on the site.

Wauconda Grade School opened in 1924, serving kindergarten through fifth grade. The original Wauconda High School, at 217 Slocum Lake Road, opened in September 1915. The building was converted into Wauconda Middle School for sixth through eighth grades, when high school classes moved to the current building that was constructed in 1962. Wauconda High is the home of the Bulldogs; its colors are purple and gold.

District 118, organized in 1961, today has three grade schools, two middle schools, and one high school. The newest school, Matthews Middle School, was dedicated in 2007 and named for former fire chief Lyle Matthews and his wife, Louise. Transfiguration Catholic School opened in 1948.

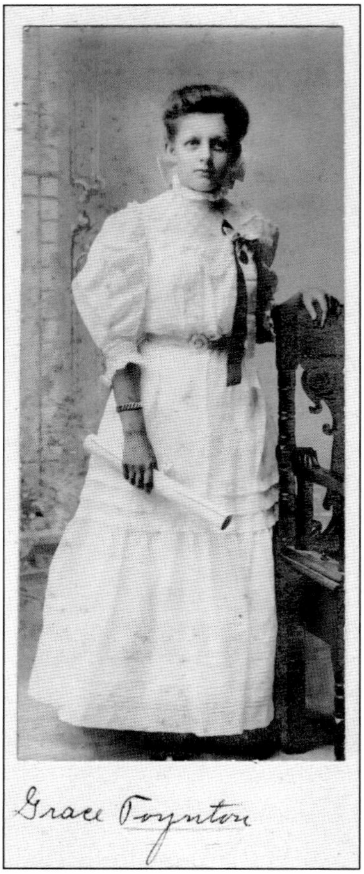

In this 1908 high school graduation photograph is Grace Toynton, whose mother gave her a Kodak camera as a graduation gift. She captured images of life and historical events in the early 1900s, such as when the first train pulled into town on May 10, 1913. She earned money by snapping pictures of local residents. She experimented with time exposures and developed and printed her own photographs. (Courtesy of Mary Ellen Thomas Perry.)

Grace Toynton (later Mrs. George Harris) and her high school classmates Bessie Clough (later Mrs. Rollin Hallock) and Mertie Kuebker (later Mrs. Homer T. Cook) pose on graduation day in 1908 with their flower girls, Wilma Farnsworth and Frances Kent. It was said that "all the boys had gotten bored and dropped out." (Courtesy of Mary Ellen Thomas Perry.)

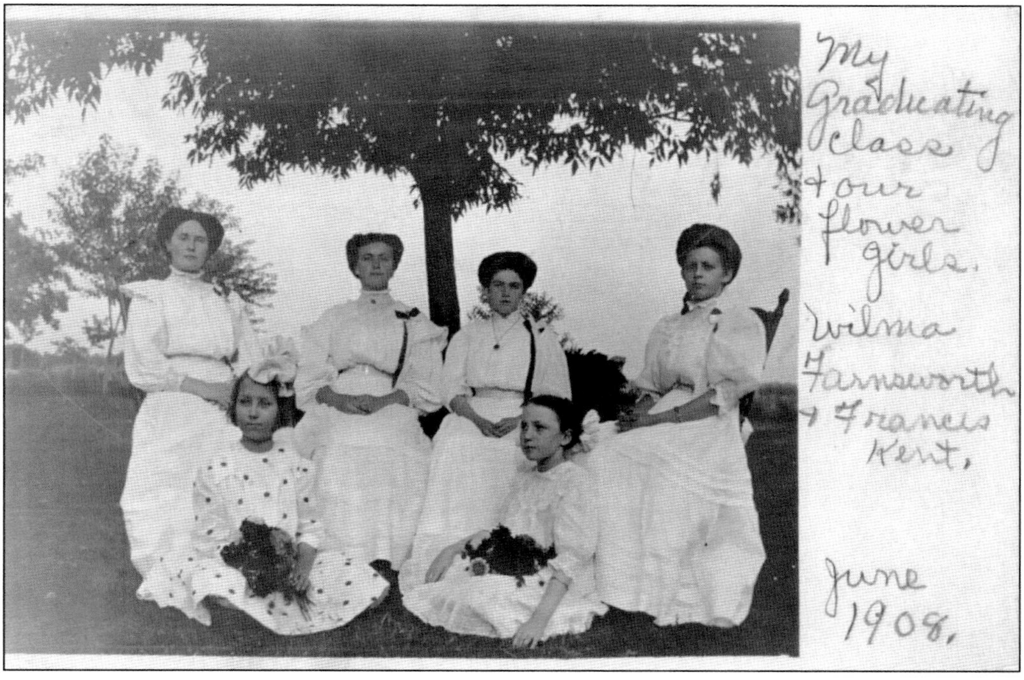

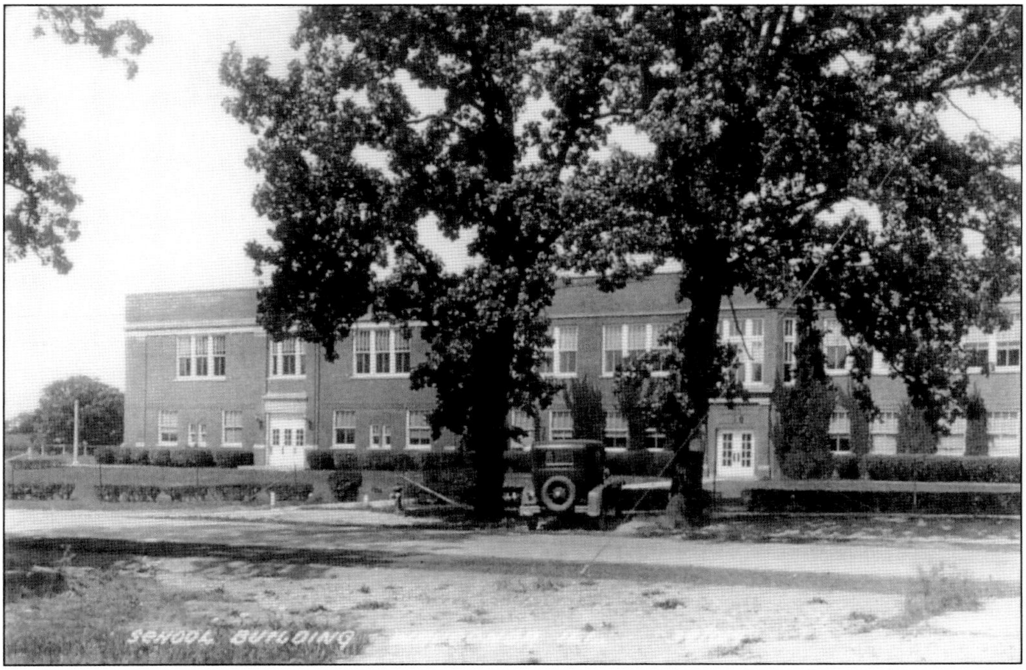

Wauconda Township High School, built in 1915, is seen with the first of two additions that expanded the school. A new school eventually would have to be built in 1961–1962. (Courtesy of Ron K. Vaughn Sr.)

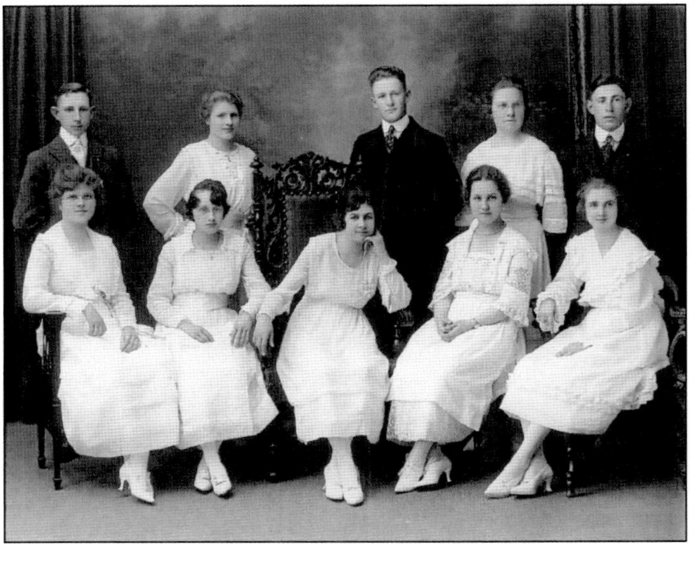

Here are the 1919 graduates of Wauconda Township High School. They were the first class to graduate after completing all four years at the school. They are, from left to right, (front row) Esther Russell, Effie Gilbert, Grace Mueller, Wilma Farnsworth (a flower girl on the left in the picture on the facing page), and Martha Peterson; (second row) Harold Brooks, Marion Hughes, James Young, Matilda Sandman, and John Olinger. (Courtesy of Cindy Francisco Bilisko.)

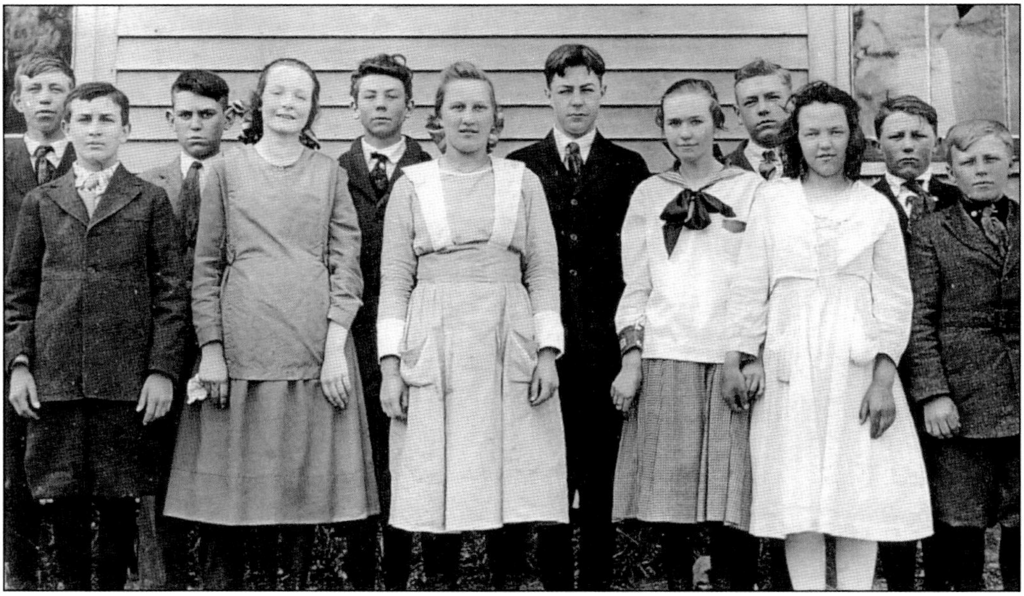

Pictured here are members of the Wauconda Academy's graduating class of 1915. Of those who can be identified are James F. Carr (first row, left), Wilfred Green (second row, second from left), Carl Fink (second row, fourth from left), and Herb Hapke (first row, far right). (Courtesy of Neville Carr.)

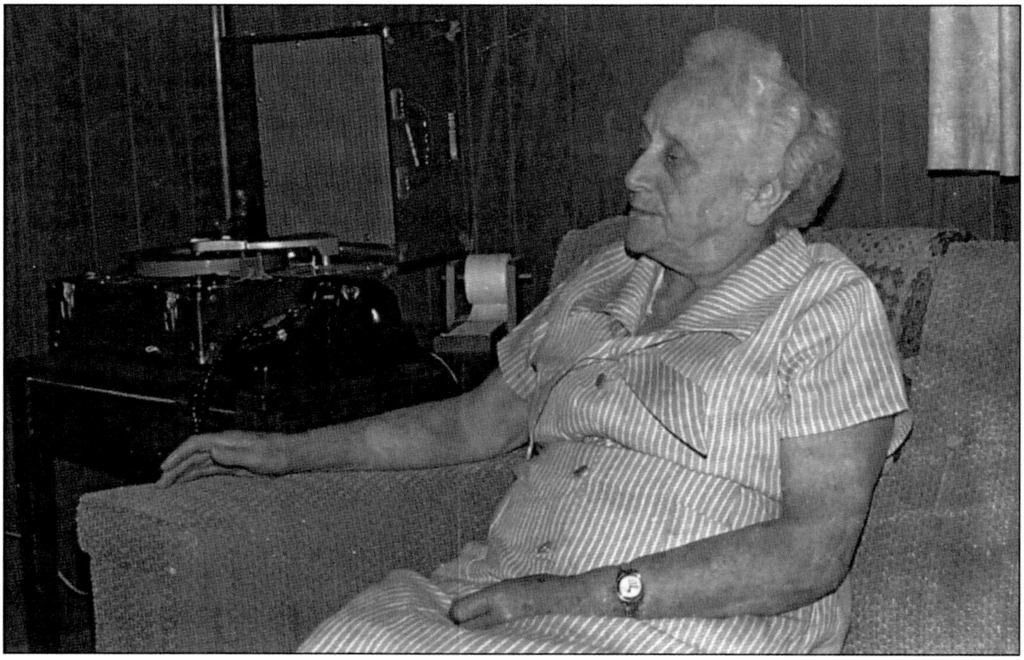

Many people remember teacher Effie Gilbert Francisco. She attended Wauconda Academy and returned as a teacher after high school graduation in 1919. In 1924, she began teaching in the new Wauconda Grade School. She married Harry Francisco and taught until their sons, Gilbert and Dale, were born. She returned to teaching but retired in the 1950s because of eyesight problems and subsequent blindness. Pictured here in 1965, she learned Braille and continued to crochet and tat. She died in 1980. (Courtesy of Cindy Francisco Bilisko.)

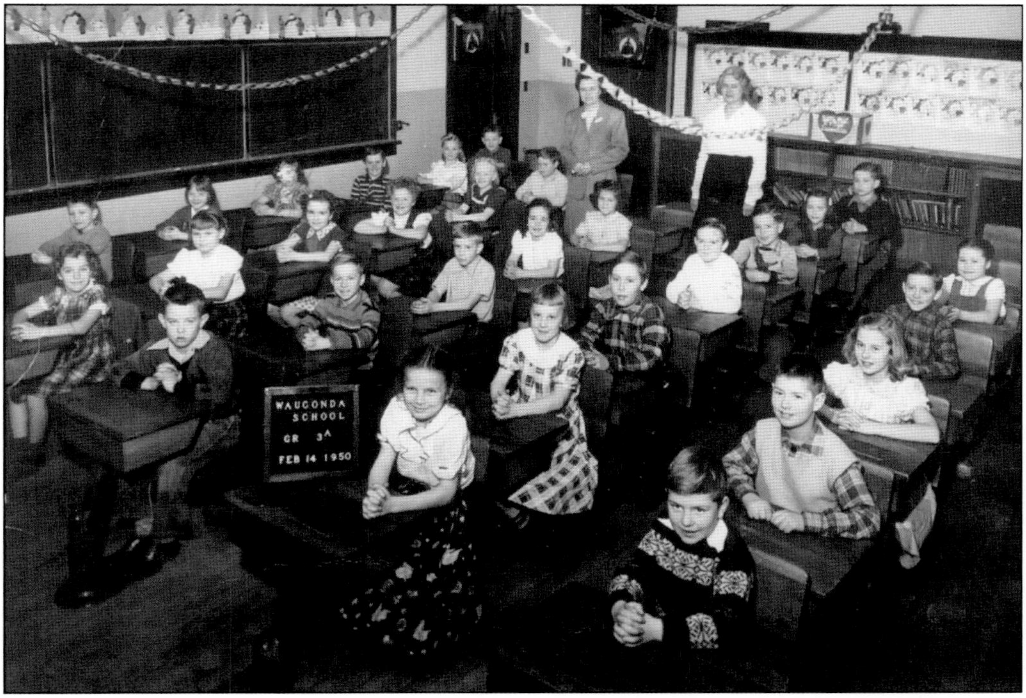

Above, the youngsters in Wauconda Grade School's third grade of 1949–1950 pose obediently. Standing in the back of the room are Principal Ruth Minto (left) and teacher Anna Gerbert. The first boy sitting under the blackboard to the far left is Neville Carr. His daughter Elizabeth Carr Buisson teaches first grade in the same classroom today. Below, Wauconda Grade School second graders perform a patriotic pageant in February 1932. Pictured from left to right are Mary Ann Ford, Henry Green, Ross Harris, Jacqueline Ross, Ruth Dobner, and Glora Jean Anderson. (Above, courtesy of Neville Carr; below, Jacque Ross Peterson.)

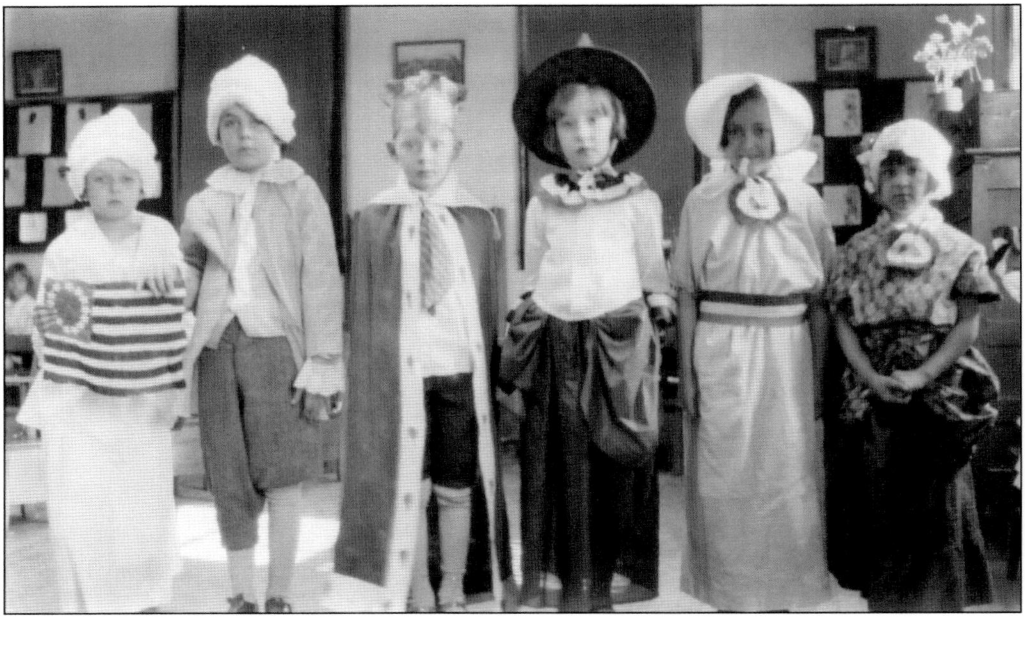

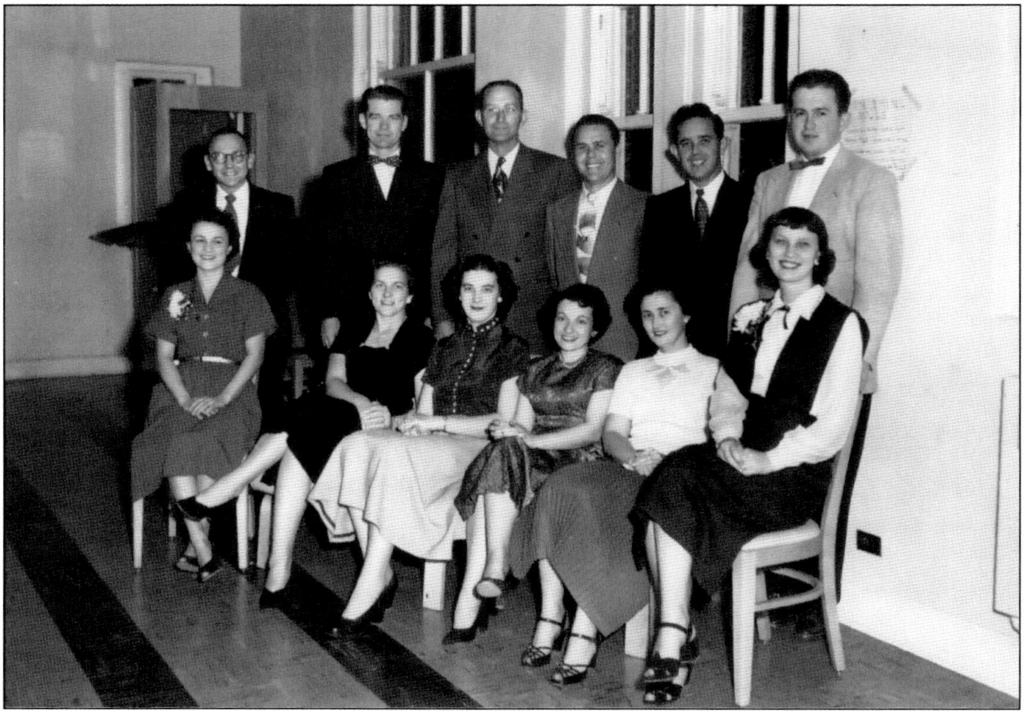

In this 1950s photograph are teachers and principals of the grade school and high school. They are, from left to right, Mr. and Mrs. Bud Holz; Richard and Gladys Warfield; Mr. and Mrs. Roy Sarff, Mr. and Mrs. John Sciacca; Elmer and Ruth Icenogle; and an unidentified couple. (Courtesy of Neville Carr.)

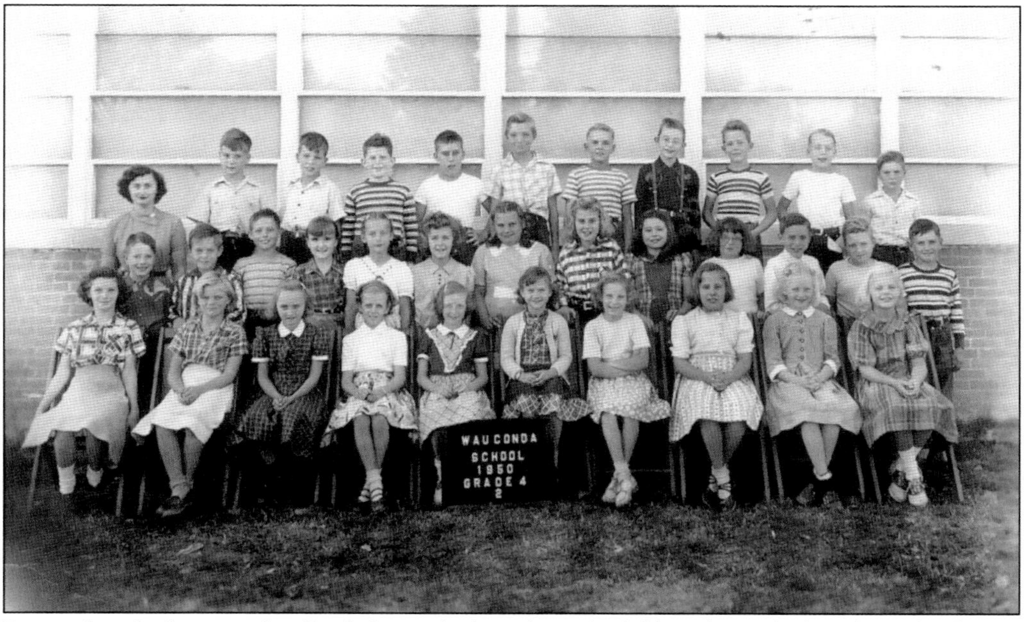

Pictured with their teacher Ruth Icenogle (standing, far left) is the 1950 fourth-grade class at Wauconda Grade School. (Courtesy Neville Carr.)

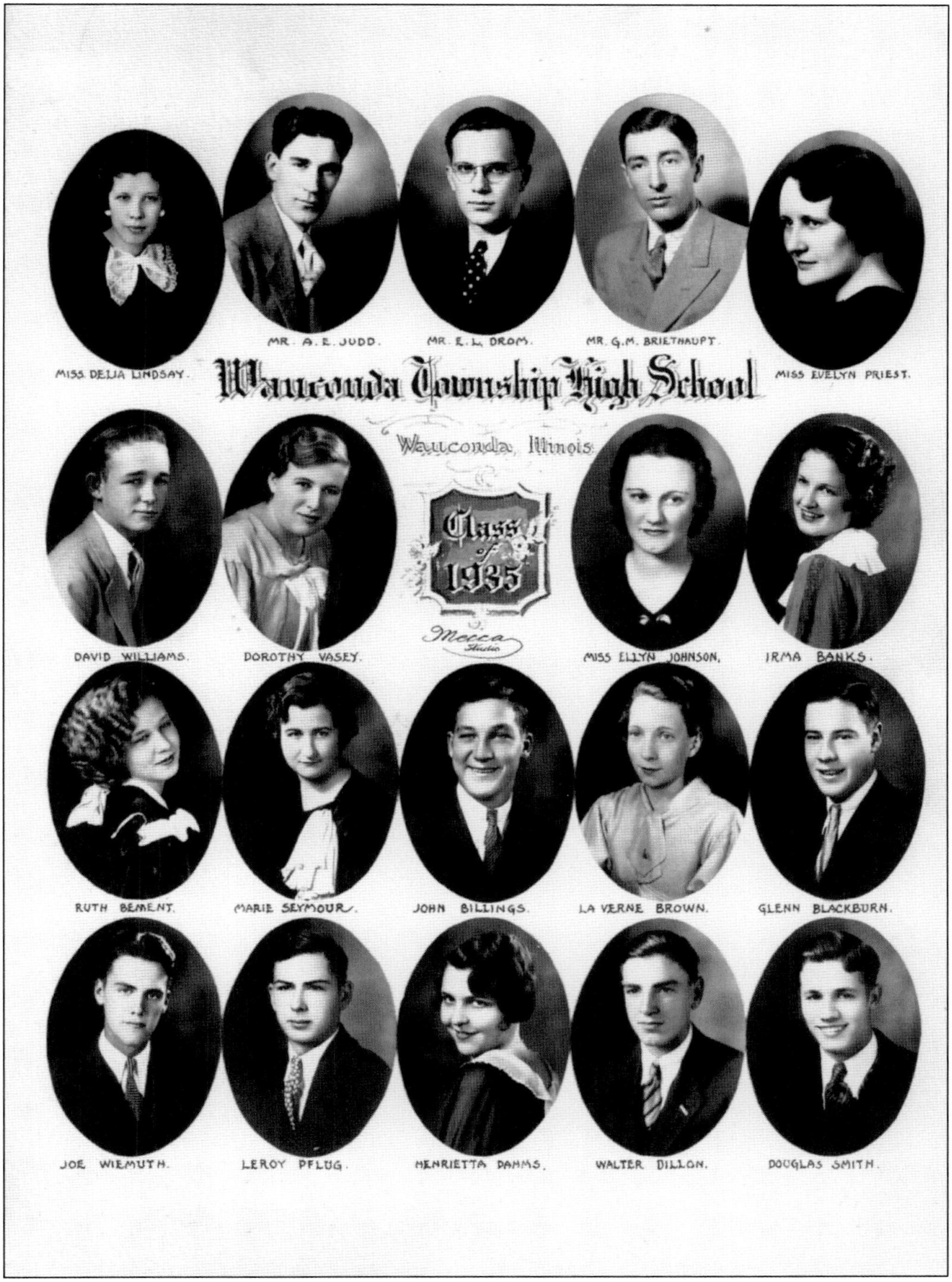

This is the official photograph of the Wauconda Township High School class of 1935. (Courtesy of Deanna Wiemuth Rogers.)

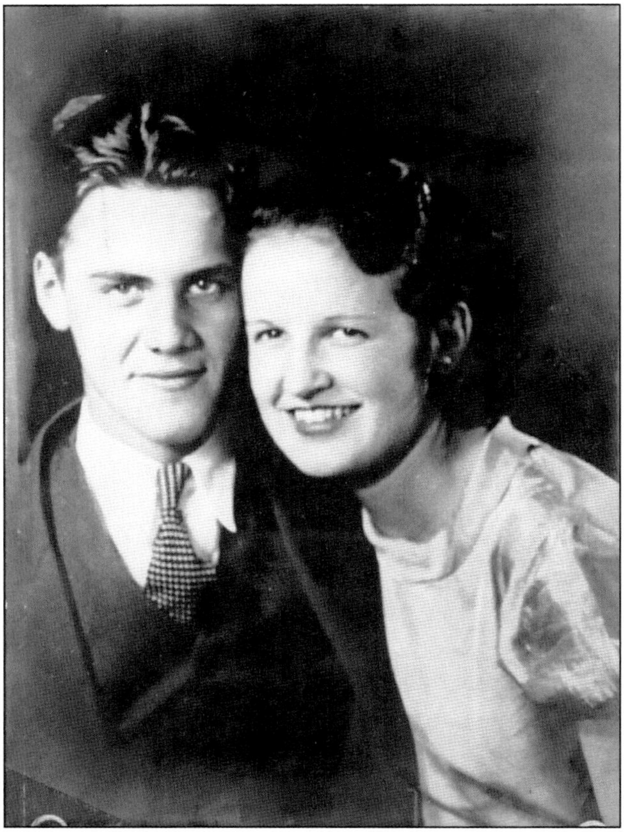

Pictured on their wedding day, March 20, 1936, are high school sweethearts Joe Wiemuth and Irma May Banks from the class of 1935. In attendance were Stanford Wiemuth and his wife, Doris Paddock Wiemuth. Burt Love officiated the service. The Banks had four children—Joseph, Deanna, Marcene, and Irma Jane—and were married 73 years. Irma died in 2009 and Joseph in 2010. (Courtesy of Deanna Wiemuth Rogers.)

The Wauconda Township High School's 1934 basketball team poses for a photograph. The only player identified is Joe Wiemuth (first row, second from right). (Courtesy of Deanna Wiemuth Rogers.)

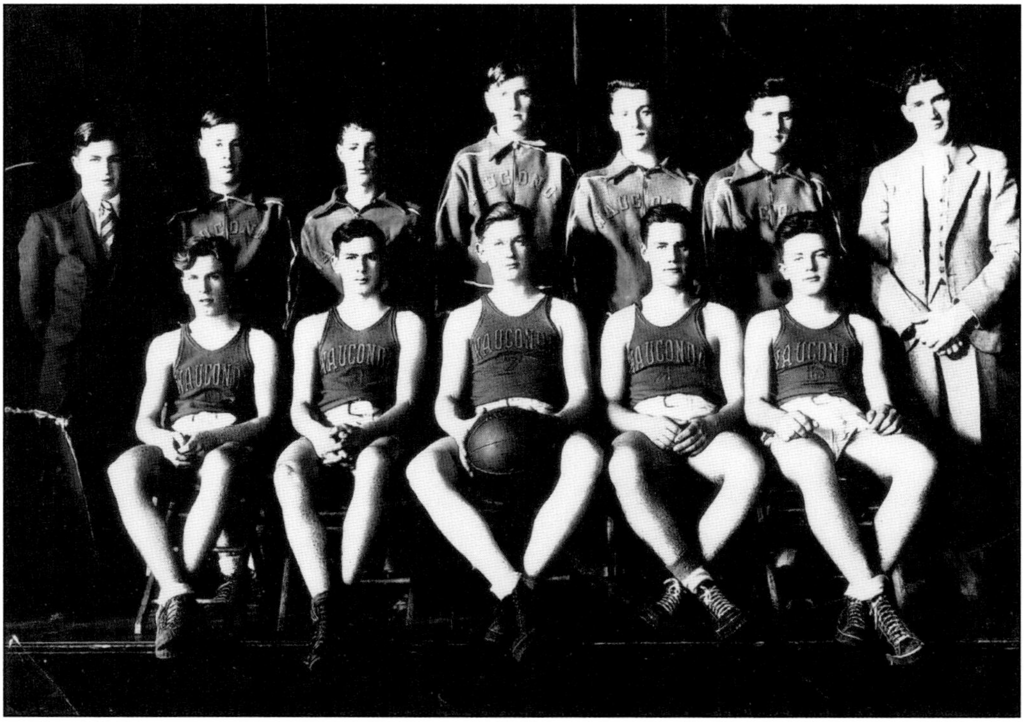

Wauconda Township High School, at 217 Slocum Lake Road, opened in September 1915. These are hallway scenes from the high school yearbook.

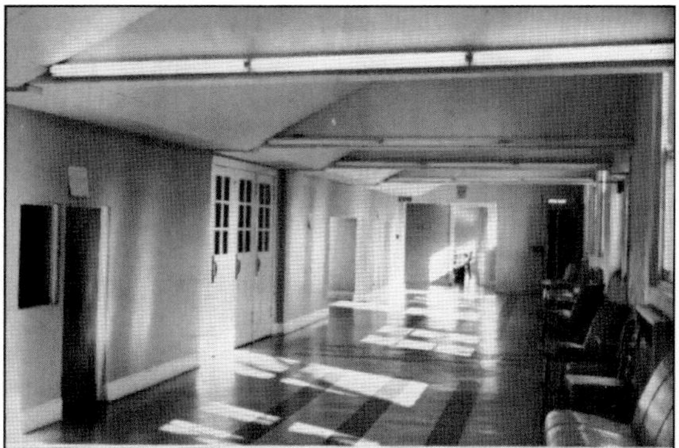

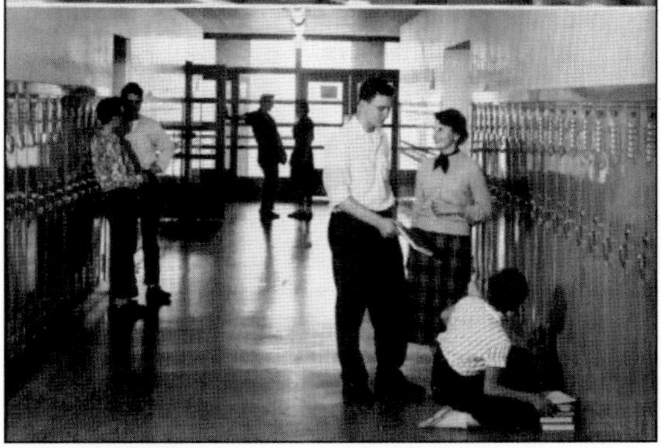

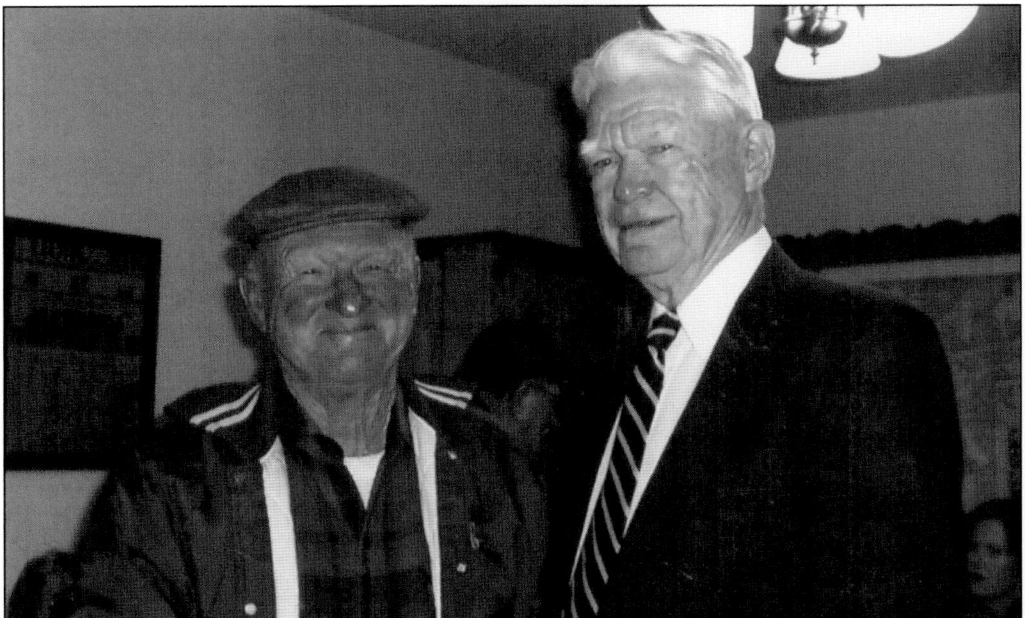

Richard Warfield (right), a farm boy during the Depression, earned master's degrees from the University of Illinois and Northwestern University. He came to Wauconda on July 1, 1946, as the agriculture teacher and principal of the high school. At the time, the school had approximately 100 students and eight teachers. Warfield went on to head the board of education and was superintendent of schools from 1955 until his retirement in 1975. Lifelong Wauconda resident Bob Reardon (left) is a former pupil of Warfield's. (Courtesy of the Federated Church.)

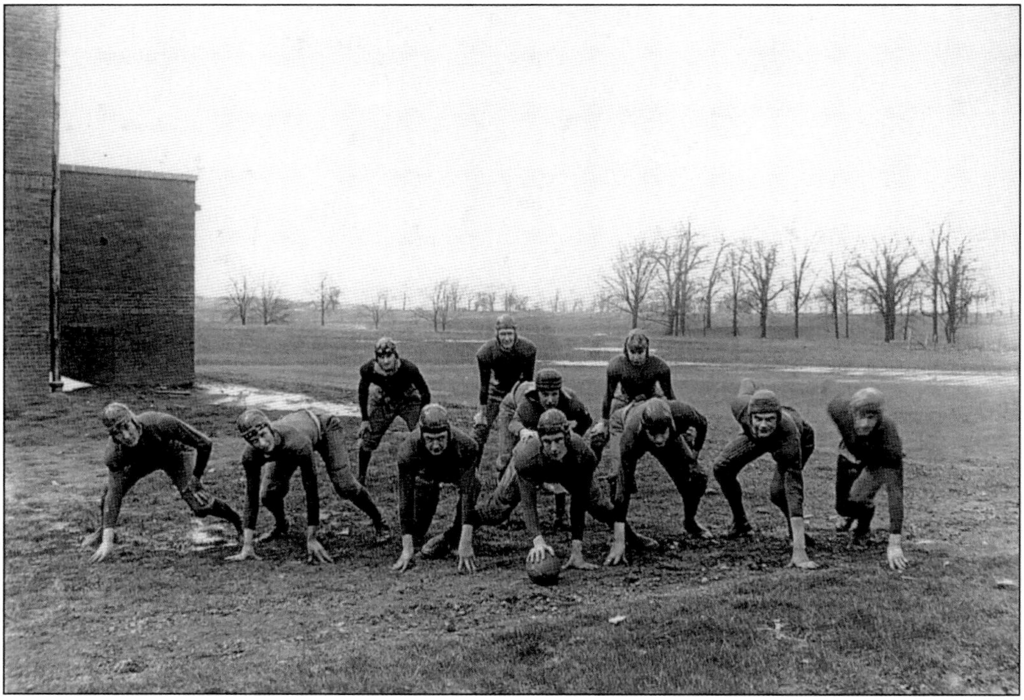

Ready for play, the Wauconda Township High School football team takes the field for the 1920–1921 season. (Courtesy of Neville Carr.)

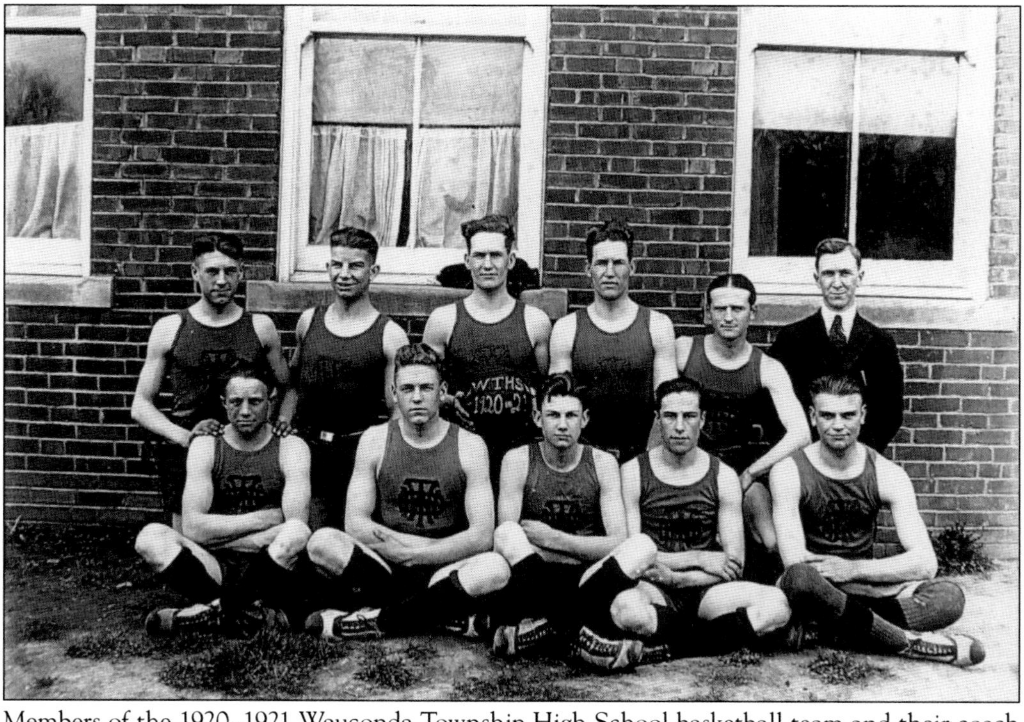

Members of the 1920–1921 Wauconda Township High School basketball team and their coach pose for the official team photograph. In the middle of the back row are the Stroker twins. (Courtesy of Ron K. Vaughn Sr.)

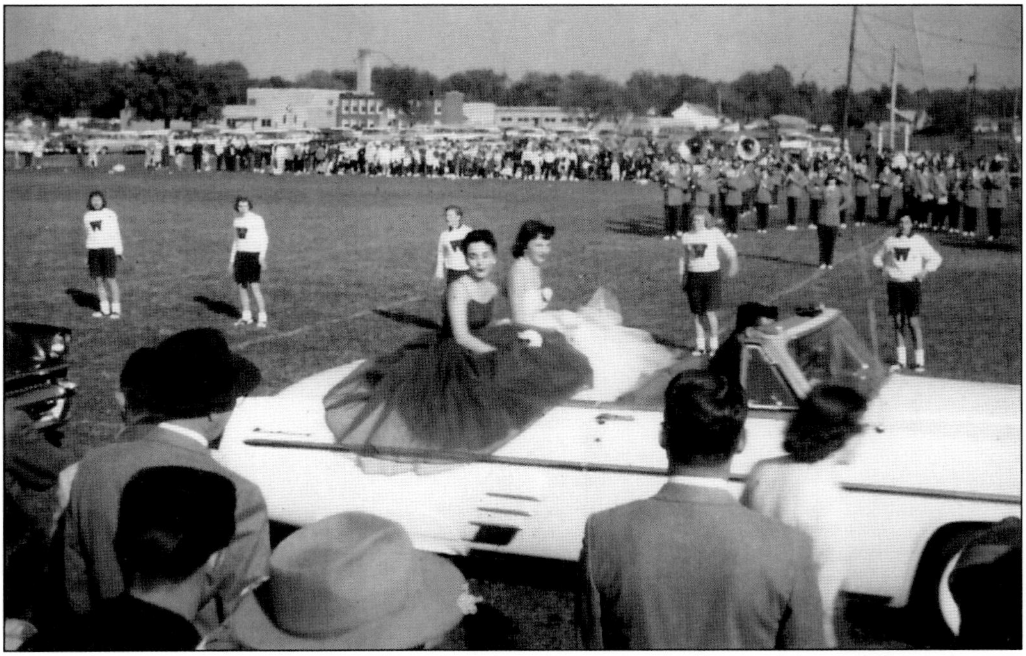

The Wauconda High School football field is a sea of activity at halftime of the 1957 homecoming game with fans, cheerleaders, and the marching band. Riding atop the cool convertible are two members of the Queen's Court: Marianne Folise (left) and Louise Kittman Hartigan. (Courtesy of Marianne Folise.)

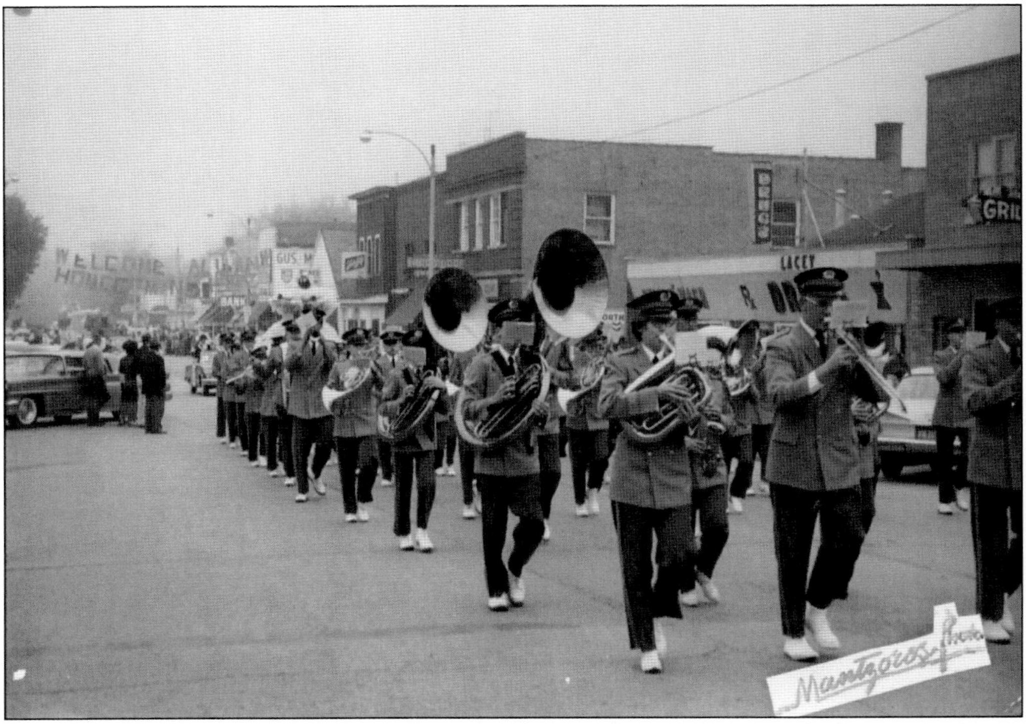

Here comes the Wauconda High School Band in the 1962 homecoming parade down Main Street. The student behind the first tuba is Ron Vaughn. (Courtesy of Ron K. Vaughn Sr.)

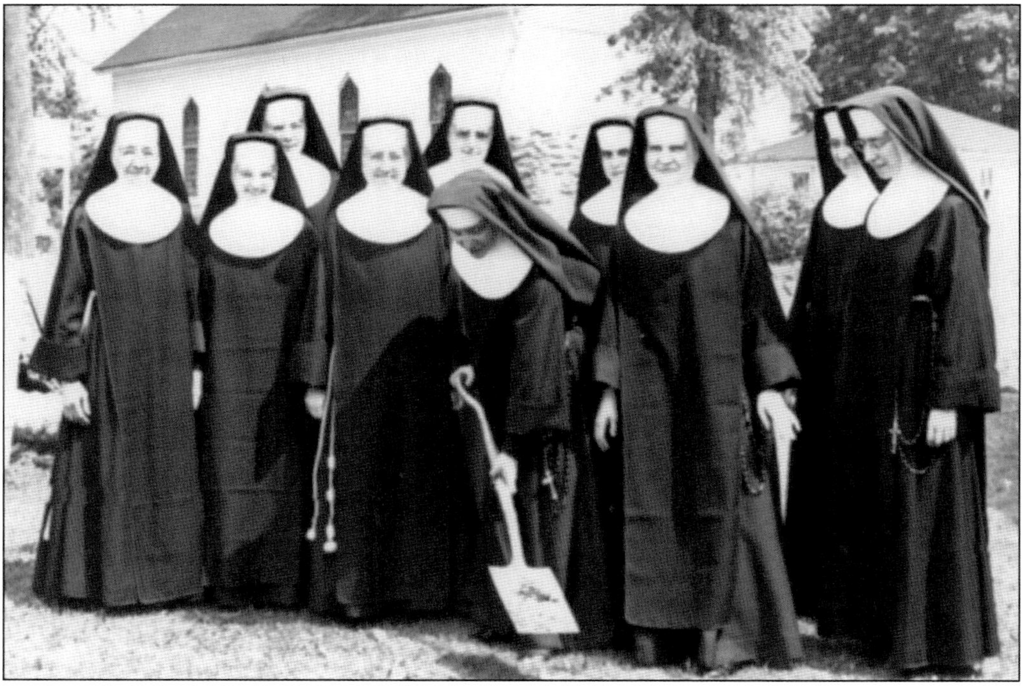

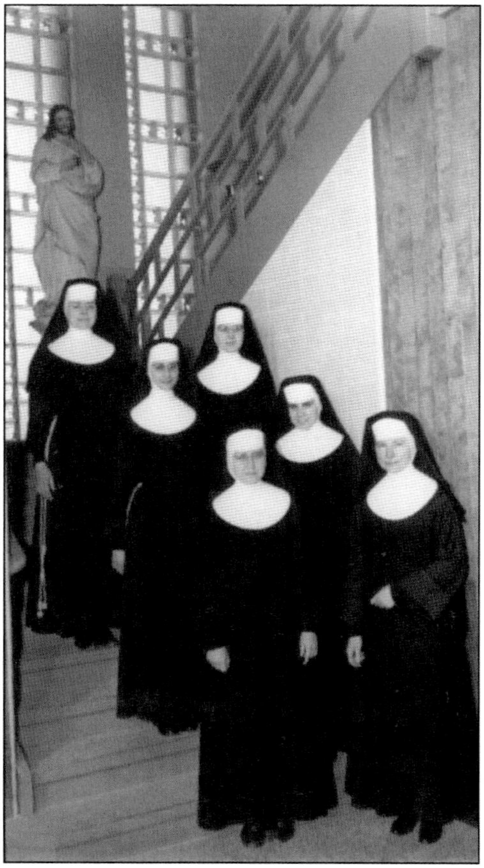

Transfiguration School opened with 27 first- to sixth-graders in September 1948 in a two-story frame building at 310 West Mill Street under the guidance of the Franciscan Sisters of Wheaton. The school and convent were in the same building. The nuns taught the children downstairs and lived upstairs. From 1949 to 1960, the school was expanded to accommodate a growing enrollment that peaked in 1964 at 564. Helping to break ground on April 2, 1950, for a new brick school (above) are (first row, from left to right) Sister Davidica, Sister Yvonne, Sister Elaine, Sister Mary Joseph, Sister Herlinda, and Sister Francella; (included in the second row) Sister Victor, Sister Bartholomew, and perhaps Sister Ruth. On September 26, 1954, ground at 315 West Mill Street was broken for another school, and on July 10, 1955, Mass was celebrated in the new quarters; in November 1955, Cardinal Stritch dedicated the combined church and new classrooms. Under the leadership of Rev. Thomas McMahon, the new parish administrator, plans for another four-classroom school were drawn up and subsequently dedicated May 1, 1960. The last sister left Transfiguration in 1979. (Both courtesy of Franciscan Sisters of Wheaton.)

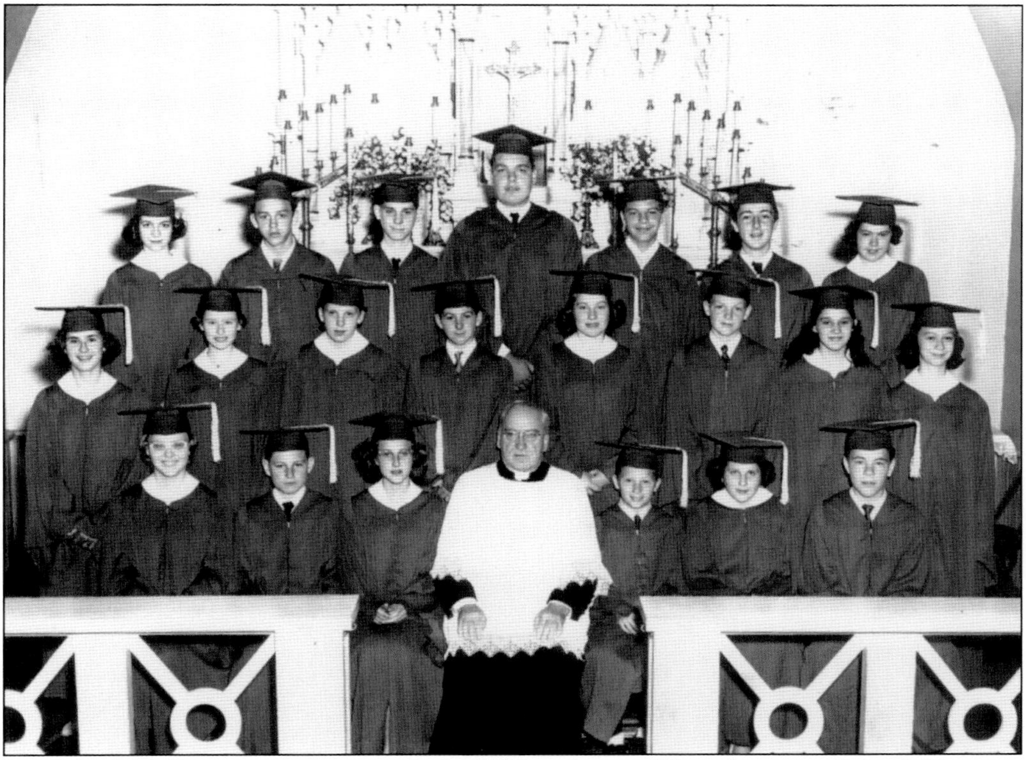

Rev. John J. Mulligan, pastor, poses with the 1955 graduates of Transfiguration School. They are, from left to right, (first row) Judy Weiler, Larry Duerling, Barbara Staniewicz, Dennis Ciesil, Ann Dumaski, and John Holm; (second row) Patricia O'Neill, Kathie Broughton, Charlene Duggan, Jim Cousar, Patricia Murphy, Jerry Neumann, Betty Ann Olsczewski, and Mary Margaret McGuire; (third row) Pat Wagner, Jim Longfield, Bill Lenz, Anthony Liska, Jerry Niemo, Tom Gibbons, and Cynthia Thiel. (Courtesy of Kathie Broughton Carr.)

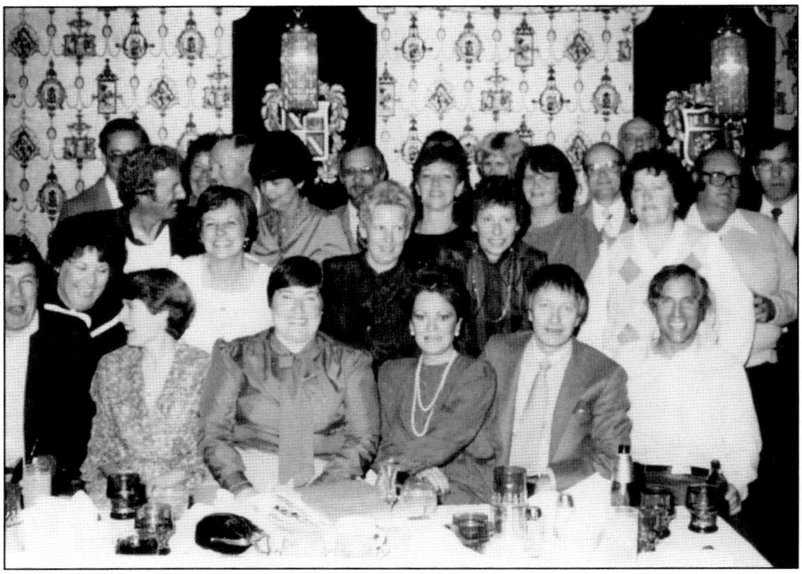

Members of the Wauconda Township High School class of 1959 get together for their 25th class reunion. Some of these faces can be found on page 101 as third-graders and 102 as fourth-graders. (Courtesy of Marianne Folise.)

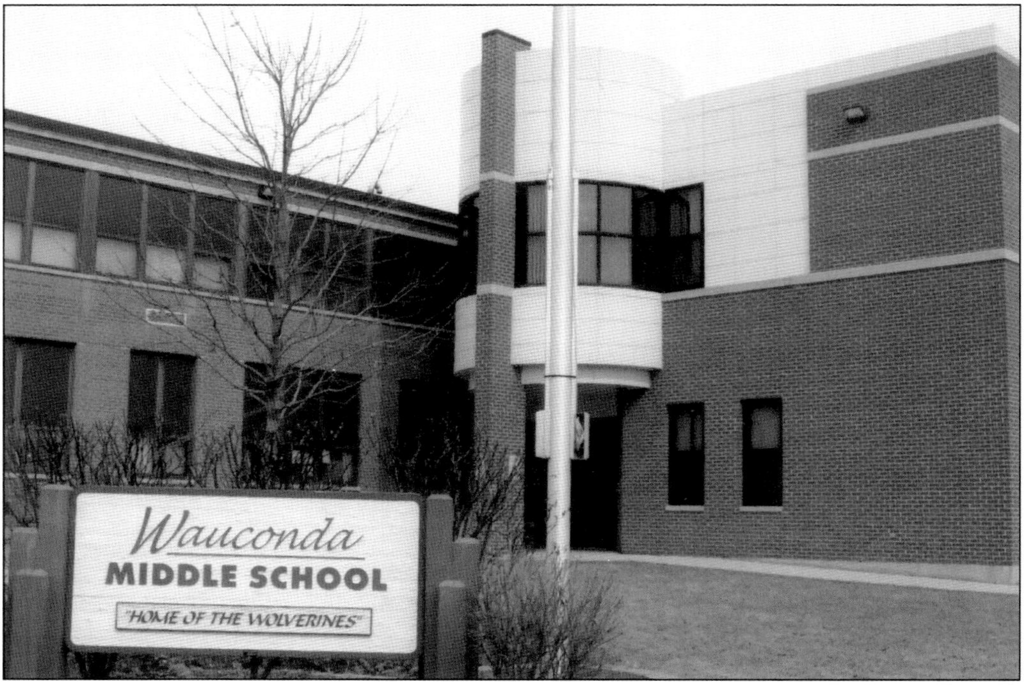

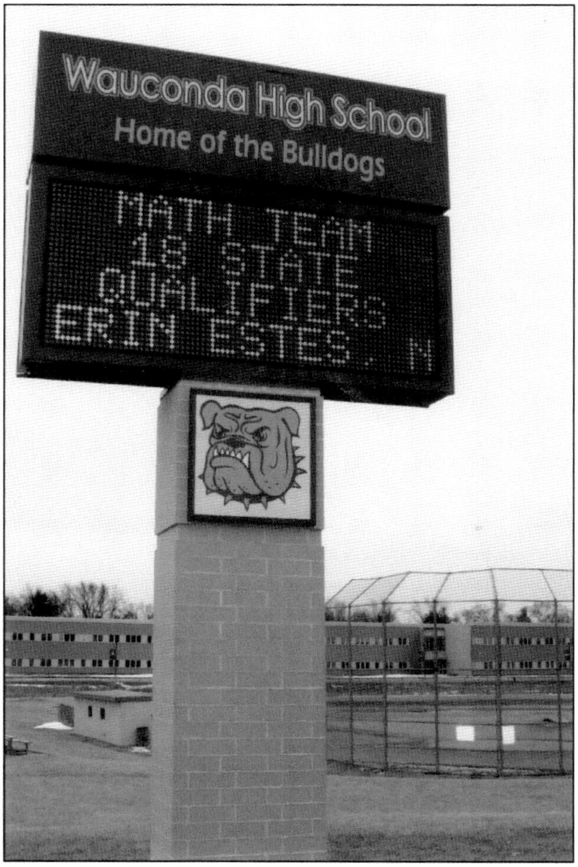

Wauconda Middle School (above) was established for the 1962–1963 school year when high school classes were moved to a new building at 555 North Main Street (at left). The class of 1962 was the last to graduate from the old high school. Its yearbook was dedicated to the alma mater "for never having cared how smart or how stupid we were; and especially for having never asked us what family we came from, what church we went to, or what we intended to make of ourselves." The word "Township" was dropped from the high school's name. (Both courtesy of Marianne Folise.)

Nine

Those Who Serve

Firefighters, police officers, military, and service club members are just some of the people who serve the Wauconda community.

Wauconda became a village on August 18, 1877, and by October 8 it had its first police official in Constable Henry Golding. In January 1878, residents approved a tax levy to build a calaboose, or local jail; thus was the auspicious beginning of public safety and crime prevention in Wauconda. Later that year, in December, the village passed an ordinance allowing the police department to arrest nude bathers and swimmers for indecent exposure. The department has been enforcing curfew since May 6, 1887, when an ordinance required children younger than 16 to be off the streets after 8:00 p.m. Roller-skating on the village's new cement sidewalks was banned on May 27, 1908.

The modern age for the department began when George Mollenkemp was appointed Wauconda's first police chief on May 4, 1939. The Lions Club purchased the first squad car on June 4, 1945, a Ford that cost less than $1,500. Today, the police chief has a team of 26 ranking and patrol officers.

The Wauconda Fire Company was formed on November 9, 1889. It became known as Wauconda-Niagara Fire Company, named for the fire equipment it used. In 1931, the Wauconda Fire Department was created and received its first motorized fire apparatus, a 500-gallon-per-minute pumper. The department had been a volunteer force until 1978, when it hired its first full-time chief, Lyle Matthews.

In Wauconda Cemetery is the grave of a Revolutionary War veteran Rueben Hill. Wauconda's men and women have served in every one of America's wars since then. By May 1918, during World War I, 40 men and one woman, Yvonne Haas, were in Uncle Sam's service. Air Force First Lt. Charles D. De Novo was decorated during the Vietnam War. He received the Silver Star, Distinguished Flying Cross, and nine Oak Leaf Clusters to his Air Medal.

Justus Bangs, Wauconda's illustrious founder, outfitted a company of soldiers for the Civil War. Some of the soldiers killed in the war, unidentified or without families, were brought to Wauconda for burial.

Service clubs also work to make Wauconda a better place. For example, Wauconda owes its gratitude to the Wauconda Woman's Club, which started the first public library.

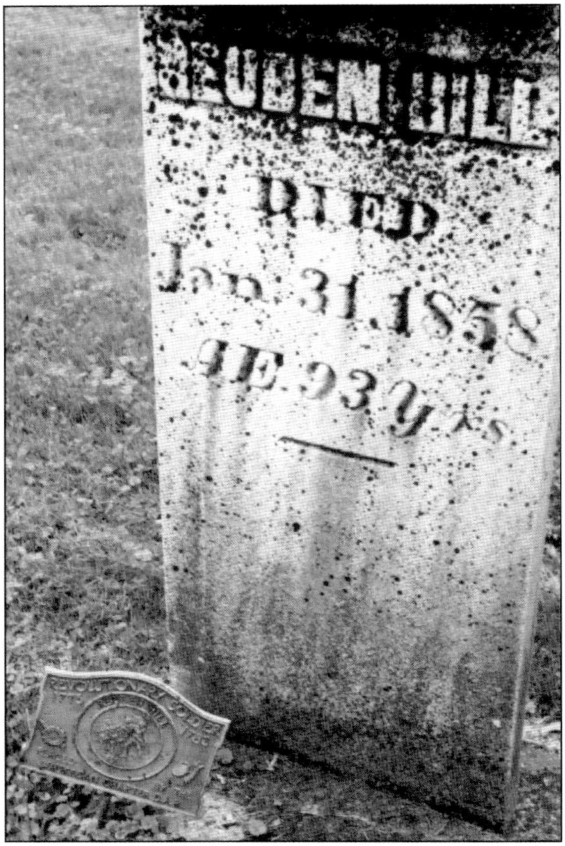

The grave of Reuben Hill in Wauconda Cemetery (left) is marked with a Revolutionary War plaque (below). Hill was born in Goshen, Connecticut, in 1765. While living in New York state, he enlisted in the Army in the fall of 1780 at the age of 15. He enlisted twice more with different companies and was discharged as a private on January 1, 1783. Fifty-one years later, he successfully applied for a military pension. About 1840, Reuben's son Seth Hill purchased property in Wauconda Township. It is probable that the entire family, including Reuben and his wife, Patience, came west at that time. In the 1850 census, Reuben and Patience, both 85 years of age, were living with their son's family. The family farm was along Route 176, south of Bangs Lake. Hill died at the age of 93. (Both courtesy of Marianne Folise.)

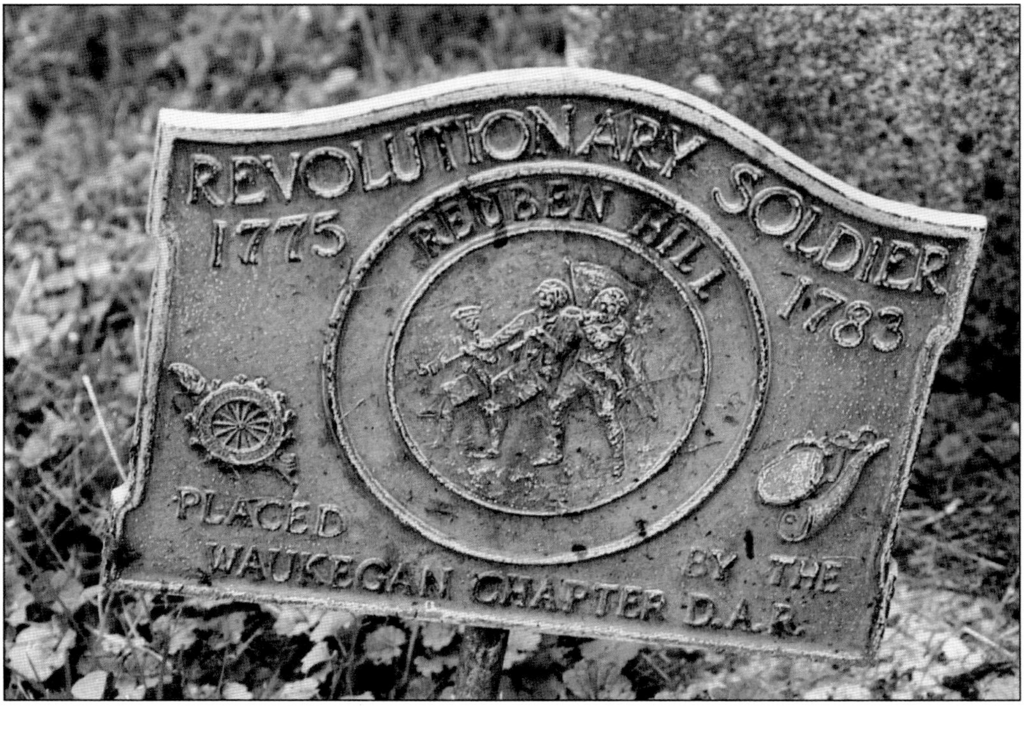

Richard "Buddy" Froehlke was killed at the Battle of the Bulge on December 20, 1944. Buddy, whose parents owned Phil's Beach, was a Wauconda Township High School star basketball player and 1941 graduate. He was a junior at Notre Dame University when he was drafted. Herman Maiman, who had a telegraph office in his general store, asked 20-year-old Jan Prior (Hironimus) to deliver a telegram to the Froehlkes on her way home from work. She first ran to the house of her friend, Geraldine Kirk (Cashmore). "I knew it was bad news because I held it up to the light," she recalled. The message stated that Bud was missing in action. (Courtesy of the Froehlke family.)

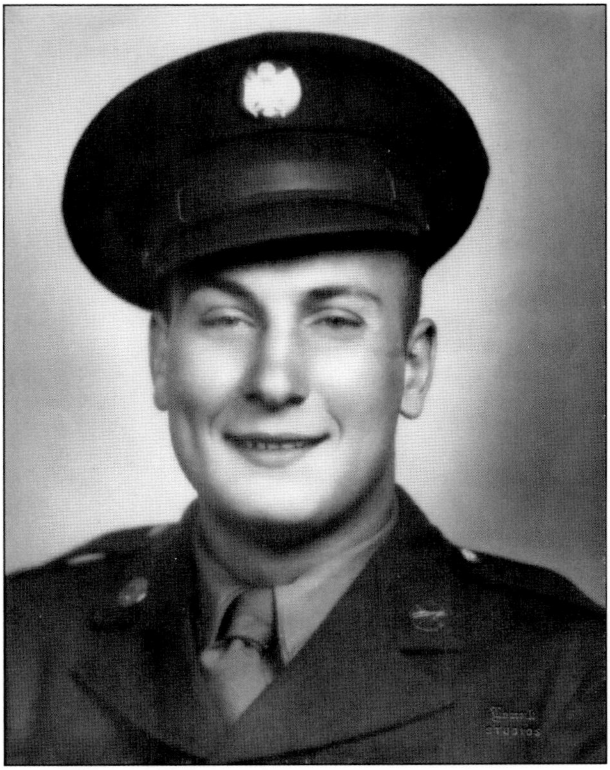

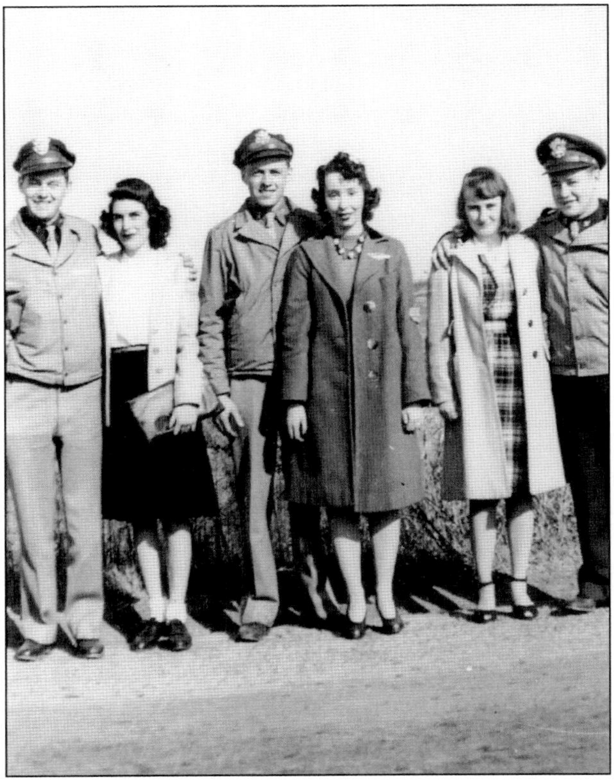

In the center are Lt. Robert Peterson and his wife, Jacque, with his copilot and bombardier and their wives in Greenville, South Carolina, before the crew left for duty in 1944. Peterson served in the 14th Air Force in China, Burma, and India. He was awarded the Air Medal and Distinguished Flying Cross. He flew a B-25 bomber. (Courtesy of Jacque Ross Peterson.)

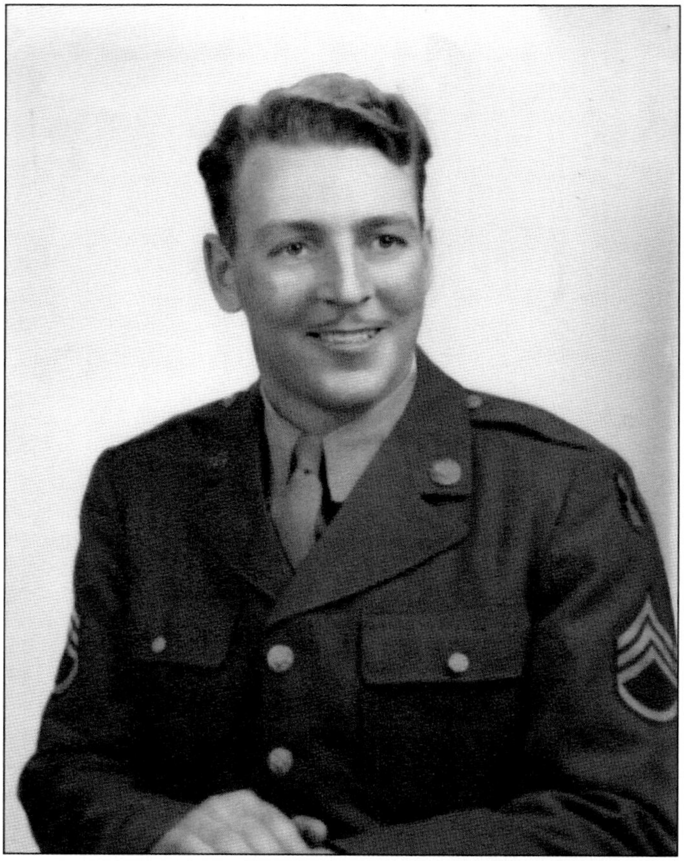

John Kuester earned a battlefield commission of second lieutenant while fighting in Europe during World War II. He lost his leg when he stepped on a land mine during heavy fighting and was awarded the Purple Heart and Bronze Star for continuing to fight alongside his men after receiving the injury that cost him his leg. (Courtesy of Richard Kuester.)

In front of the Wauconda Area Public Library is a memorial garden in tribute to the life and work of Nicole Suveges, who was killed in Operation Iraqi Freedom in Sadr City, Baghdad, on June 24, 2008. She received the Secretary of Defense Medal for the Defense of Freedom. (Courtesy of Marianne Folise.)

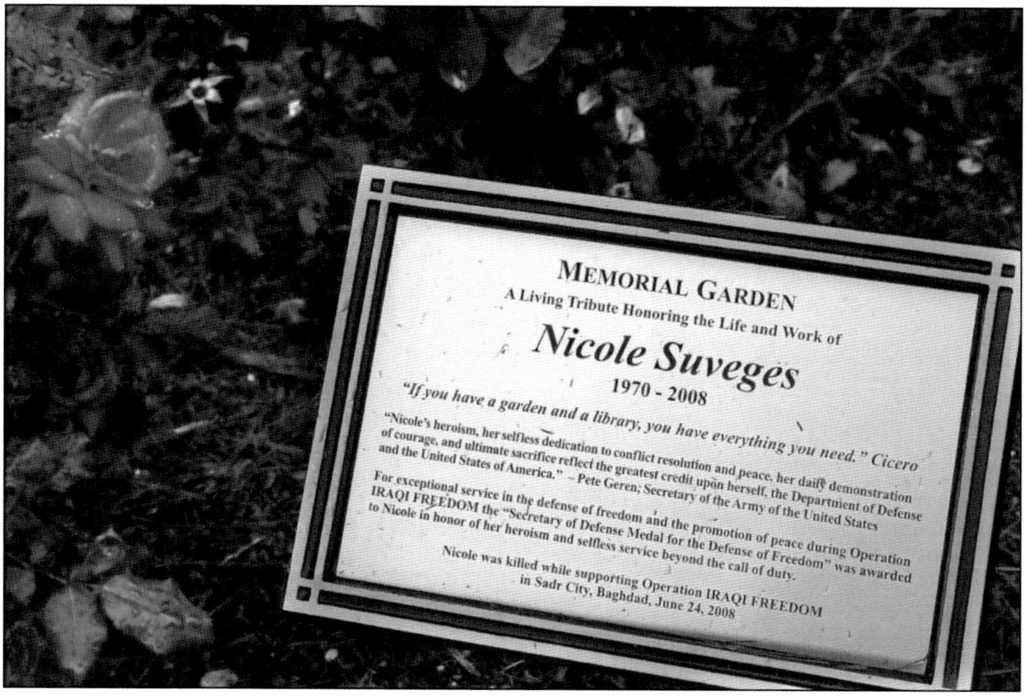

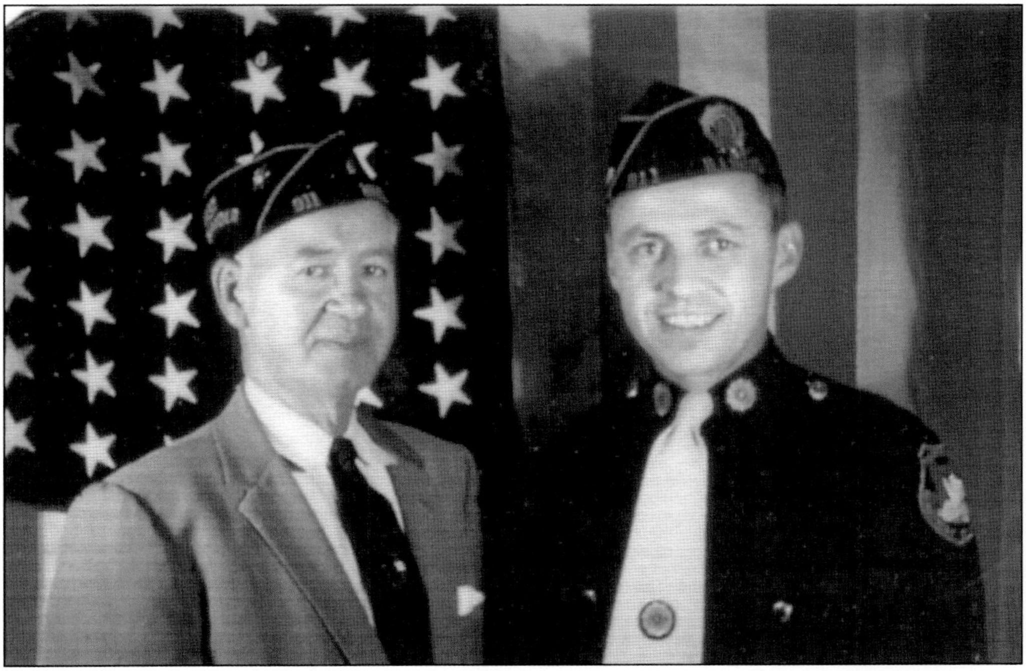

Robert Newberg (left) and Robert P. Peterson were officers of the new Wauconda American Legion Post 911. In November 1945, Peterson became its first commander. He appointed the following staff members: Gordon E. Zohorik, adjunct; Lyman Miller, service officer; Robert Newberg, child welfare; Harry Francisco, chaplain; Stanley Smith, historian; and Le Roy Pflug, Americanism officer. (Courtesy of Jacque Ross Peterson.)

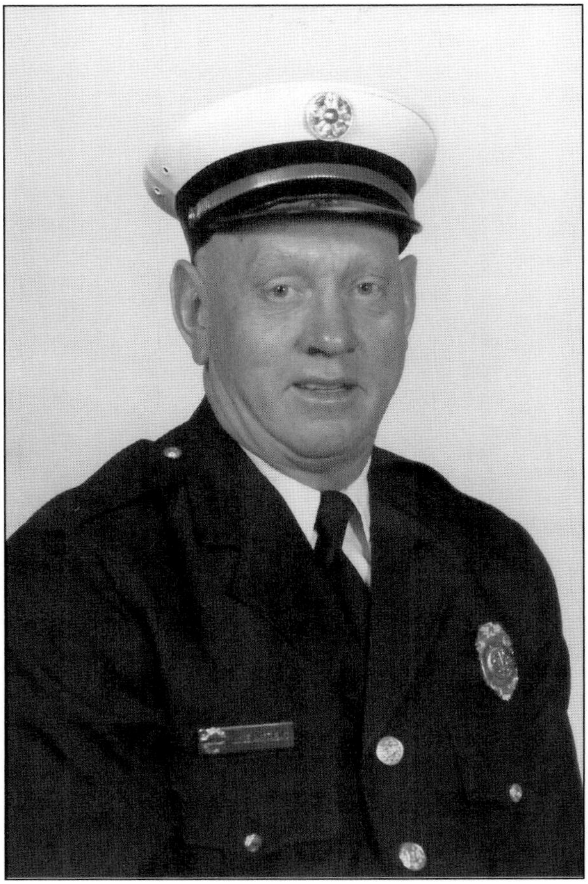

Wauconda Fire Department became a professional department in 1978, and Lyle Matthews was its first chief. He started as a volunteer in 1954 and in 1974 became volunteer chief. In 1978, the dairy farmer made a life-changing decision to become the first full-time chief, a post he held for 18 of his 42 years fire on the job. When he died on November 11, 2010, it was said his life will forever "be a reminder that there are still people with concern for others who have the courage, strength, and wisdom to bear whatever burden is placed upon them." (Courtesy of Wauconda Fire Department.)

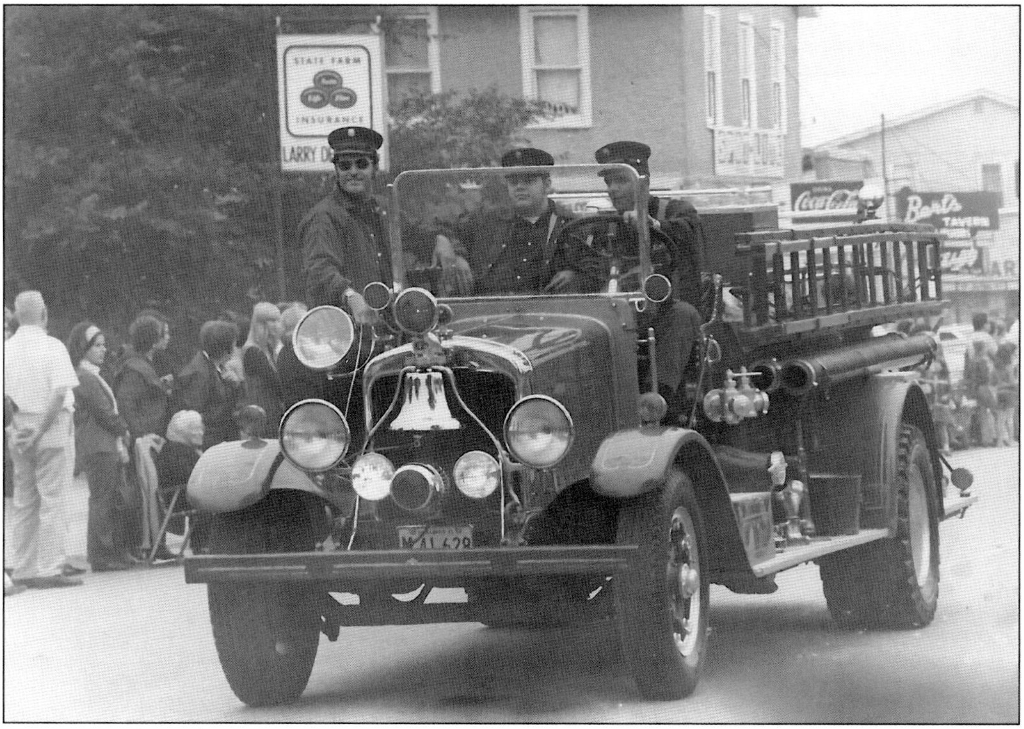

Wauconda firefighters drive Engine No. 1 in a local parade. (Courtesy of the Wauconda Fire Department.)

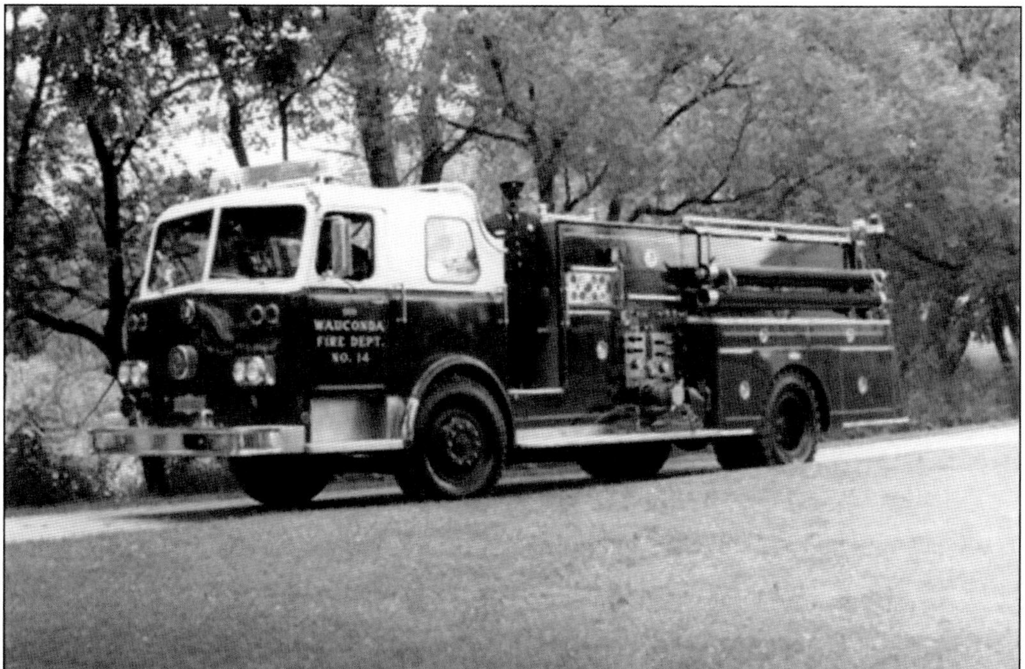

Showing off engine No. 14 from the 1950s is a Wauconda firefighter in period uniform. (Courtesy of the Wauconda Fire Department.)

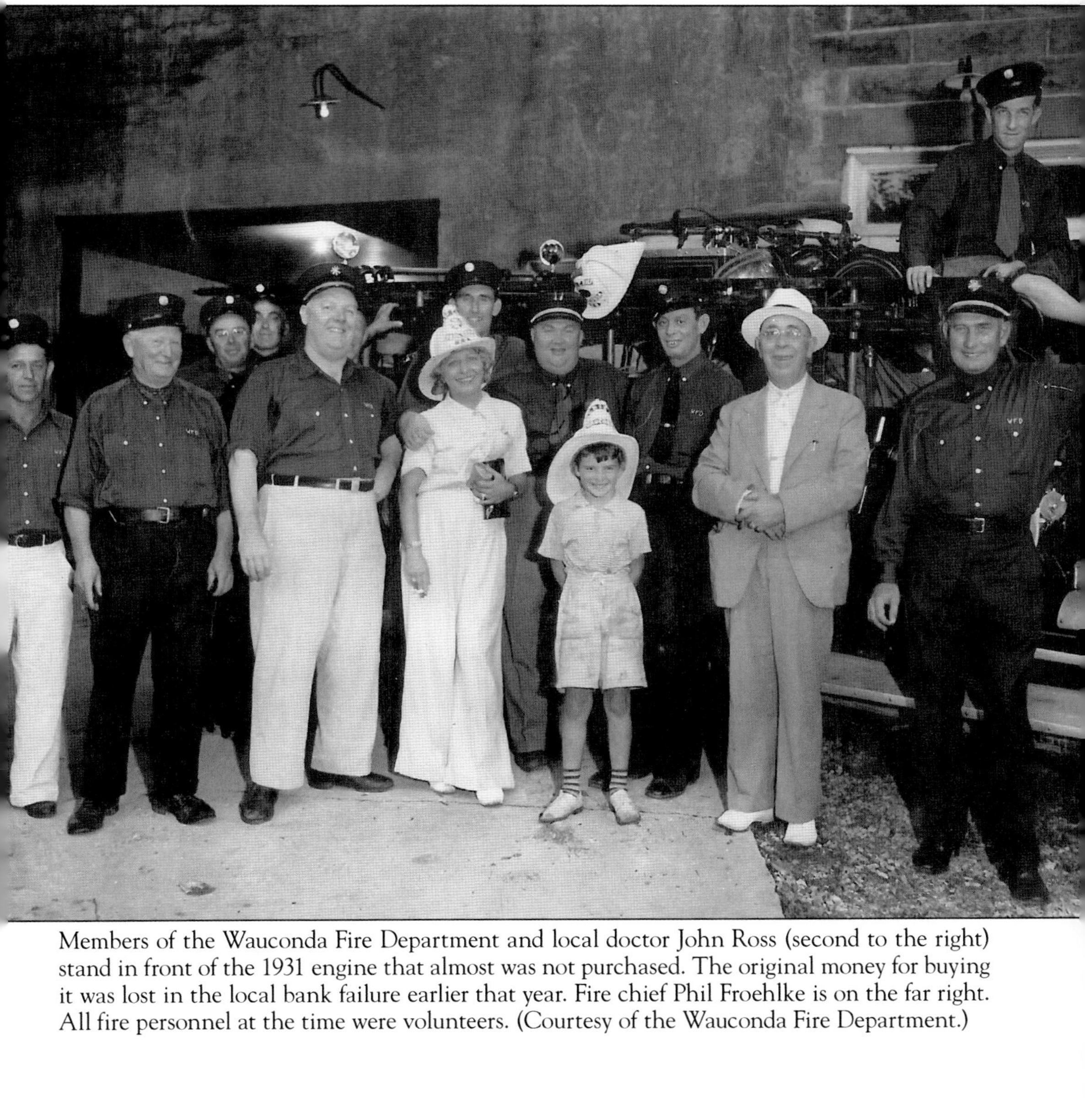

Members of the Wauconda Fire Department and local doctor John Ross (second to the right) stand in front of the 1931 engine that almost was not purchased. The original money for buying it was lost in the local bank failure earlier that year. Fire chief Phil Froehlke is on the far right. All fire personnel at the time were volunteers. (Courtesy of the Wauconda Fire Department.)

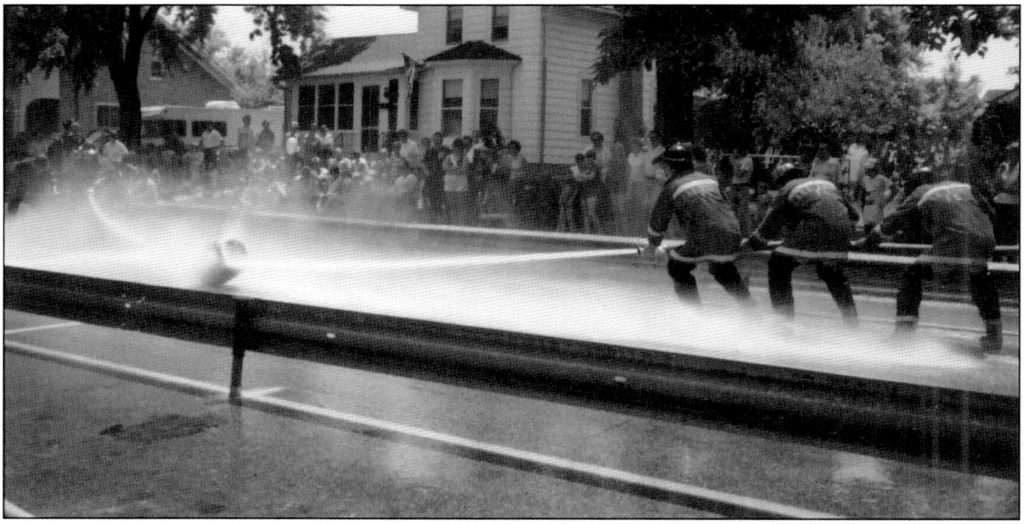

Water fights were a highlight of the Firemen's Carnivals that were held for many years in July. Departments from neighboring towns would compete to see who could move a barrel over the centerline with the force of their water hoses. (Courtesy of Elizabeth Giangrego.)

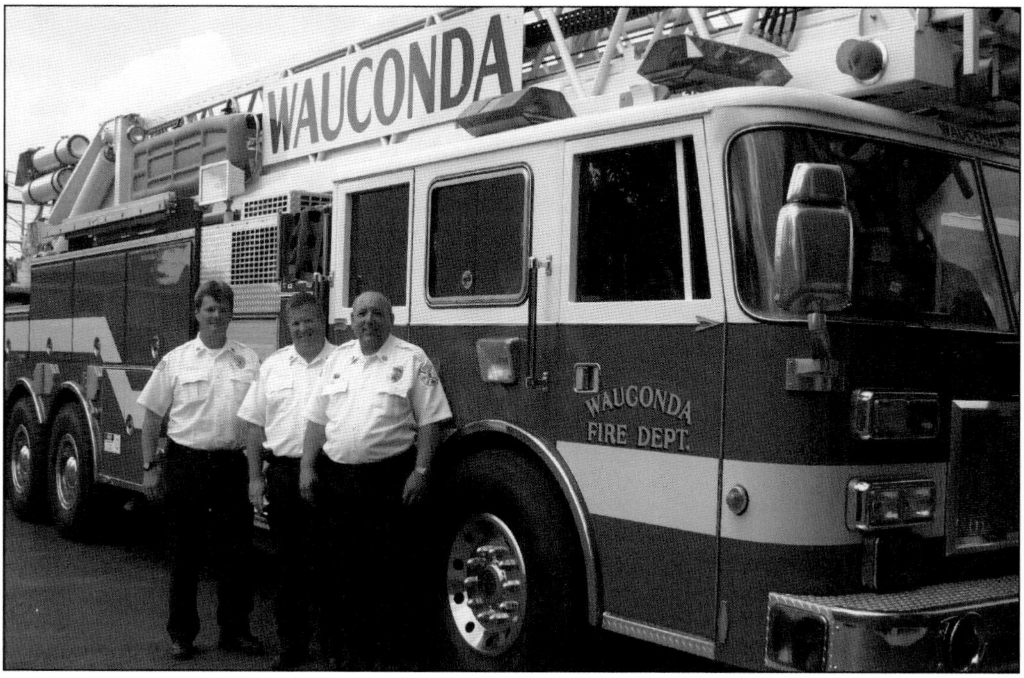

From left to right, executive officer Mike Wahl, deputy chief John Fessler, and fire chief David Dato stand in front of a very modern fire truck. Dato was named chief in 1992 and was named Fire Chief of the Year by the Illinois Fire Chief Association in 2010. (Courtesy of Marianne Folise.)

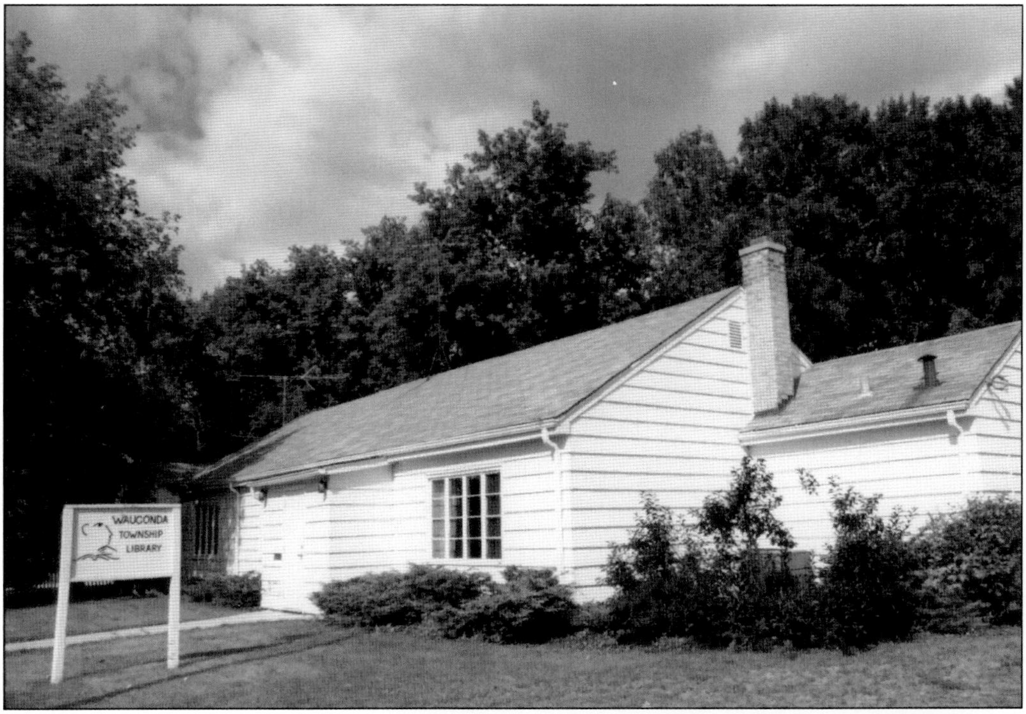

The Wauconda Woman's Club started the local library with one shelf of books in the high school in 1939. The Wauconda Township Library got its first permanent home in 1963 at 212 Osage Street in a building owned by Louise Derer. The front of the building was the library and Derer lived in the back. Now named Wauconda Area Public Library, a modern facility opened in August 1997 at 801 North Main Street. (Courtesy of Angela Catrambone.)

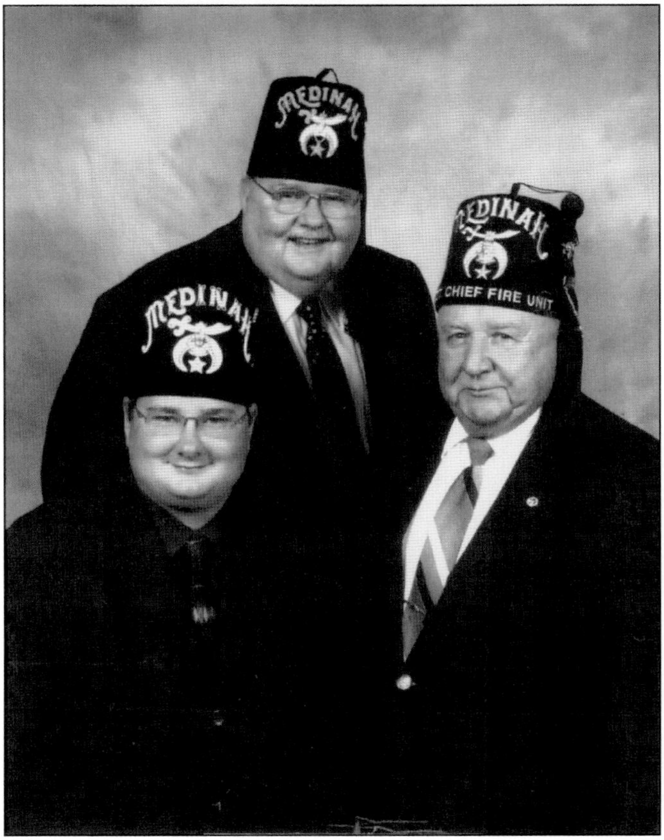

From left to right are Paul Bilisko, Richard Bilisko, and Dale Francisco—three generations of Medinah Shriners and Masons with the Rising Sun Lodge in Grayslake. (Courtesy of Cindy Francisco Bilisko.)

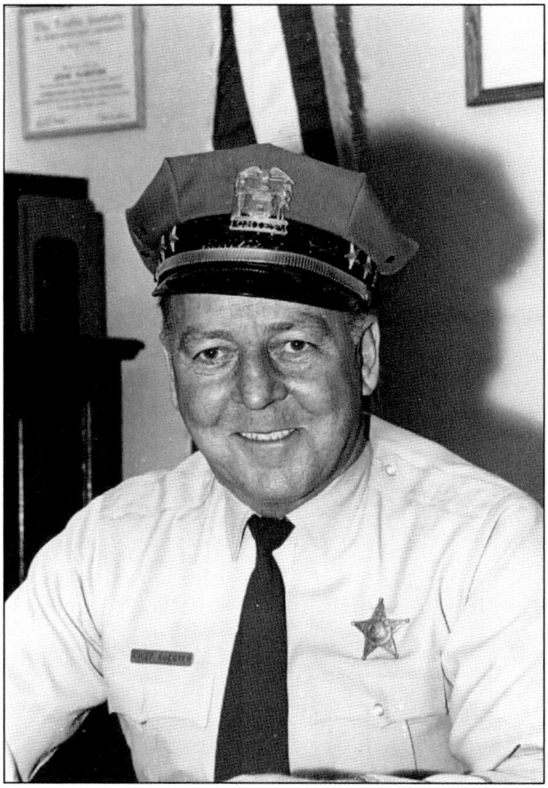

From night police officer to mayor, John Kuester (left) helped the village grow. He moved to Wauconda in 1946 and worked for the police and public works departments for 13 years before becoming police chief in 1959. In 1968, he became superintendent of public works. He knew where every sewer and water pipe was buried, as he was in town during the postwar growth spurt. Disturbed by what he saw as deterioration of the town into warring political factions in 1977, he ran for mayor and won. While in office, he won millions in grants for massive sewer improvements and road projects, and he modernized the police department and helped the fire department with its expansion plans. Kuester and his wife, Toni, are dressed in period garb for the village's centennial in 1977 (below). John Kuester Manor, a retirement home, is named for him. (Both courtesy of Richard Kuester.)

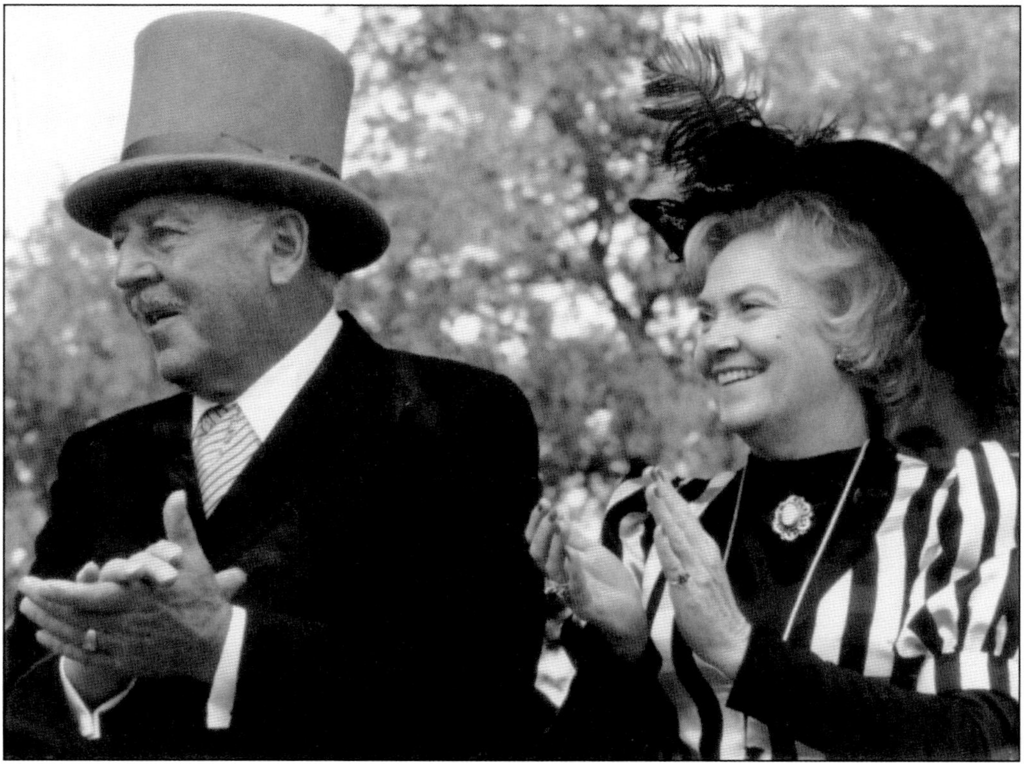

Ten

Wauconda in the News

Wauconda does not often find itself in the larger eye of the media; however, on a number of occasions it has garnered national attention. These occasions include Hollywood coming to town to film scenes for what would become an iconic movie, an atheist starting a debate with the village over its years-old tradition of placing crosses on public property; thousands gathering to throw snowballs at each other in an attempt to get into the Guinness Book of World Records, a rodeo raising the ire of animal enthusiasts, and a NASCAR race driver calling the village home.

Local residents enjoyed *The Blues Brothers*, not just because of the madcap adventures of its stars John Belushi and Dan Aykroyd, but because their beloved lake and beaches played a starring role in a couple of scenes in the movie when it was released in June 1980.

Still around town today are perhaps dozens of reminders of the 1989 battle with Rob Sherman, president of the American Atheists, Inc., who objected to the placement of crosses on village property every Christmas season.

The Lions Club thought it would be a good idea to have a snowball fight when it revived Winter Carnival in January 2005; a total of 2,936 people agreed.

The Wauconda Rodeo, which in 1994 was in its 31st year, drew the attention of animal rights advocates, charging "outrageous acts of cruelty to horses and livestock."

The village has at least one nationally known resident: Brent Sherman of NASCAR fame.

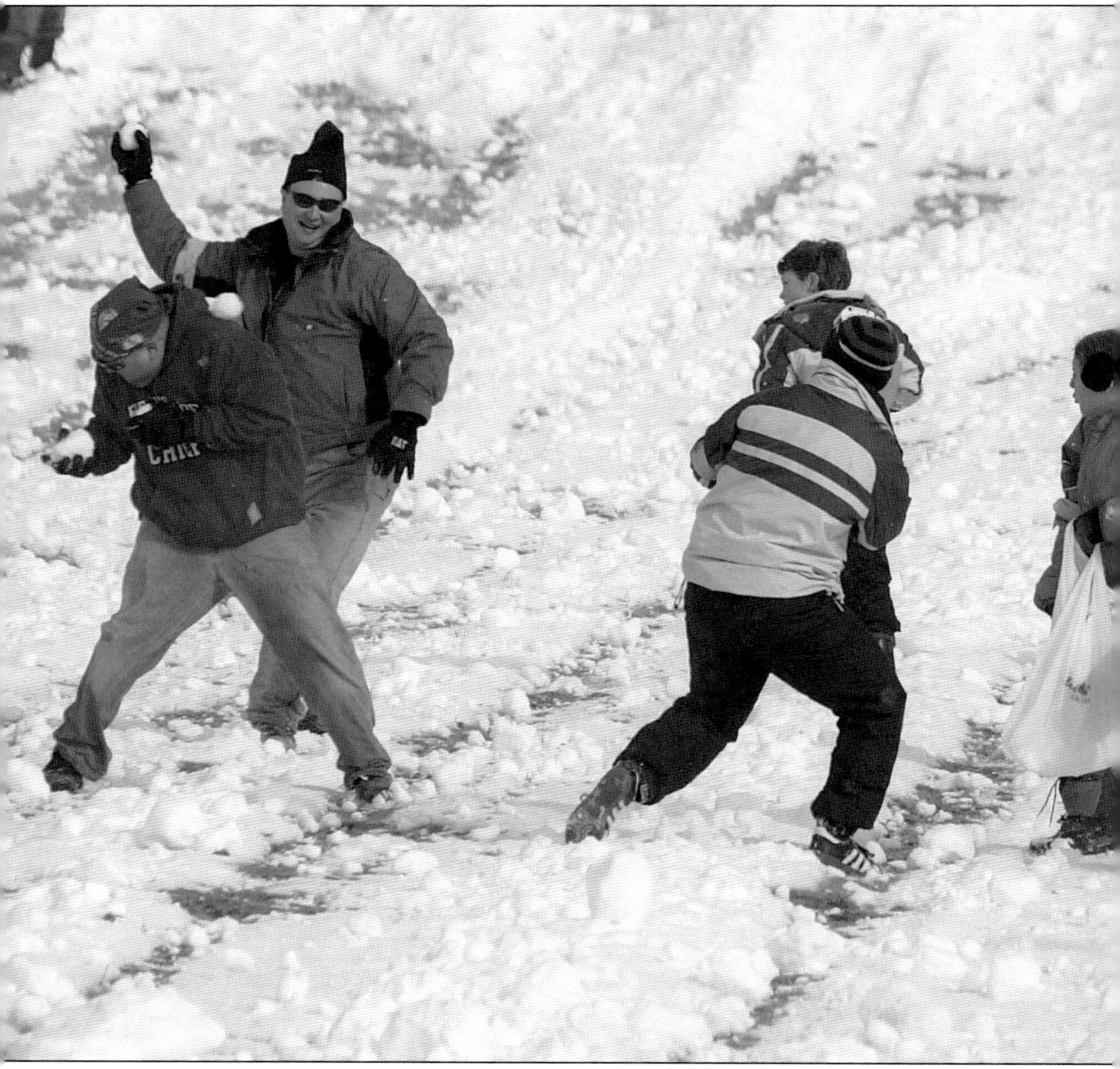

It was one for the record books—2,936 snowball fight enthusiasts gathered at Cook Park on January 29, 2005, to throw snowballs at each other. Traffic was backed up for miles, as people came from throughout the area. Some people even arrived by snowmobile. The effort broke the previous record set at a Swiss ski resort. Unfortunately, Wauconda's record lasted just over a year;

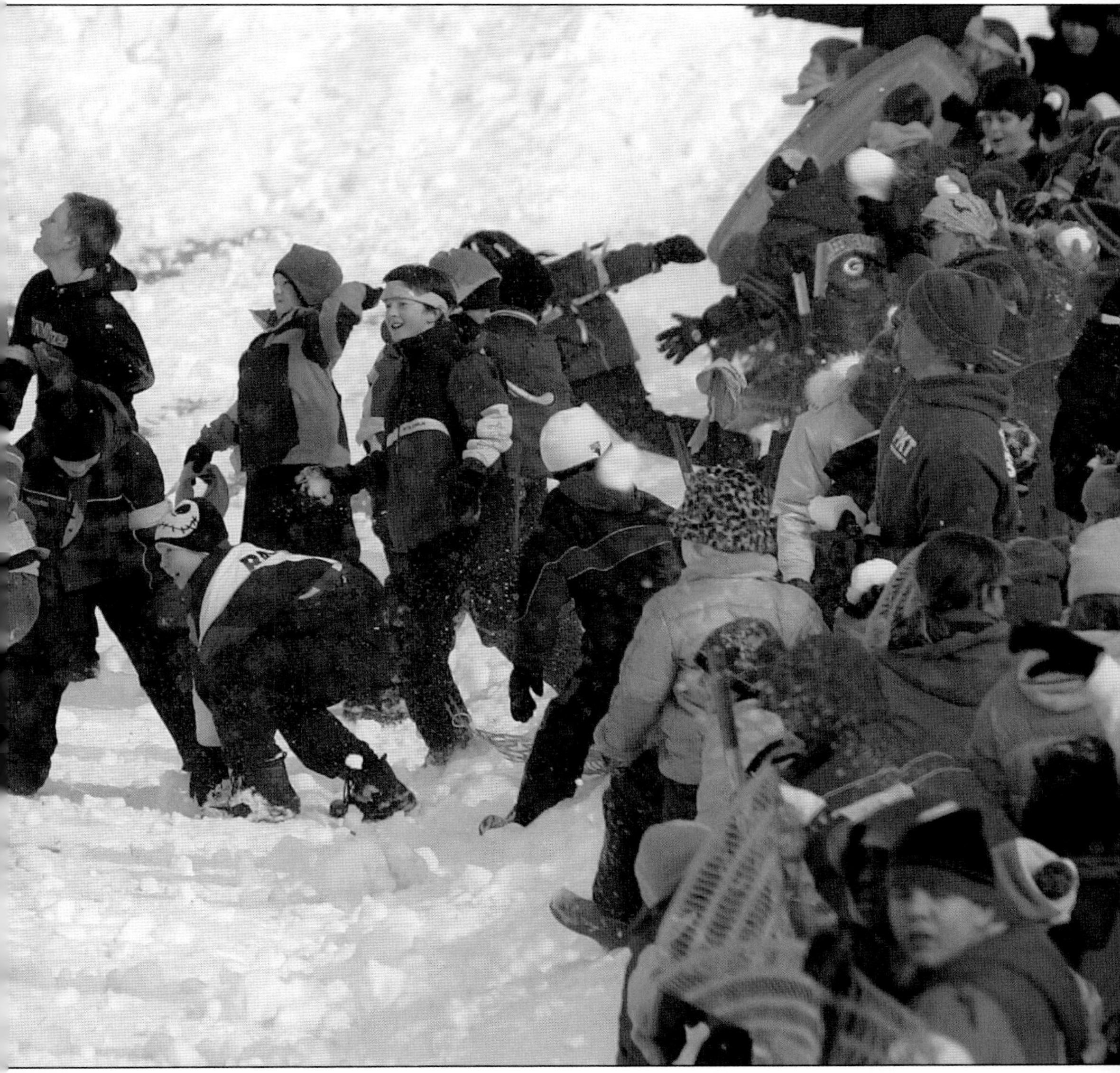

on February 10, 2006, students and alumni from Michigan Technological University, along with community members of Houghton, Michigan, broke the record with 3,749 people. They lost the title to a Korean city in 2010. (Courtesy of the *Daily Herald*.)

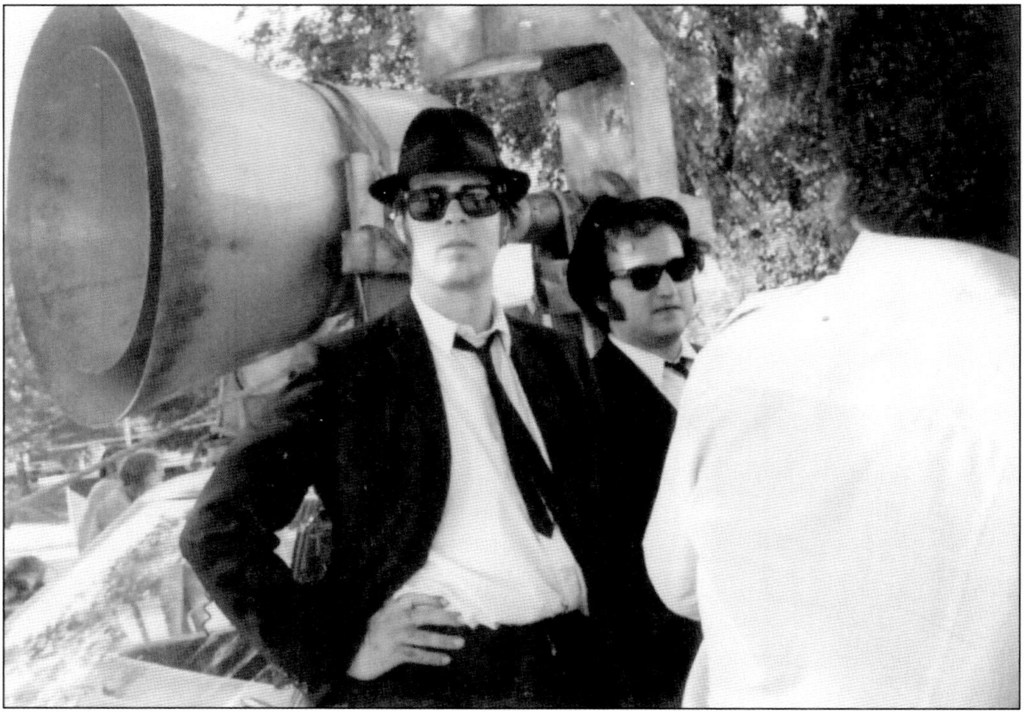

Excitement came to town in September 1979 when cast and crew of *The Blues Brothers* chose Phil's Beach and Honey Hill Beach as backdrops for scenes in the movie. Residents recall that it was a beautiful day for filming, and anticipation grew as the crew was on Route 12 filming before coming to Wauconda. The Froehlke kids—Dick, Mary, Kathy, and Mike—were chosen to be extras as were other townspeople and beach employees. Above, Dan Aykroyd and John Belushi take a break from filming. Below is the scene at Phil's Beach. (Both, courtesy of the Froehlke Family.)

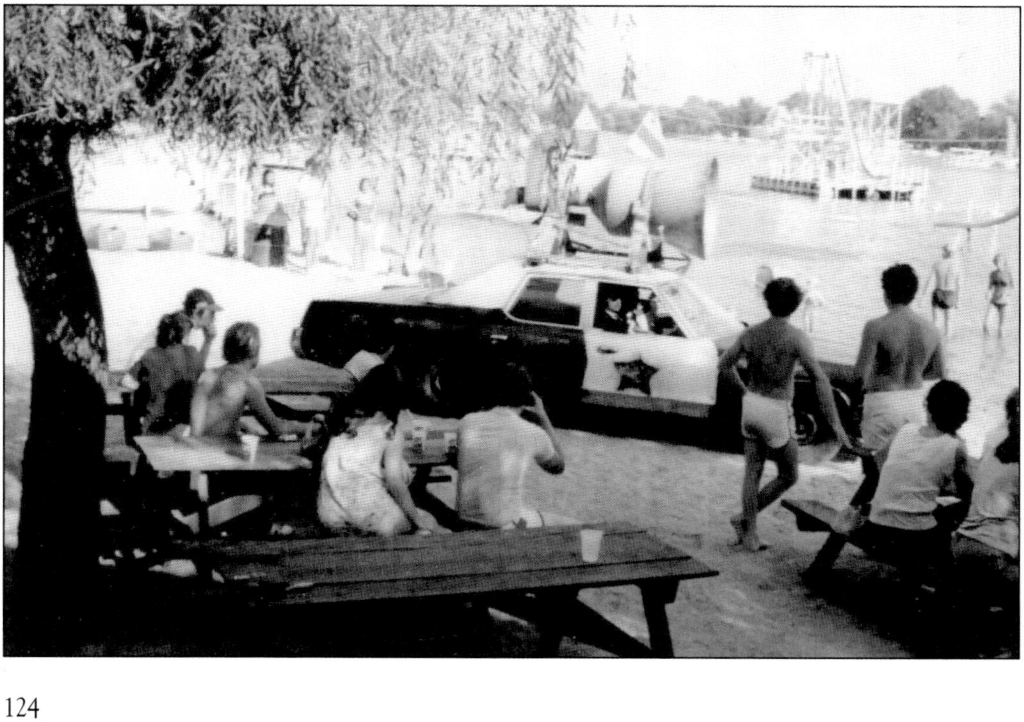

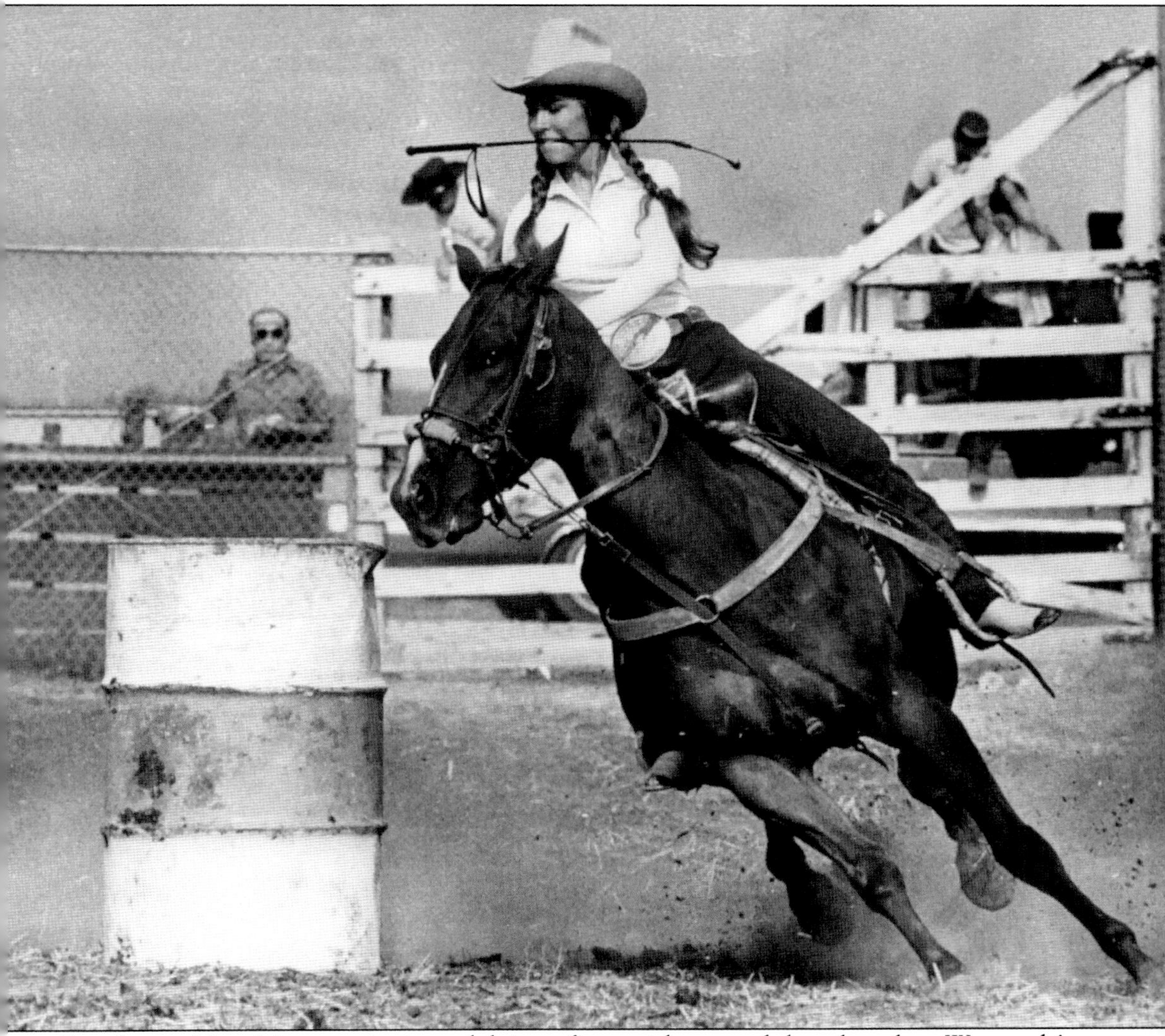

Barrel racer Mary Montrose is pictured doing a figure eight around three barrels at Wauconda's 10th annual rodeo in July 1973. This popular local event is held each year in July on the Golden Oaks Rodeo Grounds on Route 12 at Case Road. The 48th annual event was held in July 2011. The rodeo has sometimes drawn protests from Showing Animals Respect and Kindness (SHARK) and the Chicago Animal Rights Coalition for what the groups call cruelty to the horses. The groups have clashed with rodeo fans and Wauconda police several times in past years. (Courtesy of Kathy Catrambone.)

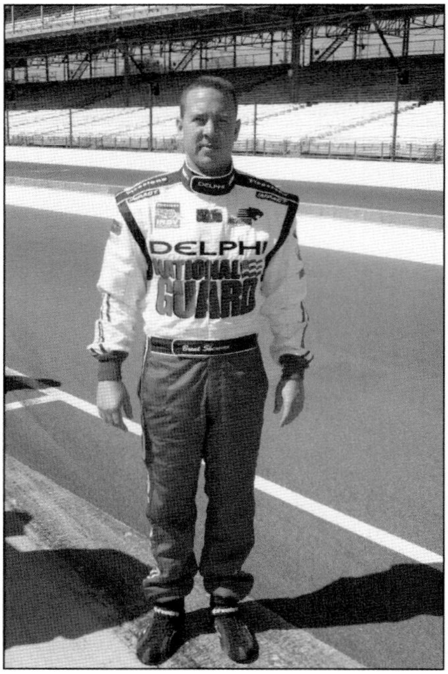

Brent Sherman is an award-winning race-car driver. Sherman, who was introduced to motor sports in the cockpit of an open-wheel car, is signed with Panther Racing after spending four years in NASCAR Nationwide and Nextel Cup Series. He served six years in the US Air Force—a stint that included four years conducting combat, surveillance, and instructional missions on an AWAC airplane. He, his wife, and their two children live in Wauconda. He is not related to Robert Sherman. (Courtesy of Brent Sherman.)

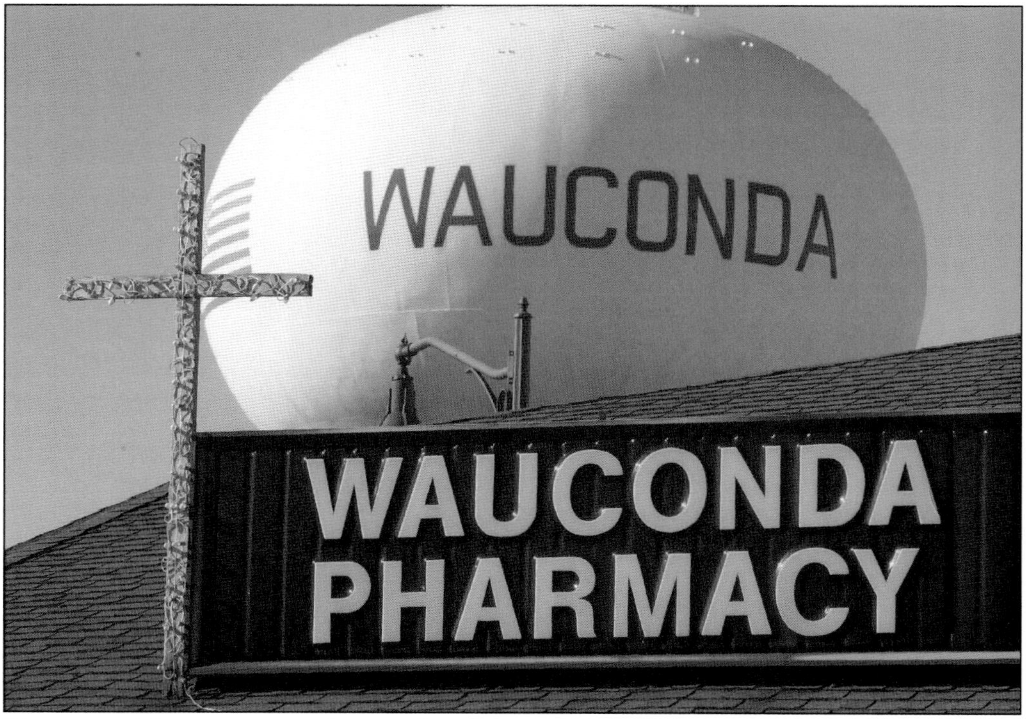

This is one of many crosses that can be seen on Wauconda businesses and homes, a lasting testament to a 1989 fight over the practice of displaying crosses at Christmastime on government property. Robert Sherman, chairman of American Atheists, Inc., objected to the crosses atop the water towers at Main and Liberty Streets and Bonner and Old Rand Roads. To avoid a legal battle that it most surely would lose, the village replaced the crosses with stars. Residents and business owners continue to display crosses year-round. (Courtesy of the *Daily Herald*.)

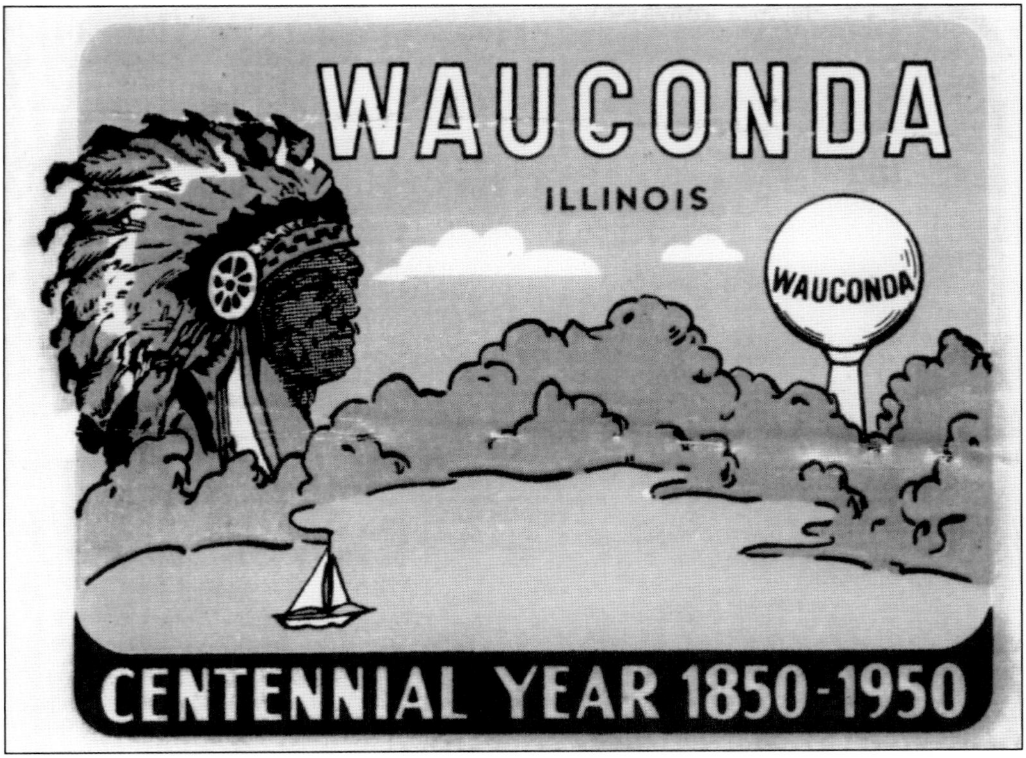

This postcard marks Wauconda's centennial year.

SELECTED BIBLIOGRAPHY

Aimers, Doris. *Memories*, 2000, 2002, 2003, and 2004. Wauconda: Wauconda Township Historical Society.

Berger, Alan. "Origins of Wauconda." *Daily Herald*, April 29, 1999.

Eaves, Rita. *The Village of Wauconda Centennial Year.* Wauconda: 1977.

Grossman, James R., Ann Durkin Keating, and Janice L. Reiff. *The Encyclopedia of Chicago.* Chicago: University of Chicago Press, 2004.

Haines, Elijah. *The Past and Present of Lake County, Illinois, Containing a History of the County.* Chicago: Wm. Le Baron & Co., 1877.

"It's More than Just a Creamery." *Wauconda Leader.* 1973.

Local History of Wauconda Township. Wauconda: 1914.

McAlister, Lynn. "Wauconda Township History Timeline." Wauconda Township Historical Society, 2007–2009.

Portrait Bibliography Album of Lake County, Illinois. Chicago: Lake City Publishing Company, 1891.

Powers, Hattie. "Student Account of Wauconda History." Illinois State Centennial. 1918.

Robinson, Carol Culp. "Schoolgirl Lens Captured History." *Wauconda Leader.* 1976.

Transfiguration Church Dedication Book, Wauconda: Transfiguration Church. May 5, 1985.

Whitney, Richard. "Old Maud." *Transportation Trails.*

Wishik, Toni. "Life and Doings of Justus Bangs: the 'Grand Old Man' of 1891 Recalls." *Daily Herald*, August 17, 1977.

Discover Thousands of Local History Books Featuring Millions of Vintage Images

Arcadia Publishing, the leading local history publisher in the United States, is committed to making history accessible and meaningful through publishing books that celebrate and preserve the heritage of America's people and places.

Find more books like this at
www.arcadiapublishing.com

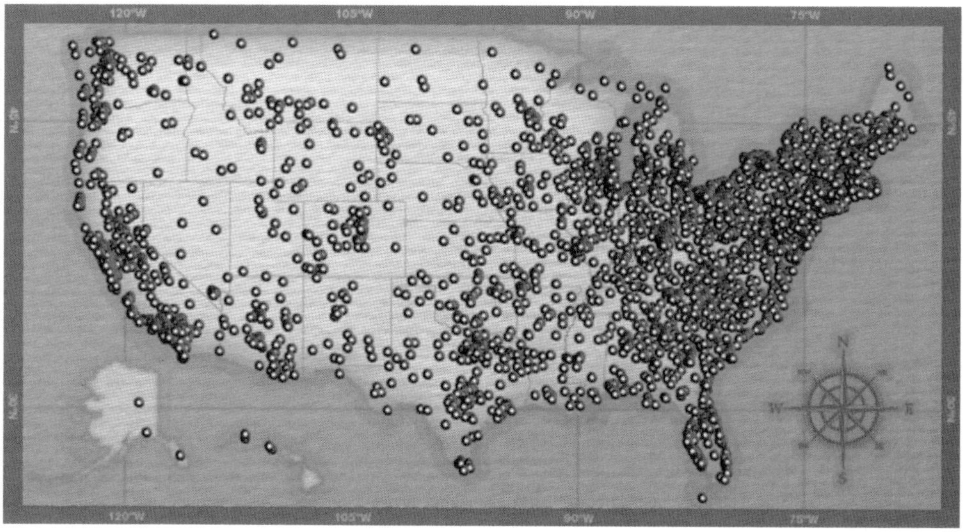

Search for your hometown history, your old stomping grounds, and even your favorite sports team.

Consistent with our mission to preserve history on a local level, this book was printed in South Carolina on American-made paper and manufactured entirely in the United States. Products carrying the accredited Forest Stewardship Council (FSC) label are printed on 100 percent FSC-certified paper.

MADE IN THE USA